£1.

RADIO PLAYS

David Pownall

RADIO PLAYS

AN EPIPHANOUS USE OF THE MICROPHONE

BEEF

PLOUGHBOY MONDAY

FLOS

KITTY WILKINSON

UNDER THE TABLE

OBERON BOOKS
LONDON

First published in 1998 by Oberon Books Ltd.
(incorporating Absolute Classics),
521 Caledonian Road, London N7 9RH.
Tel: 0171 607 3637 / Fax: 0171 607 3629

British Library Cataloguing-in-Publication Data
A catalogue record for this book is available from the British Library.

ISBN 1 84002 034 2

Cover design: Andrzej Klimowski

Typography: Richard Doust

Printed in Great Britain by Arrowhead Books Ltd., Reading.

Contents

AN AUDIENCE IN MIND

Six Radio Plays by David Pownall

For those who haven't heard David Pownall's work on air, the publication of this collection of radio plays presents a rare and welcome opportunity to sample the imagination of one of this country's most talented and prolific writers for the medium. But for those of us working in radio theatre, this publication presents a challenge. Just what exactly are we doing each time we bring a new play to the point of production. What is radio for? Are we using it to its best advantage?

To his credit, when asking me to address this publication, David Pownall's first concern was that I shouldn't jeopardise my position by endorsing views seemingly critical of current BBC attitudes towards radio drama. However, it struck me as odd that it was being left to a lone writer to extol the virtues of an art form which even the most cynical BBC Executives profess to love.

The plays in the collection are as varied, emotionally, intellectually and geographically as it is possible to be, yet they all attempt through the pure use of sound to incline towards pure meaning. For Pownall, radio provides two stark choices: either one exploits the medium's capacity for intelligent penetration, taking the audience to the complex recesses of the mind, or one opts for a tone and story to match a perceived audience. The icy reality is that radio is like litmus paper – the commonplace becomes more commonplace and the unusual becomes more unusual. The audience know this and responds accordingly.

A play like *Elgar's Third** or *Under the Table* comes not from second-guessing an audience's appetite but from the imagination of the writer with the pure idea – the poetic inspiration. The reason why Pinter and Beckett came to prominence on the radio was because, unshackled from the accoutrements of theatre or TV, their voices could ring un-neutered in the mind's ear. These writers were not driven by target audiences but by the fact that *everything* and *nothing* could be as close as an inhalation or an exhalation of breath.

I believe that we in the BBC are in danger of forgetting how heavily we rely on the pure idea coming from the writer. Corporate constraints and the sometimes desperate need to repeat past success can so easily blind us to the fact that the audience is listening to the radio because it wants to be stretched. Artistically, and ultimately commercially, it makes sense to allow that pure voice in this the purest of mediums.

Pownall's plays do have an audience in mind. It is not an inert ever-fixed conglomerate – the invention of marketeers who desperately need such conglomerates if the strategies upon which their careers are built are to mean anything – but rather a fluid and rich confusion of personalities and intellects, who are ever open to a new possibility. Individuals who consider themselves *listeners;* that is to say people who will pay attention to something their highly tuned sensors will tell them is real, is true, and is particular to their lives and emotions. The plays in this collection indicate that *this* is the audience that Pownall has in mind. People like you and me, I suppose.

Eoin O'Callaghan
Executive Producer Drama BBC
London 1998

*Published by Oberon Books in *The Composer Plays* by David Pownall, 1993.

INTRODUCTION

A friend in Brighton who was reading a novel by Mrs Gaskell, recently left a plaintive message on my answering machine, asking if I knew the meaning of the northern dialect word *threep*. Because of the context, he thought it might translate as *to gossip*, but he wanted to be sure. I rang a farmer friend in Cumbria and put the question to him. He didn't know either, but undertook to find out. He knew of a place called Threapland nearby. He eventually came back to me with an answer: *to threap* (not ee) is to argue, debate or haggle. Threapland is so called because it is land that was much argued over. As I was thinking about what to say in this introduction, and constantly running into the realisation that I strongly dislike the word *radio*, as well as *wireless* – both inadequate expressions of oral power – it struck me that a completely non-scientific, idiosyncratic substitute would be *The Threaper* – that which argues, debates and haggles.

So, from now on, each time I sit down to write a r*d*o play I'll say to myself: I am entering the land of *The Threaper*. (Threnody and reaping? Threatening and aping? SOE has it also as 'to persist in asserting something (contradicted or doubted); to affirm positively or pertinaciously; to maintain obstinately or aggressively)'. Familiar? It catches the querulous tone of the swirl of technicalised sound we live in.

It seems fair at this point to admit that I'm a clinical technophobe who has a psychotic aversion to small screens. For years I assumed the nausea to be my reaction to what was on the screen but after being diagnosed as a Horton's Alarm Clock migraineur, I realised it was not only the programmes that were to blame. Hence, my strong partiality for radio above television – and my fate to be forever shackled to enormous obsolete German office typewriters instead of computers and word-processors. But one ends up loving what is necessary, and rejoicing in the power of limitations.

Pleasures are always worth analysing, as far as they will permit. Because I listen to a lot of radio drama, and music and talks, the medium is difficult to place at a distance where sensible judgement can be exerted. The sound extension of our world is another layer, almost an atmosphere around the house. There are actors in the air, arguments linger on into silence and the middle of the night. I wonder sometimes if we are aware how powerful this influence is upon our lives. To imagine the long silences of domestic life before the advent of broadcasting is a real challenge to the imagination. They can't have been singing around the piano *all* the time.

Radio drama is the closest art to story-telling we have so its roots are very ancient. If ever a play uses solo narrative technique, I notice how the medium seems to hit its stride. Listening to Don Taylor's adaptation of the Anglo-Saxon poem *The Seafarer* recently – which took dramatisation away from the original about as far as it will go – I was struck by the authority of the told tale as the playwright pursued action or incident which could be created from very spare beginnings. Was this the art of the adaptation, or the authority of what was at its centre? Another strength, related to story-telling, is the 'Ancient Mariner' technique of having an enthralled listener within the play. This doubling of the essential connection between narrative and listener always seems to add power – as if the amazement one human being can find in the life of another is reinforced from within. Radio theatre has to buttonhole strangers in order to pour out its story.

Radio theatre is unique in the closeness between play and listener. Drama winnowed out of a strong, central plot, deep character revelation, fast changes of scene, full flavour of thought and language – these are the pure pleasures of the best radio theatre. But the true delight of the medium is in the work the listener must do within the mind – the lifting of the story fully into the imagination. It is at this stage that the natural monologue of narrative must become dialogue so a true play can be made. The story-teller fragments. One voice becomes several. These must be held in balance with no help from the physical world. Only the dialogue will carry the play and do all the necessary work.

Although directors and studio technicians do all they can to create conditions in which a kind of sound stagecraft can exist – microphone positions, sound skylines and backgrounds, atmospheres, stereo movements – these are essentially attempted break-outs from the prison of pure radio: evidence of yearnings towards the visual. However, inside the prison is a prairie – a continent – a universe – if the dialogue will allow. Any radio play that relies solely on dialogue for its journey, refusing to call in outside assistance, has a greater hold on the essential form. There is a way to provide every thought or action to a listener by the spoken word – if only the playwright can find it without resorting to audial signposting. The deeper the listener is involved with a character, the easier it is to move him around in an imaginary environment. Knowledge has its own eyesight.

My childhood war-time world was shaped by the wireless – (an odd term, I always thought, it was a world of wires!) so I rely on the ear and trust myself to interpret what it provides – not so, the eye. It was through sound I dealt with the war which dominated everything each day. Film had very little part to play. The theatre, no part at all. The truth came out of the little machine in the corner by Grandad's chair.

Churchill spoke to us from there – exhorting, sometimes confessing to disasters, bringing every child close to the nightmare in which it had been born. A taste for that danger remains. The wireless is still the oracle, though the priesthood is softer. Whenever the small machine spins a tale of threat out into the air using all the artfulness of actors and writers, a ghost of those real scenes, beneath the real sound of German bombers over Liverpool, edges into the back of my mind. Somehow I am once again wandering along the frontiers of my innocence, having to believe both the best and worst. Once I had started to write plays for radio, I slowly re-established that feeling. If anything, over the time I've been writing, it's got stronger.

～

As Martin Esslin, once Head of Drama at the BBC, stressed in his essay *The Mind as a Stage*, radio drama is very much a writer's medium. This needs some interpretation as it reveals a fact only writers can fully acknowledge. It is not that dialogue is king – nor that the Word is omnipotent – but that writers use radio in a particularly experimental, often secret way. Because it is so free with imagination and so restricted in physical reality, the mind expands in the direction writers use most when they are trying out ideas.

Radio provides a laser test. If a piece succeeds in sound only it has the inner strength to survive the clumsier, cruder forms. This laboratory use of radio drama is covert, but, to the writer it is invaluable. Of the six plays in this volume, one (*Flos*) was inextricably connected to the writing of a stage-play (*King John's Jewel*), and also part of research and development of a novel, *The White Cutter. Beef* originated in a stage-play. *Ploughboy Monday* became a film script after a producer heard it in his bath. The idea for *Kitty Wilkinson* was given me by the great radio director, Martin Jenkins; a BBC suggestion triggered *Under the Table.* This close understanding between playwrights and directors can be intensely creative provided the idea of the target audience is excluded from the relationship. Once the gun appears in the hand of the target, playwriting becomes scriptwriting – and they are not the same thing as anyone who's done both knows.

A play is essentially one thing standing in its own time, controlled by a defining action or movement of character. Its edges are its truth. Take it out of that limitation into serial form, full of intervening lapses of time, and it becomes loosened and runny, having no firmness or strength. A true play cannot be serialised. But the mass of the television and radio audience prefer drama in that form. Television abandoned the single play when Dennis Potter died. Radio still clings onto it. So, it is possible to be a radio playwright these days – but not a television playwright. In the cinema the idea of a playwright was jettisoned from the very beginning. A writer for a film has always been a scriptwriter because the power of decision over the text has never been trusted to his hands.

Having written forty-five radio plays over the last twenty-seven years – the first, I note, concerned a bid for freedom (the driver of a chain ferry over a lake freaks out, works it loose and sails away) – if I analyse what they are about, some groupings emerge. In my case, ten are adaptations of my own stage-plays – a practice now discouraged, thus reducing the audience for new work in the theatre and forcing theatre and radio apart. Of the remainder, three are about family, five about music, two are literary, eight are historical, one an adaptation of one of my novels, one an adaptation of a short story of mine, and the remaining fifteen cannot be classified as anything but radio plays in origin and execution. This mixture is broad and, for the sake of future radio playwrights should stay that way. Radio is not a form in which to encourage specialisation. Its beauty to a working writer is how its strength arrives through its service not only to itself but the other verbal arts as well.

Radio allows greater access to difficult work because the concentration on the word and its meaning can only be absolute. Sound effects constitute less than five per cent of radio plays and, though fascinating, as sounds they are to the word what the frame is to the picture – there to hold it up and set it off. There is no better means of penetrating and unfolding a text. I read Valle-Inclan's play *Divine Words* a year ago and thought I understood it until a recent radio version took me where my eyes had failed to reach. To take a thought round the back of the mind is the speciality of the spoken and written word, but a listener has to be quicker than a reader, while a watcher only registers what *is* and puts it into a pattern, never what *could* be.

~

'... some situation, emotion or experience which will be appreciated by, or rather applicable to the average mind.' No, this is not 1998 and *dumbing-down* talk. This is a man speaking in 1924, and adding a further encyclical that no radio play should be longer than forty minutes. With the recent changes in Radio 4 scheduling, one is forcibly struck how the wheel has come full-circle and we are at the beginning again and eager to make the same mistakes. R.E. Jeffrey, (with whom director-general Reith accorded) went on to say he thought clever dialogue was not necessary because 'dramatic action is *seen* in complete detail by all those who listen with close attention.' At the same time, this extraordinary management metaphysician believed radio plays had advantages over stage productions because they affected 'mentality, imagination and emotion' more deeply. This mish-mash paradox in the mind of a very powerful BBC head of drama illustrates what has been going on for the last seventy years. The art form has been the victim of its only patron and never been able to serve its real potential.

The sense of inner contradiction worsens when we realise how radio drama now only survives because that patron is still very much alive and kicking. Without the BBC, the publication of these plays would be pointless and all of them would never have been written because radio drama would have died by 1965. Imagine if cinema only had Warner Brothers, or the theatre, the RSC.

Radio plays have always suffered from being part of a mix of broadcast programmes which must balance and complement each other. They have never been allowed to exist in their own right, as a stage-play does, or a film. The mind of the listener is never aware how much the diet of his mind has been pre-arranged. The straitjacket radio drama has always worn was tailored out of a management necessity, as it was perceived in 1923 – a shattered post-war world, full of insurrectionary nightmares and political dangers.

Writers instinctively sense the chain as it is being forged, but the denial of freedom to radio dramatists from the outset was not challenged as it would have been if the theatre had been fettered to such a degree (though it suffered badly enough in that time, mainly due to self-censorship based on commercial direction). Somehow, an unwritten agreement emerged guaranteeing the biddability of radio playwrights – even those who.enjoyed higher freedoms in other forms. By the time any sense of the modern classic had evolved, the damage was done. A radical play was broadcast out of its time, shrouded in reverence, and thereby neutralised. Meanwhile, the contemporary playwright went to work under the blanket of the BBC's suzerainty.

Popularity is its own defence. New music struggles to be true to what it hears within, and to be accepted. No one composes or writes in order to be ignored. The BBC is the main champion of new music, and shoulders its risks. This defence of the difficult, unusual and alarming is also needed by radio drama which has further to go than music, having been held back so long – which is now a positive advantage. There is room for expansion and moving forward without the danger of unnatural contortions in search of originality. Having been so severely hedged in for seventy years means there is space. One of the reasons for the deep-rooted respect and affection the BBC is held in by the general population is that it protects and defends the life of the creative arts and the need for them to move forward. A few years back, along with other writers, some actors and directors, I spent a week-end locked up with Arthur Miller talking about where theatre was going in the western world. At the end, someone asked if there was one thought he'd like to leave us with. His answer was immediate and unreserved: Don't let them destroy the BBC.

~

To be at the elbow of the humanoid who first scratched a picture on the wall of a cave, or sang, or danced would have been interesting. The question: 'Why are you doing this?' naturally comes to mind. With the technical arts, this question was frequently asked. What the early film-makers and broadcasters thought they were doing is open to us – though their reasons are often as much use as Neanderthal grunts.

Their preoccupations were not with what they could do, but with what they couldn't. It was the limitations of radio which first impressed those who recognised its potential as a vehicle for theatre. What did not come to mind was the huge advantage of concentration of language and meaning which would enable any text to be penetrated as it never had before.

Appalled by the problem of writing a play for radio with all the in-built handicaps, the first author to attempt it decided to set his piece in a coal-mine with three people lost in total darkness. Richard Hughes described writing a radio play as presenting 'a blind man's world'. He could have added that in such a world, the other senses are intensified, the imagination becomes supremely powerful, and vision is recreated from within.

Beginnings are customarily a time of optimism but this was not so with the birth of radio theatre. A very cautious, self-crippling, sideways approach was made, hemmed in by anxieties about audiences and alienation should the mind and imagination be challenged beyond what was comfortable. The great advantages were not seized upon because they appeared to be intellectual – and the 1920s had become iconoclastic about thought. Joyce and Eliot were able to shake the old modes of meaning, but, as with the Einsteinian universe, their findings were thought beyond the public mind.

It would be sad to believe re-birth of ideas and advantages in the arts is impossible. Reincarnation of hope for a passed opportunity which presents itself again at a different time is not absurd, especially in the art form the Absurdists made their own. Even with the world's radio drama reduced to expression solely in this country to any real depth – the others having been effectively destroyed by letting commercial interests run riot – nevertheless, that is a very substantial seed-bed.

Drama on radio emphasises styles of thinking. The banal becomes more banal – the intelligent, more intelligent. Because the BBC, from its inception, has had an audience in mind, radio drama has always been on reins, made to perform as if it were the place where silent movies and dialogue met up and decided to behave far too responsibly.

With the adrenalin of anarchy exhausted in the other arts, the theatre of the free air can now take the lead and penetrate into places the cinema can only dream of entering – the deep complexities of the mind, fortune, time and action where mental relationships and intuitive perceptions are unfolded. What is to stop radio drama taking the plunge? All we need is the swimming-pool.

David Pownall

AN EPIPHANOUS USE
OF THE MICROPHONE

Commissioned by the BBC for the 75th
anniversary of the first play ever broadcast

An Epiphanous Use of the Microphone was first broadcast on BBC Radio 4 on the 15th May 1998. The cast was as follows:

QUEEN ELIZABETH I, Anna Massey

SHAKESPEARE, Michael Maloney

JOHN REITH/SIR TOBY BELCH, Crawford Logan

CATHLEEN NESBITT, Jane Whittenshaw

CHAMBERLAIN/CECIL, John Rowe

VIOLA/MARIA, Rory Cambell

OLIVIA, Alison Pettitt

MURIEL/STUDIO MANAGER, Rachel Atkins

FESTE/RAMSEY MACDONALD/
MASTER OF TEMPLE, Gerard McDermott

LORD CHAMBERLAIN/BACON/ORSINO/
SIR TOBY BELCH (1923 prod), Iwan Thomas

BURBAGE/MALVOLIO/
CECIL LEWIS, Christopher Wright

DIRECTION, Martin Jenkins

TODAY'S ANNOUNCER: Spring, 1923. A session at the BBC's new school for announcers at Savoy Hill.

Scene 1

(*Savoy Hill studio.*)

ANNOUNCER: This is the British Broadcasting Company. We are proud to present for the first time on radio, William Shakespeare's immortal comedy ...

REITH: Hold on, hold on Lewis. Aren't we missing a trick here?

ANNOUNCER: I beg your pardon, Major?

REITH: This isn't just the first time on radio for *Twelfth Night*. It's the first play on radio, anytime, anywhere. Must get that in somehow.

ANNOUNCER: John Reith, the first general manager of the BBC – Major is a hang-over from the Great War that ended only five years ago – instructs Cecil A Lewis, while working out the prologue to precede ...

CECIL LEWIS: William Shakespeare's immortal comedy ...

REITH: Make a lot of that word IMMORTAL!

CECIL LEWIS: Yes, Major. William Shakespeare's IMMORTAL comedy ...

REITH: Not quite that much. Bring it down a little. No. Let's try a new approach altogether. Hushed reverence.

ANNOUNCER: ... immortal comedy ... like that?

REITH: Perfect. A whisper, but with authority.

TODAY'S ANNOUNCER: Within the hour they will have put together a concise and cogent announcement, which includes reference to the date of their broadcast, May 28th, 1923 and ...

ANNOUNCER: ... the première of *Twelfth Night* on February 2nd, 1602, in the Middle Temple dining room, only five minutes walk down river from our studios here at Savoy Hill. Tonight, we feel a special kinship with the Lord Chamberlain's Men, that great company of actors, famous in our theatre's history. Across the centuries, we salute them. AVE!

REITH: Then the fanfare. That'll work very well. The lapels on your dinner jacket are too shiny. Tone them down.

ANNOUNCER: Yes, Major. D'you think the average listener will understand the Latin?

REITH: What? Ave? Don't be so patronising, man! Of course they know what AVE means. In my first draft for the announcement I had AVE AGITATE LANCEAM, Hail Shake-speare! But I took it out in case it could be politically misconstrued.

Scene 2

(*Cross to a rehearsal room 1602 – wooden boards.*)

SHAKESPEARE: Can you sing a song from written notes?

FESTE: Anything.

SHAKESPEARE: Have a go at this.

FESTE: Give me a moment ... hm-hm ... yes.

SHAKESPEARE: Take more time if you want.

FESTE: No need. I'm ready. Master Shakespeare.

SHAKESPEARE: Off you go.

FESTE: O mistress mine, where are you roaming?
O stay and hear: your true love's coming,
That can sing both high and low:
Trip no further, pretty sweeting;
Journey's end in lovers meeting,
Every wise man's son doth know.

Scene 3

(*Cross to Savoy Hill studio – all CAST.*)

REITH: Announcement is right at the heart of radio.
We announce the world to all the senses. We make ideas appear in the sky of the mind. We are the oral star. I've checked this out with the medical people: we touch the space-nerve.

ANNOUNCER: The space-nerve, Major?

REITH: That portion of the greater auditory nerve which draws from the drums, harps and canals of the inner ear our sense of whereness.

ANNOUNCER: Is that the same as *a*wareness?

REITH: Awareness is enfolded in whereness, young man. Gravity, meaning, balance and silence affect the space-nerve. As broadcasters we must get *on* that nerve and never let go.

Scene 4

(*Burst of audience laughter from a broadcast stage-show heard as if on 1923 wireless – play voices distant.*)

(*REITH's home. Sedate clock ticking in background.*)

REITH: No! No! No! Dreadful. No sense of whereness.

MURIEL: No sense of anything, John. D'you mind if we turn it off? I don't see the point of trying to listen.

(*The wireless is turned off.*)

REITH: We don't seem able to improve on it. So much noise beyond our control. Most unsatisfactory.

MURIEL: Well, thank God for silence, I say – and a good book.

(*Picks up book.*)

REITH: (*Pacing.*) My mind was on another plane. Communicators in times of severe social and political stress often seek an amoral persona.

MURIEL: One of your father's sermons?

REITH: On the passing of Queen Victoria. Changed my life.

MURIEL: When you were interviewed for this BBC job did anyone ask what you'd actually broadcast if successful?

REITH: A lot had been assumed. We must have news they said – we must have hints for housewives. We must have sport. We must have racing tips, and dance music.

MURIEL: Oh, John ...

REITH: But at one point I stopped the proceedings and drew their attention to what I had listed under 'hobbies' in my curriculum vitae. Theatre! Life-blood!

MURIEL: Lots of plays! We must have lots and lots of plays! But expertly done, my darling. You'll obviously have to start with a Shakespeare.

REITH: Of course – but done in one of our studios. Only the best talent. A new technique will be needed. I hope the profession can make the adjustment. Actors can be annoyingly idle about such things.

MURIEL: Just think of it: no more uncomfortable seats. No more fighting to get to the bar at the interval.

REITH: No having to get up and walk out if it's rubbish. Just switch it off.

FESTE: (*Sings.*) What is love? 'tis not hereafter;
Present mirth hath present laughter,
What's to come is still unsure:
In delay there is no plenty:
Then come kiss me, sweet and twenty:
Youth's a stuff will not endure.

Scene 5

(*Fade in Whitehall office.*)

CHAMBERLAIN: Now you're sure we're clear on that point?

REITH: We are, Postmaster-General.

CHAMBERLAIN: Nothing controversial as far as politics, religion or industrial matters are concerned. We don't want strong opinions, over-dramatisations, distortions of the truth. Nothing like that.

REITH: I understand.

CHAMBERLAIN: You agree very readily, Reith. Is it possible to run your company on that basis?

REITH: Absolutely, Mr Chamberlain. We simply give the facts and state the opposing cases.

CHAMBERLAIN: We will be listening carefully – very carefully.

REITH: Of course. In time we hope everyone will.

CHAMBERLAIN: Don't want this radio thing of yours falling into the wrong hands.

(Big Ben strikes three quarters.)

REITH: May I press you to be a mite more precise?

CHAMBERLAIN: We don't think it should become a platform for radicalism of any kind. Steer a middle course. Tone down the drama. Let common sense be your guide. Plain common sense – that is if you want to keep your monopoly.

REITH: What's your favourite Shakespeare play, Mr Chamberlain?

CHAMBERLAIN: Is that a trick question?

REITH: Bless you, no, sir. We have decided to take a step forward and broadcast a play of the Bard's over the air from one of our studios. I'm asking influential men of good taste for advice.

CHAMBERLAIN: Bit early, isn't it? Shouldn't you let people get used to the wireless via something less weighty? Less difficult to understand.

REITH: I think that would be a mistake. While our transmissions can only be received in London, this is the time to test intelligent public opinion. Once we reach out into the sticks they'll only favour horse races and recipes. The public will need leading. Our aim must be to bring understanding where there was once ignorance – and light where there was only mental darkness.

CHAMBERLAIN: I must remember not to pass this on to the voters of Birmingham – or Stratford-upon-Avon. I think *Othello* would be my choice.

REITH: *Othello*? You're the first person to suggest that. For some reason I had it in mind you'd be a *Measure for Measure* man.

Scene 6

(The LORD CHAMBERLAIN's office – 1602.)

LORD CHAMBERLAIN: For God's sake there's nothing to worry about. Why d'you think *Twelfth Night* might get you into trouble?

SHAKESPEARE: A precautionary anxiety.

LORD CHAMBERLAIN: I've read the whole play twice and can't see anything wrong with it. Does that calm your fears?

SHAKESPEARE: We are your company – the Lord Chamberlain's Company. We perform under your protection. I have to assume you wouldn't deliberately let us stage something that could – even *might* – cause offence.

LORD CHAMBERLAIN: I certainly wouldn't. So, put your mind at rest.

SHAKESPEARE: Francis Bacon is in favour at the moment.

LORD CHAMBERLAIN: Is he? I never pay attention to such things.

SHAKESPEARE: Bacon aspires to conquer the stage. He's very jealous of my success, and sees me as a threat to his ambitions. That *Richard the Second* business was all his doing. He used his position as the Crown prosecutor at Essex's trial to infer that because the rebels had performed my play, I was a rebel myself – which is the last thing I am.

LORD CHAMBERLAIN: Yes, he did make as much out of that as he could. But, then – it was an emergency. The danger was real.

SHAKESPEARE: It wasn't my fault Essex's rebels put the play on. They didn't even ask me – and I wasn't paid a single penny!

LORD CHAMBERLAIN: How d'you think Bacon can use *Twelfth Night* against you? It's not about a monarch being deposed.

SHAKESPEARE: Someone has already shown Bacon the play ... now he's spreading rumours it contains parallels with Her Majesty's recent unhappiness. He's urged her to come and see for herself.

LORD CHAMBERLAIN: Has he! Your play has a very simple theme – confusion in love. A common affliction.

SHAKESPEARE: Which makes everyone laugh. Except perhaps those who are suffering from excess of it – like Elizabeth.

LORD CHAMBERLAIN: Wrong on two points: one, that she'll come – two, that she hasn't got over Essex. Once he was executed, she began to heal immediately.

SHAKESPEARE: Yes, well – I don't want to be responsible for re-opening that wound – and then for the consequences.

LORD CHAMBERLAIN: Then we shall say it was written for Candlemas – the Purification of the Virgin. That lady was confused in love. Or, if she wasn't, she should have been.

SHAKESPEARE: We might get away with that, as long as the Church doesn't accuse me of encouraging Roman Catholicism.

LORD CHAMBERLAIN: Let's do it for the Candlemas feast. I'll find somewhere for you to put it on. As for the other business – stop worrying. Bacon can't hurt you. In spite of his brilliance in court, he's still an outsider.

Scene 7

(*REITH's office at Savoy Hill. Strand traffic in a street below – 1923.*)

REITH: As an experienced performer, and a leading light amongst the ladies of the stage, let me ask how seriously you take my new theatre of the air.

NESBITT: With the cinema, it's part of a wonderful expansion in opportunities for actors.

REITH: Ah, jobs. Anything beyond that? I'm told you're a thinker, Miss Nesbitt. Give me your thoughts – not your financial aspirations.

NESBITT: Well, firstly, there'll be no audience to play to. That's the main problem. We'll have to imagine them and they'll have to imagine us.

REITH: Except for hearing you.

NESBITT: Yes. But we can't hear *them*. It will be a sort of one-way traffic.

REITH: Well observed, Miss Nesbitt. That will be our struggle – to feel along with our audience. Who are they? (*Goes to window and opens it.*) If we lean out of the window and incline our eyes upwards, what that is tall, thin and erect do we encounter?

NESBITT: The mast, Major?

REITH: Quite so. And atop the mast at night?

NESBITT: A little red light.

REITH: A little red light. (*Pause.*) I see a star. A star of wonder. A star of light shining over a spot where good news is born. Where the Word is sent forth so nation can speak unto nation. Though radio cannot appeal to the eye, it is made of visions.

NESBITT: Yes, Major.

REITH: Visions for the inner eye. Have you thought about all this?

NESBITT: Oh, yes! I'm very conscious …

REITH: News, sport, endless opinionated conversation, dance music, cookery … is that all we're here for? What about what's best in you, in me, in the unborn?

NESBITT: The potential is enormous.

REITH: Let's say you're Shakespeare. You've only ever seen your work done in rough, unlovely buildings by actors in tawdry clothes. Suddenly someone comes along and offers you a way into the very heart of the home. You'd bite his hand off.

NESBITT: I'd be enthusiastic, certainly.

REITH: No more hazel nuts whizzing around. No more fidgets. No more coughers ruining the majesty of the words. Paradise! D'you believe in ghosts, Miss Nesbitt? If you do – and the Bard did – expect a visitation on the day our first drama production goes out. He will be there, beaming with delight.

NESBITT: That thought certainly helps me.

REITH: He's been waiting to go on the radio for three hundred years. He knew the artistic principle on which broadcasting must operate: 'On your imaginary forces work.' Chorus, *Henry the Fifth*. Inspire your cast with that. Dismiss.

NESBITT: Will I be producing *Henry the Fifth*?

REITH: You will be told which play we're doing in time.

Scene 8

(*To SHAKESPEARE's lodgings. Drinks being poured.*)

BURBAGE: There're reasonable things in it.

SHAKESPEARE: Good of you to say so, Dick.

BURBAGE: Bit tame for my taste – but I understand why.

(*Script being thrown down on table.*)

SHAKESPEARE: What d'you mean – tame?

BURBAGE: Well, not much happens. What have we got here? A mix-up. Few jokes. Few songs. No guts to speak of. Nothing to get your teeth into. Hm. Malvolio's quite a good part. I'll do him. You've written better, Will – but don't fret. We'll make it work for you.

SHAKESPEARE: *Twelfth Night* is dangerous – anarchic – full of people about to get out of hand.

BURBAGE: Doesn't come across that way. There's no danger for anyone. Show me where there's any danger.

SHAKESPEARE: If you feel that way perhaps you shouldn't be in it?

BURBAGE: (*Going.*) Got to give the play a chance, Will. Without me it won't have one.

SHAKESPEARE: You're an arrogant sod Burbage!

BURBAGE: And why write these big female roles. I've counted all the lines. Half of them will come out of the mouths of boys.

SHAKESPEARE: And why have I done that, Dick?

BURBAGE: So no one will take them too seriously.

SHAKESPEARE: They talk about love in error. Mistaken love. Love that deceives. Love that can bring down a state.

BURBAGE: So you say.

SHAKESPEARE: If Olivia married the youth Cesario –
who is half her age – as Essex was of Elizabeth's –
wouldn't it be a catastrophe?

BURBAGE: You're making a case now, Will. That wasn't in
your mind when you wrote it.

SHAKESPEARE: (*Exploding.*) What d'you know about what
was in my bloody mind when I wrote it?

BURBAGE: I don't want you making up explanations to
please me ...

SHAKESPEARE: Why should I want to please you? You're
nothing but an actor!

BURBAGE: Like you!

SHAKESPEARE: Perhaps. (*Calming.*) But not just an actor.

BURBAGE: That brings me to something else. My part
needs building up. I could improvise another five minutes
finding this letter. Do my short-sighted business. Drop it a
few times. There could be a wind. I could chase it. Or you
could double the length of my soliloquy.

SHAKESPEARE: It's not really a soliloquy, Dick. It's a
man reading a letter to himself, and there're interjections
from other characters.

BURBAGE: Yes. I wanted to talk to you about them. Are
they necessary?

SHAKESPEARE: I determine your stride, Dick! That's as
fast as I want you to go at that point – and remember it
is in part a comedy. Look out for the laughs. When you
make your entrance in the yellow stockings and
cross-garters there'll be a big response.

BURBAGE: If I get it right, there will. Timing!

SHAKESPEARE: Don't talk through the laughter. Wait. Let
it build, then die down, before you speak.

BURBAGE: You know a thing or two, laddy – which
I taught you. Leave it to me. Before we leave the arena ...
You know you've got a woman disguised as a man ... well,
disguised as a eunuch, though that's never followed up.

SHAKESPEARE: Viola's an innocent. She doesn't know the
difference.

BURBAGE: We'll come to that in a minute. But shouldn't there be a man disguised as a woman as well? Instead of tricking him into putting on yellow stockings and cross-garters to please Olivia, get him to dress as a woman because Olivia's a lesbian.

SHAKESPEARE: She's not a lesbian.

BURBAGE: She is. She falls in love with a woman.

SHAKESPEARE: Who's disguised as a man.

BURBAGE: As a eunuch, according to you. Make your mind up.

SHAKESPEARE: Dick, just do the play as I've written it, will you, please?

Scene 9

(*An exclusive London club. Quiet chat.*)

MACDONALD: Good of you to risk inviting me to your club, Major.

REITH: I'm flattered you accepted my invitation.

MACDONALD: It's quite an instrument you have in the BBC – not too important to Labour as yet because our members can't afford to buy your receivers – but the day will come when you can sell them cheaper.

REITH: Oh, that should be soon.

MACDONALD: I'm told the Tories have already muzzled you.

REITH: Oh? I hadn't noticed.

MACDONALD: Nothing controversial? Complete impartiality? You'll be an extension of the judiciary by the sound of it.

REITH: We won't be judging anyone Mr MacDonald.

MACDONALD: Won't you? But can you avoid it? Impartiality is a myth with things as they are. Greed has triumphed over civilisation. It has to be fought. Which includes your masters.

REITH: The Tories are not my masters.

(*Discreet clock strikes nine.*)

MACDONALD: They gave you the monopoly on broadcasting. Aren't you nervous that if Labour comes to power we'll take it away?

REITH: Not at all.

MACDONALD: You think we have a preference for strong, centralised control of information and opinion like the Soviets?

REITH: That never occurred to me.

MACDONALD: Plenty of propaganda plays and operas and poetry – art harnessed to our political programme ... all that.

REITH: Nothing could be further from my mind.

MACDONALD: With the poverty and suffering we have prevalent in our country, isn't it reasonable to throw every thing into the fight? Can we afford freedom for a few artists to indulge themselves?

REITH: You're playing Devil's advocate, I fear.

MACDONALD: The suffering I allude to is very real, Major. We are one of the richest nations on earth yet the mass of our people live miserable, deprived lives while one class profits.

REITH: I have made enquiries. I know you love the arts.

MACDONALD: Easy to say. I often think that love of that nature should be expended upon people. Many writers would agree with me – even to their own detriment. It is a shameful civilisation we live in, Reith. Read the War Poets and hang your head. Will you broadcast them as well as the Old Brigade?

REITH: We shall be in no one's pocket!

MACDONALD: Except your shareholders. You have to realise that you have been given an impossible structure by the Tories – one that will force you into their arms.

REITH: I dispute that.

MACDONALD: The Tories will never let you represent real working-class interests, you know that. Put their point of view – express their frustrations. Not much has changed in the way this country is run. It will change, though, we'll see to that, but the battle lines are just being drawn. What will the BBC offer my people?

REITH: I believe an understanding will evolve between all the British the people and the BBC – otherwise I will have failed.

MACDONALD: But every day you'll have to find something to say. Air-time will have to be filled. Now and then the truth will have to poke its head out – that could be dangerous.

REITH: What I really wanted to talk about was something much simpler: the BBC plans to put a Shakespearean play out over the air. Do you have a favourite?

MACDONALD: (*Laughing.*) You're pulling my leg! (*Pause.*) No, you're not. Had to be Shakespeare, of course.

REITH: That was a consensus I assumed.

MACDONALD: Have you spoken to Baldwin and Lloyd George?

REITH: They're thinking about it.

MACDONALD: I don't have to. It has to be *Lear*. God stand up for bastards like me.

Scene 10

(*REITH's office. 1923 traffic outside.*)

NESBITT: We have all the suggestions now, Major. Lloyd George's choice is *Henry the Fourth Part One* because it's the only play with a serious part for a Welshman. (*Pause.*) Owen Glendower?

REITH: I am familiar with the play, Miss Nesbitt. (*Pause.*) Well, after all he's been through perhaps Lloyd George is allowed to be sectarian once in a while.

NESBITT: What d'you think.

REITH: I'm one of those odd people who don't really like Falstaff.

NESBITT: No good parts for women.

REITH: Yes … a lot of our listeners will be women. We should always bear that in mind. They have their own way of looking at things.

NESBITT: I sometimes wonder if any writer since Shakespeare had noticed that. Our new prime minister's suggested *Midsummer Night's Dream*.

REITH: Ah! That I didn't expect.

NESBITT: It's useful to know Baldwin believes in fairies.

REITH: Has Ramsay MacDonald stuck with *Lear*?

NESBITT: Yes. With a footnote – remember the bastards. Far too pessimistic, surely?

REITH: I think 'howl howl howl' can wait for better days. Well, here's my quandary. I thought they might agree on *Hamlet*. We'll have to do *Twelfth Night*.

NESBITT: An excellent choice.

REITH: Have you ever wondered why it's called that, Miss Nesbitt?

NESBITT: You know, I can't say I have. I suppose I've always taken the optional title seriously – *What You Will*.

REITH: What happens on Twelfth Night in every God-fearing Christian home?

NESBITT: Well, people take down the Christmas tree – their decorations …

REITH: (*Interrupting.*) In many countries it is when gifts are given, like the three kings.

NESBITT: Ah.

REITH: *Twelfth Night* is about giving the greatest gift of all, Miss Nesbitt.

NESBITT: Oh.

REITH: Which is why it's my favourite.

NESBITT: Mine too.

REITH: Have you made many mistakes in love, Miss Nesbitt?

NESBITT: Well – I …

REITH: It's so easy to do. We know so little when we're young. Which way to go.

(*Pause.*)

I hope people will understand why I'm doing a play about love before any other. You do, don't you?

NESBITT: I think so.

REITH: Why?

NESBITT: Because after all the recent suffering and deprivation we need to know what love is these days.

REITH: I knew you were the right person to put this play on for me. Is it really a comedy?

NESBITT: If vanity, crudeness, stupidity, blindness, are comic when you set them against truth.

REITH: Which is?

NESBITT: Wanting to love and be loved.

REITH: D'you think we'll get away with not being able to deliver so much of the spirit of the play? The visual side is so important.

NESBITT: Radio can get into the heart, which is where *Twelfth Night* takes place.

REITH: You've made me easier in my mind, Miss Nesbitt. Thank you. But we still have a hill to climb. But if we do our job properly with dear old *Twelfth Night*, perhaps the day will come when our audience will have the courage to sit beside their fires and listen to King Lear's terrifying despair – bastards and all!

FESTE: (*Sings. Voice over.*)

Come away, come away, death,
And in sad cypress let me be laid;
Fly away, fly away breath;
I am slain by a fair cruel maid.

Scene 11

(*The Middle Temple dining hall as the audience is arriving – all CAST.*)

BACON: Why are you hiding, Will?

SHAKESPEARE: I'm not hiding.

BACON: Standing behind the door is an odd position for a popular author. He should be out amongst his admirers.

SHAKESPEARE: Is that why you seek me out, Bacon? Because I'm popular with you? Or because you wish to gloat?

BACON: About what, dear man?

SHAKESPEARE: I know you've read the play.

BACON: Out of interest, I did ask a friend for a glance at a script he happened to have – yes.

SHAKESPEARE: Your only interest, Bacon, is to get me into as much trouble as you can.

BACON: You're the one who chooses to write about older women mistakenly falling in love with younger men – who are not what they seem. How else is anyone at Court supposed to interpret this latest piece?

SHAKESPEARE: I didn't make up that part of the plot. It's taken straight from an Italian story.

BACON: What does it matter where you lifted if from. You decided to use it. And it's obvious to everyone what you're getting at.

SHAKESPEARE: I'm not! Is every love-scene to be a parallel of what's happened at the palace?

BACON: It's mischief. Worse than the mischief with *Richard the Second*. This time you've gone too far. You're holding Elizabeth and the institution of the monarchy up to ridicule. Your play is a treasonable libel.

SHAKESPEARE: Whatever I wrote, you'd twist it to suit your own ends.

BACON: I'd better find myself a seat. Don't want to get stuck behind a big fellow. We're going to be cramped ... hot, isn't it?

(*A commotion.*)

SHAKESPEARE: You bastard. You persuaded the Lord Chamberlain to make us do the play here in the Middle Temple, didn't you? You've turned this into a trial!

BACON: Talk to you after the show!

(*Moves off into the crowd. The audience hushes. Shuffling steps.*)

BURBAGE: (*Intense whisper.*) My God! You should have warned us!

SHAKESPEARE: What are you doing? Get back in the dressing-room before someone recognises you!

BURBAGE: You should have told us *she* was coming.

SHAKESPEARE: Oh, no!

BURBAGE: I'll never forgive you for this, Will – never!

SHAKESPEARE: I didn't know. Bacon's behind it, the crafty bastard! He got her to come.

BURBAGE: How slowly she walks. Breaks my heart. And the poor thing's dressed as a man. Does she think she's in one of your plays?

BACON: Excuse me ... excuse me ... (*Pushing his way through.*) Where is ... ah ... such a crowd, your Majesty ...

QUEEN: Don't call me that! Look away, man! Look away! And call me sir. I'm in disguise!

CECIL: (*Arriving.*) It's far too hot in here.

BACON: They obviously didn't expect such a crowd, Lord Cecil.

CECIL: Must we have so many candles?

QUEEN: They're for Candlemas – to keep the feast. Be quiet and sit down! We'll sweat it out. Pooh! The stench of all theses bucks in this heat is disgusting! None of them have changed their clothes since Christmas.

CECIL: Shall I clear a space?

QUEEN: And leave me sat in the middle of it for all to gawp at? Use your brain, man! (*Pause, then in her head.*) If Shakespeare has dared to mock me in this play I don't want them watching to see how I take it. How can anyone find such love laughable? The pain of betrayal ... the public humiliation ... the poor old bitch couldn't keep her man ... she bought him but couldn't control him ... past it! Bacon better hadn't be right! If he is, Shakespeare will hang!

FESTE: (*Sings – Act 2 Sc 4.*)
Not a flower, not a flower sweet,
On my black coffin let there be strown;
Not a friend, not a friend greet
My poor corpse where my bones shall be thrown.

Scene 12

(*The rehearsal studio at Savoy Hill.*)

OLIVIA: ... Get you to your lord;
    I cannot love him: let him send no more ...

NESBITT: No! No! Much too loud, Enid!

OLIVIA: It's like dribbling into a drain-pipe! Really,
    I think you should find someone else. I'll never be any
    good at this.

NESBITT: You'll be very good, darling. It just needs a
    certain control we're not used to. It'll come.

OLIVIA: Then help me. Tell me what to do.

SIR TOBY BELCH: That goes for all of us, if I'm not
    mistaken.

MALVOLIO: Come on, Cathleen. Tell us what to do.

NESBITT: Good Lord, I can't really ... I'm struggling
    myself. We'll have to feel our way along.

SIR TOBY BELCH: What's going to make a good radio
    actor in your book?

NESBITT: Too early to tell, Henry. I go out and listen to
    scenes I'm not in over the speakers, but until we can
    record it, I'm really grasping at straws. I think you all
    sound marvellous, honestly ...

SIR TOBY BELCH: Don't soft-soap us now. It's quite
    unnerving not to know how we sound. We're performing
    in a vacuum.

REITH: (*On approach.*) That's not a bad way of looking at it,
    Mr ... er ...

SIR TOBY BELCH: Caine – Henry Caine. With respect,
    sir – that's no good to an actor. Like Nature, we abhor a
    vacuum.

REITH: Ah! But you must square up to the void and create
    an imaginary space: and, in that space, put one auditor!

OLIVIA: That lets me out. An audience of one?

REITH: Are you telling me that when you're on stage
    you're acting for all the people in the house? From my
    understanding, great actors aim at one person in the

audience, then universalise. That one person might as well be a microphone – someone who'll pick up every nuance, every meaning, and carry it to others. Come on. Rehearse the scene with me standing in as the microphone. Keep your positions. (*Pause.*) Well come on.

OLIVIA: I can't imagine you as a microphone, Major not in the terms you've described.

REITH: (*Coldly.*) You'd oblige me by doing as I ask Miss Rose.

OLIVIA: (*Very upset.*) I can't do it!

REITH: Miss Nesbitt, will you calm this person down. Tantrums are not my forte.

OLIVIA: That won't be necessary. (*Pause.*) You are a microphone, Major. You are the universe.

REITH: Proceed.

NESBITT: (*Quickly.*) Let's go from 'How does he love me?'

OLIVIA: How does he love me?

NESBITT: With adorations, fertile tears,
With groans that thunder, with sighs of fire.

OLIVIA: Your lord does know my mind; I cannot love him:
Yet I suppose him virtuous, know him noble ...

REITH: (*Abruptly.*) Thank you. Miss Nesbitt, I'd like to see you in my office straight away. (*Goes.*) Dismiss.
(*Door opens and closes.*)

MALVOLIO: (*Under his breath.*) Trouble!

FESTE: Dismiss! What does he think we are!

OLIVIA: (*In tears.*) I *was* trying!

SIR TOBY BELCH: (*Consoling.*) Of course you were ... (*Out.*)

Scene 13

(*REITH's office.*)

NESBITT: I know she can do it, Major (*Shutting door.*) She'll come round ...

REITH: I thrive on challenges, Miss Nesbitt – and I like what I do to mean something. Because of the visual

humour, *Twelfth Night* is the most difficult of
Shakespeare's plays to adapt for radio.

NESBITT: I hadn't thought about that. I've simply been too
busy trying to work out the logistics.

REITH: Well, I have to think of everything Miss Nesbitt.
Never mind the acting – what about the sound effects?
How will we do the storm, for instance?

NESBITT: Storm? What storm?

REITH: I don't want any crude theatre techniques – sheets of
tin and all that. We must use our equipment intelligently.

NESBITT: The storm has already been and gone by the
time the play starts, Major.

REITH: What? (*Pause.*) He uses storms so often one gets
very mixed up. That's right. The shipwreck is in the
past. The brother and sister have been cast up on the
shore of Illyria. But don't we have the play *because* of the
storm?

NESBITT: Well, I suppose one could argue ...

REITH: Very interested in *because*, Miss Nesbitt. The BBC
will always be interested in *because*. We will have a storm
effect as a kind of overture with someone blowing into
the microphone.

NESBITT: But won't having a storm upset people? People
who know the play.

REITH: Only academical pedants. A storm is an elemental
experience. Everyone's been in a storm. Everyone's been
knocked about by Nature. You must have been.

NESBITT: Yes, Major, I have.

REITH: Ramsay MacDonald made the connections for me.
You see – I had a very happy war. That had affected my
perception of how most people remember it. But we
cannot broadcast grief and bitterness. It has to be
channelled through great art. Therein lies the fusion of
happiness and misery, Miss Nesbitt – the binding of the
storm.

NESBITT: Now you've explained, Major – I think it's a
lovely idea.

REITH: A brushstroke of sound is all we need to start our play. Then, out of chaos and mayhem comes calm ... music ... reflection ... love. D'you catch my drift?

NESBITT: Oh, I do, I do!

REITH: The charm of the language. The power of simile and metaphor and oxymoron. The rhythm of human life beating through the decasyllabical blank verse. We must cut the play by an hour.

NESBITT: An hour!?

REITH: At your full rehearsal, I'm told the running-time was two hours fifty minutes, was it not?

NESBITT: But a whole hour!

REITH: We won't hold their attention.

NESBITT: Perhaps we could read it faster?

REITH: No – no gabbling! The wireless has many distractable folk among its listeners. They don't have either the background, the education, or the inclination to stay two hours and fifty minutes, even with such excellent company as Shakespeare.

NESBITT: Shall we call it Sixth Night?

REITH: Go for the essentials, Miss Nesbitt.

NESBITT: And what are those?

REITH: Ah, now you're being difficult.

NESBITT: No, I'm not. But cutting an hour ...

REITH: Every actor knows the heart of the play they're in.

NESBITT: Even if it's been hacked to pieces?

REITH: The world's greatest playwright will fall apart if a few words are lost? Come, come. There are many things we have to change to bring him up-to-date. Do we still have boys playing the female roles? Do we perform in the open air in the afternoon with no lighting and no costumes? This is a new medium, Miss Nesbitt.

NESBITT: I agree – but this will be the first play ever to go out on radio. Do we want to make butchery part of the business right from the start? Might we not be setting the very worst kind of precedent? People will want to write special plays for this medium. Is this the best way to provide encouragement? If we dismember Shakespeare, what might we not do to a newcomer's work?

REITH: Shakespeare has survived all this time without you as his defender, Miss Nesbitt.

NESBITT: But as what? We've only just got the original texts restored after centuries of mutilation? I'm not sure anyone's seen Shakespeare since the English Civil War – not as he truly is.

REITH: (*Irritated.*) Ah! You want me to make the cuts! Bring me the text! I can be ruthless. This is theatre for *all* the people, not a few.

NESBITT: No, no, Major. I'll do it, but under protest. The play falls into two themes – one comic, and one romantic. Where should the sacrifices be made?

REITH: A bit of both. Keep the love. Keep the laughter. Find what most engages the ear, not the eye. And move it along at a fair old clip!

NESBITT: An hour's an awful lot, Major. I'm not at all sure I can do it. We both love *Twelfth Night* so. You said …

REITH: Fifty minutes then. There's fifty minutes excess verbiage in any play. All *you* have to do is identify what's surplus to requirements.

FESTE: (*Sings. Voice over.*)
I am gone, sir,
And anon, sir,
I'll be with you again,
In a trice,
Like to the old Vice,
Your need to sustain.

Scene 14

(*Green Room at Savoy Hill.*)

MALVOLIO: Fifty minutes! The play will end up a thing of rags and tatters.

FESTE: He's out of his mind!

NESBITT: Old Staring Eyes doesn't think people have the stamina any more. Two hours is the absolute listening limit.

MALVOLIO: At school *Twelfth Night* is sanitised so we're not corrupted: if we listen to it when we're grown-up, it's shortened so we don't get bored. Are these now the two great principles of the Christian west?

Scene 15

(*The Middle Temple dining hall. A storm rages outside.*)

QUEEN: D'you know what this play is about, Cecil?

CECIL: Love – again!

QUEEN: You'd think there was nothing else to inspire our poets.

CECIL: They keep going back to it.

QUEEN: The piss of a lecher is ice water.

CECIL: If it please.

QUEEN: Watching a play about love must be quite a penance for you with your fondness for whores.

CECIL: Forgive the contradiction, but they are my favourites. I dislike histories because they are always little more than a patchwork of old lies. Tragedies are overblown and ridiculous. Comedies, in the main, I find fatuous. But a good, witty play about love passes a couple of hours very flavourfully.

QUEEN: And afterwards you believe you are loved?

CECIL: Oh, no, no. I'd never be that stupid.

QUEEN: What, then, have you gained?

CECIL: Relief from worse plays I might have been at.

QUEEN: (*Laughing.*) Go to. Bring me the author.

CECIL: Who am I bringing him to? He's already terrified, I hear. He suspects Bacon is scheming again.

QUEEN: As if I'd listen. Tell him an admirer wants him and if someone *is* going to die, I will not watch.

CECIL: If it makes you anxious, perhaps we should go now? There can be no guarantee that something won't remind you.

QUEEN: Bacon assures me *Twelfth Night* is light-hearted.
It's about the foolishness of lovers. No blood is shed.

CECIL: The destruction of my lord Essex was not only by
means of the axe.

QUEEN: How cruel of you to mention his name.

CECIL: He is wherever *you* are at the moment. His fate
originated in his folly – his vanity, ambition, stupidity –
all of which I'm sure you'll see tonight in another guise.

QUEEN: How can you be so sure?

CECIL: Because it is part comedy. I must caution you about
Master Bacon and his recommendations. He is a very
ruthless, self-seeking man.

QUEEN: Like everyone else around me. Wasn't giving the
nod for *Richard the Second* to be put on an inflammatory act?

CECIL: Not when it was written, but the occasion made it
so. Did Essex ask for anyone's permission to do anything
during those days of madness? Shakespeare knew
nothing of the liberties taken with his *Richard II.* We must
only blame what is blameable.

(*Outside the storm rises – cross into:*)

Scene 16

(*Room at Savoy Hill. Door opens.*)

REITH: May the editor of the immortal Bard be interrupted
in her deliberating?

NESBITT: I'm finding it a dreadful business, I must confess.
(*Door closes. Movement of furniture as he takes another chair to the
desk.*)

REITH: Where are we? Oh, dear. You're only on Act One.

NESBITT: I'm having to do it word by word, Major.

REITH: That's not the way. Cutting through anything is a
matter of decision-making – red-tape, corners, defensive
positions ... you have to take a line at least, preferably
the movement of one small idea ... Hmm, let's see now ...
Here! Later in the scene we have Malvolio sounding off
... nine lines, and eight from Olivia ... that could all go.

NESBITT: And a lot of the plot with it! That's the first time we learn about Malvolio's self-love and ridiculous pride.

REITH: But we find out later, don't we?

NESBITT: But the audience need the information *now*. That's why Shakespeare put it there.

REITH: I have a suspicion, Miss Nesbitt, that one of the ground rules of radio is the longer the speech the less it will be listened to. Too many words. Are we agreed – these go?

NESBITT: (*Boiling over.*) Then why are we attempting the play at all? That's the way he writes! With words!

REITH: Miss Nesbitt – remember out of chaos and mayhem comes calm. We need to fillet the text. To keep what's best and dispose of what's unnecessary.

NESBITT: And what right have you to do that?

REITH: What right did Shakespeare have to create his play? One he *assumed*. And we must do the same. Now, we'll leave those two long speeches since you think they're so important, but ...

(*Pages rapidly turned.*)

... here's a perfect example of what we can do without ... a big section of this scene ... What's all this nonsense? '... thou spokest of Pigrogromitus, of the Vapians passing the equinoctial of Queuebus: 'twas very good I'faith. I sent thee sixpence for thy leman ... ' They'll think we're mad if we broadcast that kind of gibberish. (*Out.*)

Scene 17

(*The Middle Temple dining hall. The storm blows outside. The audience chats as it waits for the play to start.*)

QUEEN: I am told that hidden inside any play you write there is another play. The trick is – how to find it?

SHAKESPEARE: That is said of many authors.

CECIL: I'm assured all ends happily.

QUEEN: To those who are ending unhappily that may not be much comfort. Don't be downcast. You're being teased.

SHAKESPEARE: To please you is my desire and hope.

QUEEN: What are you writing now?

SHAKESPEARE: Something based on an old Danish history.

QUEEN: Danish? Who is it comes from Denmark?

CECIL: King James of Scotland's wife, Anne.

QUEEN: We must think of Anne. Her man-loving husband hoped to succeed me here. What happens in this Danish play?

SHAKESPEARE: A young prince, Hamlet, sees the ghost of his father who tells him to revenge his murder.

QUEEN: Must all murder be revenged? My mother, Anne, was murdered by my father. Cut off her head. No revenge for that. A playwright might work one out – if he had the guts. But I'd handle it very carefully if I were you. Then there's the murder of someone's name – what of that? What revenge should be taken? (*Pause.*) So, your prince sees a ghost. I'll be a ghost soon. What d'you think of that?

SHAKESPEARE: I dare not think of it at all.

QUEEN: You dare think of anything – but you'll be subtle and secretive about it. I know you. Now, this ghost play whose writing haunts this play, has its own ghost. You must believe in them a lot. Are there any ghosts in this play we're about to see?

SHAKESPEARE: Er… no.

QUEEN: You had to think about it. I've been told it's about love.

SHAKESPEARE: That is so.

QUEEN: Who is in love?

SHAKESPEARE: Many people are in love.

QUEEN: Of what rank?

SHAKESPEARE: Er … a duke … a steward, with himself …

QUEEN: What women?

SHAKESPEARE: A serving-woman … a castaway, who's nobly born … a young widow.

QUEEN: I heard there is a duchess.

SHAKESPEARE: That's the young widow.

QUEEN: Ah. So no queens?

SHAKESPEARE: None.

QUEEN: Do all these lovers suffer?

SHAKESPEARE: They do, but in such a way it must not be taken too seriously.

QUEEN: You must be an artist of great ingenuity if you can take the seriousness out of suffering and leave anything worthwhile behind. Lord Cecil would trade all the world's beauty for a whore's inner thigh. Is there suffering in that?

SHAKESPEARE: Let me answer for him: limitation is suffering. The acceptance of limitation is freedom. (*Pause.*) There's no need for you to add to that, is there?

QUEEN: I find it very amusing to contemplate the idea that while you're with me at this moment, somewhere in your strange mind you're busily writing a play to please the queen who hopes to come after me.

SHAKESPEARE: Oh, no, Majesty!

QUEEN: Wouldn't you say it's too much of a coincidence, Cecil? He's writing a Danish play which will be ready for when I die? Make this Hamlet young, handsome and Frenchified. That's how King James likes them.

SHAKESPEARE: Is this still teasing? I am Your Majesty's most loyal subject.

QUEEN: There's no such thing. If Essex could betray me, anyone can! – even you! I'm suffering in this heat! Open the windows!

SHAKESPEARE: If we do that, all the candles will go out.

QUEEN: I'm dying! Is that what you want?

SHAKESPEARE: If we could move you to where there's ...

CECIL: Open all the windows!

(*Sound of people rushing around.*)

SHAKESPEARE: Stop them! Shield the candles!

(*Many windows being opened. The storm roars in. Shouts. Laughter.*)

(*Pause.*)

(*The storm abates.*)

SHAKESPEARE: (*In his head.*) Now you're inside Chaos.

QUEEN: Everything's gone dark! I *am* dying! I must speak ... settle the succession ... Cecil! Where are you?

CECIL: Here.

QUEEN: Get a clerk. Must dictate my will.

CECIL: I know, by my faith, this is not the time of your death. Trust me.

QUEEN: Now I'm cold. Hold me. It's terribly quiet.

CECIL: Shut all the windows and start the play!

(*Several large windows closed.*)

MASTER OF TEMPLE: But the actors will be in darkness.

CECIL: What difference will it make to them? She needs the play. Begin at once. That is an order!

MASTER OF TEMPLE: (*Moving to where SHAKESPEARE is.*) Master Shakespeare, we are commanded to begin.

SHAKESPEARE: Don't be ridiculous! No one can see anything!

MASTER OF TEMPLE: Let them stand and give their lines!

SHAKESPEARE: But their moves? Their expressions? Their gestures? Everything will be lost.

MASTER OF TEMPLE: We'll just have to imagine those for ourselves, won't we? (*Moves away.*)

SHAKESPEARE: (*To himself.*) I won't have this!

(*People bumping into each other. Some laughter. A chair is knocked over. Oaths.*)

BURBAGE: Is that you, Will?

SHAKESPEARE: There's a curse on me. I know it.

BURBAGE: Get the candles lit, for God's sake!

SHAKESPEARE: Everything will be ruined! (*To himself, seething.*) God damn that mad old bitch! Why couldn't she have stayed at home?

BURBAGE: Steady on!

SHAKESPEARE: Why don't you get on with it and die?

BURBAGE: Shut up, Will!

SHAKESPEARE: She's destroying my play!

BURBAGE: Who was the idiot who had the windows opened?

CECIL: Whoever's preventing the play from starting will
    answer to me! If anyone does not recognise the sound of
    my voice, come over here and find out who I am!

SHAKESPEARE: It's not possible! We can't do it!

CECIL: Who's that?

SHAKESPEARE: The author. It's out of the question!

CECIL: Come over here!

   (*Sound of SHAKESPEARE blundering across.*)

QUEEN: You said your play is about love.

SHAKESPEARE: It is so ... but ...

QUEEN: What's strange about love in the dark? Does it
    frighten you, Master Shakespeare?

SHAKESPEARE: No, ma'am. But there're parts of the play
    cannot work without being seen.

QUEEN: Don't talk about those. Make us work for our
    understanding. I'm most interested in what you have to
    say about love.

SHAKESPEARE: It's a play about mistakes – people
    falling in love with what they think they see.

QUEEN: They are deceived?

SHAKESPEARE: Yes.

QUEEN: So, Bacon was right. It is about me.

SHAKESPEARE: No. It is ...

QUEEN: (*Interrupting.*) Who has been more deceived in love
    than I?

SHAKESPEARE: We will do the play as you wish. Please
    forgive the additional imperfections that will arise.
    Could we wait for just a few candles to be re-lit, for the
    sake of entrances and exits.

QUEEN: No. Let them do it in complete darkness. My
    darkness.

SHAKESPEARE: As Your Majesty commands. (*Calls.*)
    Beginners! Music!

   (*A concert of viols strikes up, plays, stops.*)

QUEEN: They play as if they can see. Do any of us need
    our eyes, except to be beguiled?

ORSINO: If music be the food of love, play on;
   Give me excess of it, that, surfeiting,
   The appetite may sicken and so die ...
QUEEN: (*Sharply.*) Ah! No death.
ORSINO: That strain again! It had a dying fall:
QUEEN: Ah! More death and so few words yet spoken!
SHAKESPEARE: Only touched upon ... passing references
   ... (*Under his breath.*) Come on, start the music again!
   (*The concert of viols strikes up.*)
ORSINO: O, it came oe'er my ear like the sweet sound,
   That breathes upon a bank of violets,
   Stealing and giving odor!
   (*The QUEEN sighs.*)
   Enough: no more:
   'Tis not so sweet now as it was before.
   (*Music stops.*)
QUEEN: (*To herself.*) 'Tis not so sweet now ...
ORSINO: O spirit of love! How quick and fresh art thou ...

Scene 18

(*Savoy Hill studio. In background door opens and closes.*)
ORSINO: O spirit of love! How quick and fresh art thou ...
REITH: Sorry I'm late. I know you are just commencing
   with the first scene but I have some thoughts I wish to
   share with you as actors. Miss Nesbitt – I haven't been
   entirely honest with you.
NESBITT: Major, we've had to come to terms ... Let's not
   go over all that again, please.
REITH: I couldn't be completely straightforward until
   we'd approved the cuts. Thank you so much for your
   understanding. Our dictator here at the BBC will
   always be the clock. Now, I called this meeting in order
   to infuse enthusiasm and bind the bleeding wounds of
   the text. We are not Philistines here.
SIR TOBY BELCH: I think the text has been improved, sir.
   Far too many old jokes.

REITH: Question: How dare I, a mechanical engineer by profession, take a spanner to Shakespeare?

FESTE: You're the boss.

REITH: Yes, I am Mr Hayes – but apart from that. (*Pause.*) Would it occur to you that a man who's built locomotives is good at making things work?

FESTE: If a play were a locomotive I think you'd have a very good argument.

REITH: Both take us from A to B. A play's plot is a set of rails. Enough of that. Because it's Shakespeare's most subversive piece of work, its cutting edge must be as sharp as possible. When the middle classes hear their old favourite this time, it will penetrate their minds as it has never done before. They'll *hear* its meaning, having never *seen* it before.

MALVOLIO: Will you share that thought a little further with us?

REITH: It is Shakespeare's attack on the visual. What the play says is: never trust the evidence of your eyes. Do not be deceived by appearances.

FESTE: Is that so subversive? It sounds like common-sense to me.

REITH: Shakespeare was a prophet. He knew one of the senses would betray mankind. Anything to do with the eye has been under suspicion for three hundred years. Every philosopher worth his salt has shared Shakespeare's scepticism about the value of the visible.

NESBITT: We would prefer to be positive, Major. Some of us look forward to working in the cinema as well.

REITH: Is that acting? I've always thought of it as skating on the thin ice of superficiality, sentiment and handsome profiles. The cinema will lead us into the desert, but the radio, intelligently managed can be our guide to the oasis. (*Studio sound-proof doors open and close.*)

FESTE: Now, that's what I call a pep-talk. Before he opened his mouth I thought I knew what I was doing.

NESBITT: Well, he's putting our work into a larger context – which is his job. I can't say I go along with him, entirely ...

MALVOLIO: If it's the most difficult of all Shakespeare's plays to make work on radio, why did he choose it?

SIR TOBY BELCH: He told you. It's a challenge: and, as actors, we must rise to it.

FESTE: Easier said than done. One can't help thinking there must be a basic technique for acting on the air but I haven't the faintest idea what it is. I'd better find out soon because the old skinflint's got me playing three parts!

OLIVIA: I'm simply going to seduce the microphone.

MALVOLIO: That's it. Do what you do best, eh, darling?

OLIVIA: Oh, do shut up! Have you got any better ideas?

STUDIO MANAGER: (*Talk back.*) Can you come into the cubicle for a moment, Miss Nesbitt?

FESTE: Did anyone hear the excerpts that young Gielgud chap did with Ben Webster from the Scottish play? Made me feel most odd.

SIR TOBY BELCH: Why, for God's sake? It was perfectly straightforward.

FESTE: Made me think about desperation differently. Sounded almost a new play. 'Out, out, brief candle' put me back in the war.

SIR TOBY BELCH: I don't think about the war if I can help it. I certainly don't want it in my work.

OLIVIA: Banquo's bloody ghost bring back memories?

SIR TOBY BELCH: Lay off!

STUDIO MANAGER: (*Talk back.*) Stand by to rehearse!

OLIVIA: Only asking why you can't bear cross-references. A normal mind does it all the time.

MALVOLIO: No such thing. Every mind is abnormal in my book. But I'll tell you what worries me – Act Three, Scene Four can never work on microphone in a thousand years. My big scene too.

NESBITT: (*Coming into the studio.*) Listen everyone. Note from the studio engineer. Please remember to turn the pages of your scripts over very carefully. These microphones are so sensitive.

OLIVIA: Ah, poor things!

(*Laughter.*)

Scene 19

(*The Middle Temple dining hall.*)

VIOLA: There is a fair behaviour in thee, captain;
　　And though that nature with a beauteous wall
　　Doth oft close in pollution ...

QUEEN: Oh, Robert ...

VIOLA:　　　　　　　　　　... yet of thee
　　I will believe thou hast a mind that suits
　　With this thy fair and outward character ...

QUEEN: Oh, Robert ... why?

SHAKESPEARE: (*Whispering.*) How is she taking it?

CECIL: She sighs.

QUEEN: O, Robert, Robert ... forgive me.

CECIL: Cover your ears, man. Let us not listen. She's up on Tower Hill on the day Essex was beheaded.

SHAKESPEARE: (*In his head.*) Sharing her displeasure with that reptile Bacon is the only satisfaction I'll get. (*Pause.*) *Hamlet* lies half-done. Who'll mourn for him, never mind the headless Essex?

MARIA: ... you must confine yourself within the modest limits of order.

SIR TOBY BELCH: Confine! I'll confine myself no finer than I am ...

(*Some laughter, not too positive.*)

　　... these clothes are good enough to drink in ...

SHAKESPEARE: (*In his head, bitterly.*) Which clothes?

(*More laughter behind SHAKESPEARE's line.*)

SIR TOBY BELCH: ... and so be these boots too ...

SHAKESPEARE: (*In his head.*) O, very fine boots!

SIR TOBY BELCH: ... and be they not, let them hang themselves in their own straps!

(*Big laugh.*)

SHAKESPEARE: (*In his head.*) Why are they laughing at what they can't see. (*Pause.*) Why do I fear a death I don't know? She is laughing with the rest.

(*Laughter then cross into the QUEEN laughing alone.*)

FESTE: (*Sings. Voice over.*)

When I was and a little tiny boy,
With hey ho, the wind and the rain,
A foolish thing was but a toy,
For the rain it raineth every day.

Scene 20

(*REITH's office – Savoy Hill.*)

REITH: What's this Miss Nesbitt? A deputation?

NESBITT: We've had such arguments over what we need to talk to you about, we thought it best if a few of us came. I hope you don't mind. (*Door shuts.*)

REITH: No, no. Sit down, sit down. Tell me what's on the collective mind.

NESBITT: Well, we've rehearsed, and tried to imagine ourselves as listeners ...

REITH: Good.

NESBITT: Perhaps Mr Waring should explain?

MALVOLIO: Well sir, we can't make the best scene in the play work. It happens to be mine. As Malvolio ...

REITH: Don't tell me which one that is. I already know. You can't create a moment of comic triumph by swaggering on in yellow hose and cross-garters if no one can see them. And you can't have one of my announcers saying: Enter Malvolio in yellow hose and cross-garters. Too obvious.

MALVOLIO: Exactly.

NESBITT: We know Shakespeare sets it up in the preceding scene that Malvolio is going to do this, but even so, it doesn't seem to be enough. We feel the play might – could – fall flat on its face.

REITH: And you haven't been able to solve this little problem?

SIR TOBY BELCH: No, sir. That's why we've come to you. We're snookered.

REITH: I thought as actors you'd crack it between you. Ah, well.

NESBITT: You won't cut the cross-garters, will you? I couldn't bear that.

REITH: On this Miss Nesbitt, I'd rather cut my own throat.

Scene 21

(*REITH in bed with his wife, MURIEL. A bedside clock ticks.*)

REITH: Muriel, you awake?

MURIEL: Of course.

REITH: You sense my disquiet?

MURIEL: What's troubling you?

REITH: I don't like to admit defeat – but the actors came to me with a problem I can't solve. I've consulted professors, everyone I can think of. They can't help.

MURIEL: Then you must be honest with the actors.

REITH: Honest? When they look up to me so much, Muriel? I mustn't lose the impression of infallibility.

MURIEL: Tell me the problem, John, then we can go to sleep.

REITH: We call it the Act Three, Scene Four question. How can Malvolio make his crucial entrance in yellow hose and cross-garters if no one can see them?

MURIEL: Yes, I'd thought about that. The humour does rather hinge on that scene.

REITH: Defeat, you see. We'll never be able to show anything, *ever*!

MURIEL: Just like your father couldn't, John. That didn't mean he'd failed his congregation, did it?

REITH: What? You wonderful woman! (*Kisses her.*) Thank God I married the oracle!

Scene 21

(*The Middle Temple dining room. The QUEEN's sighs and laughter alternate.*)

SHAKESPEARE: (*In his head.*) Listen to her. In the darkness she swings from sorrow to laughter and back again like a branch in the wind. When the play's over, where will her mind settle?

QUEEN: O, droll! Droll!

SHAKESPEARE: If I believed it was her honest need that playwrights live as cowards, I'd never pick up pen again. Why should any man with wits and strength choose to undermine his visions and waste what Nature puts his way?

QUEEN: A palpable hit!

SHAKESPEARE: Must remember that for *Hamlet.*

(*Laughter.*)

BURBAGE: If thou entertainest my love, let it appear in thy smiling: thy smiles become thee well: therefore in my presence still smile, dear my sweet, I prithee.

(*Loud laughter.*)

CECIL: (*Whispering.*) Master Shakespeare, the influential old 'gentleman' begs for an opportunity to get his breath back. Let us have an interval ...

BURBAGE: Jove, I thank thee: I will smile ...

(*Laughter.*)

BURBAGE: I will do everything that thou wilt have me.

SHAKESPEARE: Has she been laughing?

CECIL: Yes. It's a long time since she has done that. Congratulations! Tell the actors to break off at a suitable point and we will light the candles.

(*Cross into hubbub at the interval.*)

BACON: Do we need the stage, Lord Cecil? Costumes disappoint. Scenery is silly. Most actors are ugly. We'd get less annoyed with the theatre if all plays were performed in the dark, perhaps?

CECIL: I get the impression it's one particular playwright who annoys you, Bacon.

BACON: Not as a playwright, my lord. Only as a meddler in matters of state. Ah, Will, my dear man – well done. You have taught us not to trust our eyes tonight.

SHAKESPEARE: What to trust, and who not to trust, is well learnt, Bacon.

CECIL: Which is what this play is about, I believe. Am I right?

SHAKESPEARE: My lord, we have half of it yet to go.

CECIL: Then, I'll decide at the end.

BACON: Oh, I don't need to stay that long. I have business to attend to. It's obvious what will happen. Could I have a word with ... er ...

CECIL: She's resting. I'm afraid Bacon. *And* smiling.

BACON: If we cannot trust ourselves to love with some discrimination – where are we? The enemy of good sense is instinct. Augustine urges us to understand the inner beast and strictly tame it. (*Goes.*)

CECIL: There goes a disappointed man. (*Laughs.*)

SHAKESPEARE: But still a dangerous man.

QUEEN: (*From a little distance.*) Cecil!

CECIL: (*Moving over to her.*) I'm here.

QUEEN: Put out the candles. Let us carry on with the play.

Scene 23

(*Savoy Hill studio. The CAST chat and murmur.*)

REITH: Good evening, gentles.

CAST: Good evening, Major.

REITH: I've just come in to do my opening storm, then I shall leave you to it.

STUDIO MANAGER: One minute to go, sir. (*Talk back.*)

REITH: I played Malvolio at school, you know? It's a part for a tall man ... Who's playing Malvolio?

MALVOLIO: Still me.

REITH: You're far too short for anything but radio. What a boon the new medium is for men handicapped as you are. And I've solved Act Three, Scene Four. Radio drama will always be in two acts: an act of faith and an act of imagination.

MALVOLIO: Is that all?

REITH: To keep the arts human and not divine, each one has a curse upon it – painting is shallow, statues are cold, music is vague. Radio drama has the yellow hose and cross-garters problem.

MALVOLIO: Well, thank you for trying, Major.

REITH: You're not convinced?

MALVOLIO: Of the impossibility – yes. Ah, well.

REITH: And where are all things possible? On that stage in the mind.

MALVOLIO: Don't worry, Major. I'll have to grin and bear it.

REITH: Answer me this – when you come to Act Three, Scene Four will you, as an actor, be wearing cross-garters?

MALVOLIO: Well ... I'm not in costume, am I? I'm standing here with a script in my hand. (*Pause.*) I see what you mean.

REITH: With your inner eye – you see what I mean, you mean?

STUDIO MANAGER: (*Talk back.*) We're about to start. Just a little closer to the microphone, please, sir. When you step away, tread softly.

REITH: How does a storm tread softly?

(*Muted laughter.*)

STUDIO MANAGER: (*Talk back.*) Ssssh. Going ahead in five seconds Mr Lewis 5 – 4 – 3 – 2 – 1 –

ANNOUNCER: *Twelfth Night*, by William Shakespeare.

(*REITH blows into the microphone and creates his storm.*)

Scene 24

(*Cross to REITH's home and MURIEL listening to the storm on the wireless.*)

MURIEL: (*To herself, tongue in cheek.*) Utterly convincing, darling. Is there anything you can't do?

ANNOUNCER: In a part of the past, a great storm at sea has wrecked the ship carrying a well-born brother and sister. Unbeknown to each, both have survived, believing the other to have perished. Their names are Viola and Sebastian.

(*Music. Purcell's 'Amphitryon'.*)

MURIEL: (*To herself.*) Act Three, Scene Four. How on earth are they going to do it?

OLIVIA: Go call him hither.

(*Sound of MARIA leaving.*)

OLIVIA: I am as mad as he.
If sad and merry madness equal be.

(*Footsteps approach.*)

MALVOLIO: Ho-ho-ho-ho!

OLIVIA: Smilest thou?

MURIEL: What's the difference between a smile and a laugh? (*Laughs.*)

Scene 25

(*The Middle Temple dining hall.*)

OLIVIA: I am as mad as he,
If sad and merry madness be. How now Malvolio?

(*Footsteps approach. Groans.*)

BURBAGE: Sad, lady! I could be sad: this does make some obstruction in the blood, this cross-gartering ...

(*Burst of laughter.*)

SHAKESPEARE: (*In his head.*) They've cut three lines, the bastards! (*Pause.*) But it worked, somehow. It worked.

(*Cross on laughter into applause.*)

Scene 26

(*A private room at the Middle Temple.*)

QUEEN: You have proved to us that the voice is our purest and most potent part. I'm going on somewhere to listen to some music. Come with me.

SHAKESPEARE: If I may have a moment to speak to the actors ...

QUEEN: Don't keep me waiting too long.

Scene 27

(*On the way to the dressing room.*)

CECIL: Come here!

SHAKESPEARE: My lord Cecil?

CECIL: You are not to speak of where she takes you, on pain of your life.

SHAKESPEARE: Where ... my lord ...

CECIL: (*Moving away.*) The Queen will not be there, only the woman.

Scene 28

(*The dressing room. Excitement, laughter.*)

BURBAGE: Have you spoken to her, Will?

SHAKESPEARE: Yes.

BURBAGE: What did she say?

SHAKESPEARE: How handsome you are in the dark.

BURBAGE: Don't be funny. I thought they'd all walk out. But they stayed. They liked it. And they couldn't see a thing!

SHAKESPEARE: I have to go with her. She's waiting.

BURBAGE: Where's she taking you?

SHAKESPEARE: I don't know, exactly.

BURBAGE: Don't like the sound of that. Are you sure she liked it?

SHAKESPEARE: What are you hinting at?

BURBAGE: Well, at the interval I heard a couple of courtiers talking about what she used to make Essex do when they were alone. She was nearly seventy and past it, really. He was half her age and couldn't get enthusiastic. So she made him put on yellow hose and cross-garters and dance about for her.

SHAKESPEARE: Aaaah!

FESTE: (*Sings. Voice over.*)
> But when I came at last to wive,
> With hey, ho, the wind and the rain,
> By swaggering could I never thrive,
> For the rain it raineth every day.

Scene 29

(*A carriage in motion.*)

QUEEN: Francis Bacon is a brilliant man but I'd never listen to him on what to see. I can never like him, not after he destroyed Essex at the trial as the Crown prosecutor. He was too good at it. No, I came to your play for company and found even more than I'd hoped for.

SHAKESPEARE: I cannot say how happy that makes me.

QUEEN: It's about time someone put me in a play. When I'm dead I expect all the carrion-eaters to be dipping their pens in my blood, but it's much better to be explored alive, don't you think?

SHAKESPEARE: All my work is yours.

QUEEN: How did you know about the yellow hose and cross-garters?

SHAKESPEARE: It's a very strange thing, but I can't remember.

QUEEN: Gossip, probably. Thinking about it – if I'd actually been able to see at that point, it might have been too painful. The man Burbage doesn't have the looks my Robert had – though Malvolio has features of his character. Vanity. Oh, how vain he was. How did you put it? 'If I please the eye of one, it is with me as the very true sonnet is: 'Please one, please all.'

SHAKESPEARE: Er ... if IT please, not I ...

QUEEN: No matter. It was well-aimed.

SHAKESPEARE: I would not have you think that.

QUEEN: Oh, don't be so craven, man! Haven't I made a fool of myself many times and risen above it? Haven't my love's labours been lost? Hasn't this shrew been tamed? As I like it isn't how I got it.

Scene 30

(*A private chapel. John Shepherd's 'Gaude, Gaude, Gaude Maria' is being sung.*)

QUEEN: For the sake of the state, the church, and the people, it is forbidden to listen to these pure sounds. But, now and again, I find I have to, even at the risk of being called a papist. Just as I had to love at the risk of being called an old fool.

SHAKESPEARE: Is this being sung just for you?

QUEEN: It's a long-kept passion. This music was made for Candlemas. For the Purification of the Virgin. So, I say it's for me. But I'm the one who forbids it. Since I'm sitting here with you listening we must ask – are we in England?

SHAKESPEARE: I know exactly where we are.

QUEEN: No. We're still in your Illyria where there are laws and punishments but they're all make-believe. You cannot deny this music no matter what your Church says.

SHAKESPEARE: John Shepherd would have been happy to hear this, after all that's happened.

QUEEN: I thought you'd know the piece. My father loved it. My brother banned it. My sister used it. And I have buried it where it can be found. Pray your work doesn't suffer the same treatment at the hand of princes.

SHAKESPEARE: Amen.

(*Fade music.*)

FESTE: (*Sings. Voive over.*)

A great while ago the world begun,
With hey ho, the wind and the rain,
But that's all one, our play is done,
And we'll strive to please you every day.

The End.

BEEF

Giles Cooper Award 1981

For Michael McKay

Beef was first broadcast on BBC Radio 3 on the 9th of April 1981. The cast was as follows:

CUSACK, Richard Leech

MAEVE, Fiona Victory

CON, Garrett Keogh

CUCKOO, Gerard Mannix Flynn

ALI, Sean Caffrey

FERGUS, James Donnelly

JANET, Anne Haydn

DIRECTION, Ian Cotterell

An abattoir yard. Fade in the buzzing of an electric razor. The buzzing stops. There is a click and the sound of the cuttings being blown out of the razor.

CUSACK: Good people, good morning! If I used a cut-throat razor on meself this morning it would live up to its name. It was a wild old time in Dublin last night. Missed the last bus home and slept here at the abattoir, my place of work, having my own key as a trusted man. A question for you: would someone who made his bed in a slaughterhouse be haunted by the ghosts of cattle?

(A key turns in the lock of the personnel door in the big yard gate.)

Ah, that'll be Mr Sheehan. No flies on him, I can tell you.

(The door opens, then closes with a bang. But the lock is not set.)

Good morning, Mr Sheehan.

CON: Morning Cusack! What do you make the time?

CUSACK: A quarter past seven.

CON: What's happening then? Where's the rest of the lads?

CUSACK: Give yourself time to arrive, Mr Sheehan ...

CON: Everyone should be getting ready by now. We have a busy day ahead of us.

CUSACK: Don't start getting het up now. Relax for a minute. Mr Sheehan, you know that we've been doing these Sunday overtime shifts on worn-out cattle all this year and, nothing daunted, you called another for today of all days.

CON: The whole of Irish industry can't grind to a halt just because the Pope's here, you know.

CUSACK: Oh, agreed! But on Friday there were mutterings from the locker room when I put it to the lads that they might turn out this morning.

CON: I did anticipate resistance from the genuinely devout churchgoers; i.e., none of them. They wouldn't turn down eight hours at double-time twelve weeks from Christmas, not these greedy beggars.

CUSACK: Mr Sheehan, as I was circulating in the city last night, traipsing round from house of religion to house of religion in search of peace, I bumped into the lads, many of them on their knees, and I got the impression that none of them had the slightest intention of reporting here for work this morning.

CON: Are you saying that we haven't got a shift?

CUSACK: The great mass that the Pope held in the Phoenix Park was just too much for them, and the little masses that followed well into the night obliterated all sense of practical reality.

CON: Is everyone who's employed here an alcoholic or something?

CUSACK: Oh, be fair, Mr Sheehan. You've been working them hard lately. They haven't had a day off for months.

CON: They get paid don't they? What more do they want?

CUSACK: You must be making a packet out of this work we do on the side. Couldn't you give the staff a backhander once in a while?

CON: That's neither here nor there, is it? Are we working today or not?

CUSACK: All, right. I just thought I'd mention it. Don't worry. I fixed everything.

CON: With no labour? Who's going to do the job? You and me? Listen, those two bulls we've got coming in are colossal creatures, old as the hills, tough as nails. It will take every man we've got to handle them.

CUSACK: Mr Sheehan, everything is under control. Last night I moved around in the twilight world I favour for a Saturday night out. I like a wander into the old haunts that haven't changed for centuries. The talk is good and the music unparalleled. You can get any job you like done down there. All you have to do is put the word out on the grapevine.

CON: Don't tell me you mean casuals?

CUSACK: Fine men, in general. Devils for work.

CON: Christ almighty, Cusack! You can't use casuals in highly-specialised slaughtering! I need trained men!

CUSACK: And you'll have them. I put the word out that only experts need bother to turn up.

CON: What about the union? They'll go mad.

CUSACK: I squared it with the union. They're not bothered. They say that if our lads don't want the overtime and it's an urgent job, then we should use temporary labour.

CON: I'm very doubtful, Cusack, old son. It strikes me that you've made a mess of the arrangements.

CUSACK: I haven't. Everything will be all right.

CON: You know this contract is for our biggest customer.

CUSACK: The importance of the job has not escaped me. I wouldn't disappoint a British pet-food company for the world.

CON: If we let them down ...

CUSACK: Unthinkable. Unthinkable. Would I heap more pain and frustration on the heads of people with licensing laws like they've got?

(*The sound of a newspaper being unfolded and shaken out. Pause.*)

CUSACK: Your Sunday newspaper is a thick and juicy one, plenty of colour in it today.

CON: I like to keep up-to-date, as you know. No doubt your own choice of literature is more mind improving.

CUSACK: Literature? D'you think I'd call this literature? Never!

(*The pages of a book being riffled.*)

CUSACK: Solid sex and violence. Not recommended for children or those of delicate sensibilities. To be kept away from those who cannot stand the sight of blood, like yourself.

CON: Lay off, will you Cusack?

(*The newspaper being shaken with irritation.*)

CUSACK: Who else would the authorities make boss of a slaughterhouse over my head.

(*The book being riffled.*)

CUSACK: You should try reading this book, perhaps, Mr Sheehan. It might improve your knowledge of the world today, even though it was written way back. It's an old Irish fantasy called *The Cattle Raid of Cooley*. It will make you laugh, so it will. It's all lies and exaggerations, lies for the enjoyment of idiots.

CON: Idiots like you?

CUSACK: Idiots like me? No, idiots like all of us, Mr Sheehan, all of us.

CON: I'll stick to my paper, if you don't mind. (*Pause.*) Well, it looks as though the Pope has become a national hero overnight. The man is a veritable star. I see he's off in the old helicopter to the monastery at Clonmacnois this morning.

CUSACK: Did you get to the mass in the Phoenix Park yesterday?

CON: No, I watched it at home on the box. Very moving. I admire this Pope tremendously. You could feel the integrity and radiance coming out of him, and that being said by a man with no religion. I tell you, he has the power and charisma to change the political situation in Ireland right now. There's a great mood of optimism running through the country.

CUSACK: You're right. It was there last night until closing-time.

CON: The gunmen will be listening and watching everything that he does and says on television. It will affect them, you'll see.

CUSACK: The gunmen? Whoever thought they watched TV? Their behaviour would be ten times worse if they did. I think they'd be a lot better off with a good read of the old *Cattle Raid of Cooley*.

(*The book is riffled. The uproar of drunks at a distance.*)

CON: Will you listen to that? People going off to early morning mass in that condition. Is it any wonder that some of us turn to science for comfort?

CUSACK: Atrocious behaviour. Quite unforgivable.

CON: Do you know, they calculate that by the time the Pope leaves he will have been seen, in the flesh, by three quarters of the people of Ireland?

CUSACK: And here you have the consequences roaming the streets.

(*The uproar of drunks getting nearer.*)

CON: Straight out of the boozer into the church.

(*A rattle of bones.*)

CUCKOO: Death, blood and fury.

CON: Aaah! Get away! (*Pause.*) Where the hell did you spring from?

CUCKOO: I did the jump over the poisoned stroke and made it a little higher than usual. I think I'll have to open that door.

CON: As soon as you like, my friend, then get out of here.

CUCKOO: White bones, staring sockets, flowers in skulls. What a morning.

CON: On your way then, and good luck to you.

(*The sound of the door in the gate being opened.*)

CUCKOO: Come in, come in.

ALI: Is this the place, Cuckoo?

(*Chinking, rattling. Pause.*)

CON: Good God!

CUCKOO: This is the place.

FERGUS: Good. I've carried this for enough.

(*The sound of a big bundle being dropped with a crash. It rattles.*)

CON: Hey, don't put your stuff down now. You're not stopping. About turn you lot and out!

(*Chinking, rattling. A little mild laughter.*)

CON: Look, I'm instructing you to get off this property! You're trespassing! (*Pause.*) Well, don't just stand there with your mouth open, Cusack, do something!

CUSACK: What, exactly?

CON: Get these piss-heads out of here.

CUSACK: All right, all right. It's only a bunch of lads having a laugh. What would you say you were, eh?

Mods, rockers, skin-heads, or just travelling people?
Don't get excited now, Mr Sheehan. Leave them to me.
Now, what would a collection of obvious vegetarians like
yourselves be doing in a place of this nature?

ALI: There's an important job that needs to be done. We're
here to do it.

CUSACK: What kind of a job?

ALI: Slaughtering.

CUSACK: Mr Sheehan, I think we have been found by the
casuals.

CON: No, I'm not having that drunken rabble in here.
Go on, hop it!

CUSACK: Do you know the work?

ALI: As good as anyone ever did.

CUSACK: Cash in hand. No question asked. I think these are
good lads, Mr Sheehan. I like the look of the four of them.

CON: No, definitely! They're filthy dirty.

CUSACK: A good scrub and some disinfectant will cure
that. Once we've got them in the white coats and the
white wellies with the rubber gloves on they'll be
unrecognisable from ordinary clean and decent people.

CON: They stink. These clothes are falling off them.

CUSACK: Oh, we can't afford to be choosy today,
Mr Sheehan. Now, will you supervise them directly,
yourself, or shall I appoint a leader from within the
group?

MAEVE: I'm already their leader, and don't you forget it.

CON: It's a woman under all that clobber! A bloody woman!

ALI: Maeve will supervise.

MAEVE: Naturally, Ali, naturally.

CON: I'm not having a woman working here!

MAEVE: What have you got against women? Not your
weapon I'll be bound.

CON: That's it! Enough is enough.

CUSACK: Leave it to me, Mr Sheehan. I'm sorting it out
for you, aren't I?

CON: I don't know what's got into you today, Cusack.

CUCKOO: (*Chanting.*) Heroes dealing death like cards!
Heads hacked off, blood spurting, Swords crashing, men screaming,

CON: All right, all right. My clerk here will settle this. It's in your hands, Cusack.

(*Slight fade.*)

CUSACK: Well, you're a sight for sore eyes, my friends. I'm glad you could make it.

MAEVE: We made the beginning, Cusack. It is only right that we should make the end.

CUCKOO: I heard the Pope give the druid's snapping-mouth and the high hero's scream down in Drogheda yesterday.

ALI: It was a great moment, Cuckoo, wasn't it, my boy? Yes, he demanded a change in us all. Speaking in a voice of thunder which could be heard for miles, he shouted that the old times were over. Then he flew into the air, roaring and swaying in the wind.

FERGUS: You know how long we've waited for peace, Cusack. No one will believe it but the hero longs for nothing else, so he can rest and dream of the old days. He does not want his deeds repeated. Isn't that so, Ali?

CON: I'm leaving it to you, Cusack, old son, just as you said ...

MAEVE: The bulls are on the move then?

CUSACK: At first light this morning they started out.

MAEVE: I can feel the land tensed up, waiting for the brunt of it.

CUSACK: It will be a blow of catastrophic proportions.

CUCKOO: (*Chanting.*) The great brown bull of Ulster,
The huge white bull of the South;
Ravens have followed them always,
Women have grieved while filling
Their hoof-marks with tears
Where they roam are the roads of blood.

CON: Cusack, old son ... make a move, eh? Out, if you don't mind. Now. Immediately ...

FERGUS: (*Chanting.*) The field of slaughter bloomed red with body-flowers, white with bone-blossoms blue with staring eyes, green with bile, brown with bowel; all the colours were there to entertain the ravens, kindle the kite's appetite.

CUCKOO: There will be such a shuddering! Such a shaking! Great feats of strength! (*To CON.*) Would you like to see me do the hardest feat of all? Stepping on a spear in flight, then straightening erect on its point.

CON: Lad, I'm sorry for you. You're wasting your breath.

CUCKOO: Climbing up a spear then performing a dance on its point without making the soles of the feet bleed? It's easy when you know how.

CON: Is it indeed? No doubt you're the only man in the world who can strike a match on wet soap. Push off, will you?

CUCKOO: We're not wanted, Maeve. All that journey for nothing. They don't want us. What do they care about the bulls?

MAEVE: We'll do what we came to do. Help him. Don't let him get into his doom-slide. Come now, Cuckoo. What do we care if we're wanted or not? Did we expect a great reception when it has all been spent on the Pope? We just have our task to perform.

CUCKOO: Who will watch us? Who cares?

MAEVE: History will care, and the future.

ALI: Come, rest your head, Cuckoo. Remember how hard it is to be a hero in your own time, never mind someone else's.

MAEVE: His hair is as rough as a winter thorn bush. Well, we brought something of our own with us. They last well, these lice. Your hair is teeming with them Cuckoo ...

CON: Oh no, lice! In here! We'll have to go through the whole place with a fumigator ... Do something, Cusack! They're crawling with vermin!

MAEVE: The big ones are helping the little ones over the gaps between the hairs. Why, here's a crowd camped

just above the curve of your ear. They're lighting fires,
cooking meat, posting sentries ...

ALI: Oooooh, Cuckoo, I can see a hundred heroes in here
arming themselves before dawn, strapping on harness,
rubbing grease into their chariot-axles. Whay! Here's a
gang of stone-slingers, whirling away in your head. Get
ready to duck!

CON: Cusack!

CUSACK: Sssssssssh! You're taking a risk with yourself,
Mr Sheehan.

CON: Bloody vermin! They'll be leaping all over the
premises. Look, Cusack, old son, these ruffians are a
health-hazard. Get rid of them!

(*A low, constant musical humming.*)

CUCKOO: We should go back, Maeve. It won't work.

MAEVE: It will, I promise you. We will do it, together.
Don't despair, Cuckoo. Your strength will still be needed.
True courage is in short supply.

CON: Don't let the bastards fall asleep! We'll never get rid
of them. They're not relatives of yours are they? Those
nephews from Galway?

CUSACK: Oh, we all have a spot of their blood in our
veins, Mr Sheehan. Aren't we all heroes on the sly, when
no one is looking? But treat them carefully. They're not
in a mood to be fooled with.

CON: Neither am I. As manager of this place ...

CUSACK: Come off it, will you? All that's out in the open
now. You stand exposed. Don't forget, I know ... I know.
There are more lice in your mind than there are in his
head. D'you know what the staff call you?

CON: I don't. Nor do I care.

CUSACK: Can't you face a little truth like that?
(*Pause.*)

CON: Cusack, old son, er ... I can see that I've upset you
somehow. I must admit, I don't know why ...

CUSACK: They call you 'Slackarse'.

CON: Good of them. Cusack, old son, is it anything to do with that salary increase I put you up for but you didn't get. Now that wasn't my fault ...

CUSACK: Don't worry. I remember your heroic battle on my behalf. Mr Sheehan, your in-tray is a gaping void and your out-tray is a yawning chasm. In between is the Desert of Eternity.

CUCKOO: Cusack, Cusack ... I don't like this place. I don't like the smell. Couldn't we ambush the bulls on the road? Look at it ... none of the colour and encrustation of the old spots of sacrifice. It doesn't feel right. For death, it's too clean, too clean.

CUSACK: (*To CON.*) I will make a confession to you. If you were a man of any religion I might stand a chance of being believed in the sin which I must reveal. But you, with your analytical mind, will merely become incredulous, not being trained to the lewd and impossible as is the ear of a priest. Amongst my sins there is one that is paramount. It towers above all the others. It is an unnatural sin. It is a sin that creates more sin, in envy. There is no worse sin in the world, and I have suffered for it. Without blessing, without permission, by a twist of Time and Nature, I have lived over eight hundred years.

CON: Eight hundred years? Quite a night you must have had, Cusack, old son. You might have said you were still motherless ...

CUSACK: Don't look my age, do I? Want to know my secret?

CON: Behave like a prick if you want to, but I've had enough! Now, this is your last chance, Cusack. I'm giving you a direct order. Help me get these people out of here.

CUSACK: No.

CON: Right. I'm putting you on a formal charge of refusing to obey a lawful instruction.

CUSACK: I couldn't care less, but here's the right form for you to fill in. Three copies, remember. And don't forget to press hard with your biro or it doesn't come through.

FERGUS: Maeve ... will we ever get back?

MAEVE: No, Fergus, my love. Once we've done the job and the air has been cleared, I think we will fade away.

FERGUS: Where to, Maeve?

MAEVE: Some bone-yard somewhere. Peaceful enough. The idea is for us to be forgotten about. Cusack has told you, Fergus, heroes like us are redundant. We have to get out of the way. Death is best for us four.

ALI: But the great druid, the flying John Paul who stands on a spear and straightens erect on its point, surely that man is a hero? Look at his hands. Look at his head. Look how he circles the world checking his honour like a farmer checks his fence-posts.

MAEVE: Ah, he is a true hero of today, Cusack says. On his back he does not carry harness but ideas. In his hands he has no weapons, only the record of his talk. In his eyes are mirrors to reflect the questions. He does not prophesy, nor visit oracles. He shouts only the known words.

FERGUS: Could we try again, Maeve? (*Pause.*) Oh, I've made you sad.

CUSACK: You must forgive them if they slip and slide in your scientific brain, Mr Sheehan. Like new-born infants, they're covered in mild, metaphorical jelly, incapable of standing still and making Anglo-Saxon sense. Pity them. The ground was never steady under their feet. All impulse you see. No plan, except for today, and I sketched that one out for them.

CON: So you are responsible?

CUSACK: Oh, you know how responsible I am, Mr Sheehan.

CON: You and me will have things to talk about once this is over. I think all I can do now is phone for the police.

CUSACK: Fair enough.

CON: Well, perhaps I'll give it a bit longer to sort it out. But I'm not laughing, Cusack, old son, not laughing at all.

CUSACK: I should hope not. Me and my friends are very serious about what we're doing.

CON: Which is what, exactly?

CUSACK: In all your reading up there in the office while the killing was going on under your feet but out of your mind, did you ever get round to any yarns about the Irish heroes of old, such as I've got in my book?

CON: I can't say I did.

CUSACK: Well, you might be equally indifferent to meeting them now – Queen Maeve and King Ali of Connaught, Fergus her lover, betrayer of Ulster, and Cuckoo – the hero of Ulster. Now, I'm eight hundred years old and I don't feel a day over forty, but they're knocking on two thousand – hence the smell.

CON: The smell I believe in.

CUSACK: They were the authors of their own deeds. What actions they took rattled in the air until it got hot and radiant. The reverberations never died away in Ireland, not from the first century until the Normans came. People kept them alive by word of mouth only. Now me, I was unemployed at the end of the twelfth century – always a traditionalist, you see – and my parents put me in the monastery at Clonmacnois on the east bank of the Shannon. Hired as a man of prayer, I found myself frustrated as I had no faith in Anglo-Norman Christianity and couldn't open my mouth to an alien god. One day the Bishop of Leinster found me idling around and said, 'Give that lazy sod something to do.' 'What?', says the brother in charge of me. The Bishop thought for a minute and then said – conscious as he was of the great cultural changes taking place and the danger of the people losing their identity – 'Let him collect and write down the full text of the *The Cattle Raid of Cooley* from the lips of the peasants.'

CUCKOO: I had a house made from human heads. All my windows were made from the hip-bones of queens and my lintels from the thigh-bones of priests. That was what people said of me, and that was what was true.

CON: Who would waste time doubting it? (*Pause.*) Cusack … I don't think you're yourself today. I know you have a

habit of picking up strange companions in your
wanderings on a Saturday night, but bringing them to
work is well past my sense of humour.

CUSACK: You interpret my old routines correctly. I am
a lonely man. I do love a drink and a talk, and I do get
enthusiastic about new friends. All this I admit. Ask my
landlady. (*Pause.*) But these are the heroes.

MAEVE: What time are the bulls due?

CUSACK: Eight o'clock.

MAEVE: And you're sure they're the ones?

CUSACK: The White Bull of the South and the Brown Bull
of Ulster.

MAEVE: Did you tell the drivers that if they get the bulls
here on time there'd be largesse in it for them – the use
of my friendly thighs?

CUSACK: Maeve, what would stop them speeding and
taking chances with their cargo if I told them that?
They're simple men.

MAEVE: I want the scheme to work, Cusack. We didn't
come here for nothing.

CUSACK: I've done everything I could. Do you think the
Pope will understand a tribute like this? He's not one for
sacrificing beasts on altars.

MAEVE: Ach, come off it. Everybody is.

CUSACK: The carcases are intended for the British
dogmeat trade. You don't mind that?

MAEVE: Let the flesh look after itself. It's the thought
behind the sword that counts. The lives of those two old
bulls will go out like a pair of summer storms. They'll
do the job, put the pressure in the right place.

CUSACK: But how will I persuade this dimwit that we're
telling the truth?

CON: Christ, Cusack, old son – you hate me, don't you?
All these years I've spent sticking up for you and this is
the thanks I get ...

CUCKOO: Fight him. Weapons. Blood. Hacking.
Heads flying. Revenge. Watch the crows peck out his

eyes. Put his head over your door to smile for ever. Hate will get you high up. High up. Yaaah!

(*The door in the gate opens and then bangs shut.*)

JANET: Oh, I was looking for Mr Sheehan ...

CUCKOO: This is the country where I would rest my weapon.

JANET: Are you talking to me?

CUCKOO: Would you lend me the loan of your apples?

CON: Er ... over here, Miss Soames. Sorry about this ...

JANET: I apologise for the intrusion, Mr Sheehan. I was passing so I thought I'd check that everything was all right with our order. Everything is all right, is it? No problems have arisen, I hope.

CON: Well, the beasts haven't arrived yet.

JANET: Haven't they?

MAEVE: We're all waiting for them, impatiently. This man will tell you. He's lucky to have us.

CON: These people are nothing to do with me, Miss Soames. They're just trouble-makers. You know, last night the whole of Dublin was on its ear. They just came in off the street. I'm sorry.

JANET: Well, I hope you manage to get rid of them soon. My company is looking forward to the order being met in a satisfactory manner. Being importuned by vagrants will not be accepted as a reasonable excuse.

MAEVE: Vagrants? Do you think we haven't got a home to go to?

JANET: I hope everything works out, Mr Sheehan. I'll ring you in the morning when your premises have been washed out. Ten o'clock at number three dock.

MAEVE: Why is this woman leaving us so soon? She interests me.

JANET: I'd like to go now, if you don't mind.

FERGUS: Maeve wants to get to know you better.

MAEVE: Bring her over here.

JANET: Put me down, you brute!

MAEVE: Look at the hips on her. Now, would a child get through here, never mind an army?

JANET: Get off me! Mr Sheehan!

CON: Hey, cut that out! You, woman, leave her alone!
(*Three swords being drawn.*)

FERGUS: Don't you address the queen as *woman*. Unsay that!

CON: Look, there's no need for ...

FERGUS: Unsay it!

CON: Sorry, sorry. Now, will you put your blades away? Now, somebody must tell us what's going on.

JANET: It's obvious, isn't it? I know what I'm dealing with. Well, should we get down to business!

CUSACK: Business, Miss Soames?

JANET: Of course.

CUSACK: What business?

JANET: Look, I've been expecting something like this to happen for a long time. My company has always known that having an office in Ireland is risky. We've been prepared. The personnel department has issued a pamphlet with clear instructions to all staff as to what steps we should take and how we should behave.

CUSACK: Miss Soames, you're misjudging these characters here. All they've come for is to do a slaughtering job.

JANET: You have taken us hostage. What else could it be? (*Pause.*) It has all the signs. (*Pause.*) You have taken us hostage, haven't you?

MAEVE: I think the woman wants us to say yes.

CUSACK: A pamphlet is a powerful thing.

JANET: The first step is for me to ascertain what you want from us. In writing, if possible ...

MAEVE: Well, Cusack does all the writing for us ...

CUSACK: Miss Soames, you're a natural born extremist, you know that?

JANET: You are holding us here, aren't you?

CUSACK: Long enough to pass the time of day, that's all ...

JANET: That's what they all say. You wouldn't tell us that you intend to keep us here for ever. Now, come on, let's get down to it. What are your demands?

CON: All I can get out of them so far is that they want to work on the carcases for your consignment.

JANET: The bulls for this morning?

CON: That's right. They want nothing else out of life. See what I mean?

JANET: They're keeping us here so they can kill bulls? Everyone will think they're mad.

CON: Useful in court later on. It's a cover so they can plead insanity.

JANET: I insist on knowing! Are you from the IRA? The UDA? The UDF? The UFF? The UUU?

MAEVE: Is that a spell she's chanting? Are you chanting a spell at me? Don't act the druid if you haven't got the powers.

JANET: Why be so secretive about it? It's not fair! We must know.

CON: Cusack, for Christ's sake, find out what they want. We're not going to resist. If they're going to hold us hostage that's fine ... these things can be arranged ...

JANET: He's with them. There's no point in asking him for help.

CON: Cusack? Never. (*Pause.*) In spite of appearances I think the man is still loyal to me. He's been indoctrinated. It's tragic.

CUSACK: Don't get us wrong now. Mr Sheehan, I've reached the natural end of my employment here. There must be some other sucker in Dublin who could come along and run this place while you play the gentleman slaughterer, pretending the job isn't there. Failed his degree in Physics at Trinity, didn't you? You never got over the shock, did you Mr Sheehan? It induced a strange paralysis of the nine-to-five nervous system.

Butchery is below him. And blood? That's something you use to encourage the growth of tomatoes.

JANET: We intend to co-operate in every way possible. Please, let us all keep calm. I have had instructions from my company head office that I am to avoid heroics ...

CUCKOO: Yaaaah! Scream! Sword-edge and sloped shield! Thunder-feat!

JANET: Stop him yelling at me!

CUCKOO: I'll show you the spurt of speed, the stroke of precision! With massive stroke-dealing sword I'll hack bits as big as babies' heads off those bulls. I'll strangle them with their own dewlaps!

CUSACK: All right, Cuckoo. They'll be here soon. Don't get impatient.

CUCKOO: Lumps like boulders I'll hack *off*!

JANET: He's a psychopath! Do something about him!

CUSACK: He's not interested in you. Did I tell you that I was eight hundred years old?

JANET: Will you please stop beating about the bush and tell us why these friends of yours want to kill our bulls so much?

MAEVE: Your bulls? What are you talking about?

CUSACK: Maeve, these two did arrange to buy the two bulls, not knowing what they were. You know what Irish farmers are like about the age of their stock.

JANET: But why do you have to come here for them?

ALI: Because this is the only place that people can sacrifice a beast these days. Anywhere else and there'd be trouble. It's quite a complicated business and it has to be done properly if it is going to work. The place has to be thoroughly prepared, the altar decorated in the correct manner, the right prayers have to be said, songs sung, music made. And, of course, the beasts must be killed with the necessary ritual otherwise the whole thing will fail.

JANET: Thank you for explaining all that to me. And what is the sacrifice for?

ALI: To help the Pope bring peace to Ireland, which is what everyone seems to want.

JANET: Well, I don't know what to say. What do you think, Mr Sheehan?

CON: Do you mean, will it work? I don't see why not. A bit of sacrifice doesn't do any harm, so we're told.

CUSACK: It improves the stock of political causes like roses thrive on horse manure.

MAEVE: You two have never seen a blood-stained altar, have you? Never seen the red fog rolling out of the bull's entrails into the clear air. We were brought up on it as children.

ALI: You can do a lot with death which you can't with life.

MAEVE: And our druids were thoughtful men, men who could take the initiative, like this Pope. Ours would try anything – anything – to get rid of a plague or a piece of bad luck which was affecting the people. They'd turn themselves inside-out, experiment, take chances with their own lives. I've seen druids who've fallen asleep at the altar, covered in blood, having sacrificed every sort of living creature they could until they found the right one. Sometimes it was as small as a mouse or a wren. They never gave up. (*Pause.*) We get the idea from all this show and shouting, that if this visit doesn't work, the Pope will think there is nothing else to be done. No one has told him about the bulls, you see. He doesn't know that they're still roaming around. (*Pause.*) He hasn't made them a part of his calculations.

CUSACK: Miss Soames, I still get the feeling that you're not with us body and soul. And even Mr Sheehan doesn't seem entirely convinced. So I will have to reveal all, down to the last detail. Today we are going to create what Ireland needs most. It's nothing very complicated. A child could understand it quite easily. You could work it out yourselves. (*Pause.*) What Ireland needs is a great natural disaster.

CUCKOO: Wham! Wham! Wham! Wham!

CUSACK: Irish disasters in the past have always been without flair or drama, having at their middles either vegetables or the seven virtues. But no natural cataclysms – nothing that just came out of the earth or the sky. Well, we're going to remedy that. I bet you can't guess what it is?

CON: Lagging far behind you, Cusack, old son, far behind you.

CUSACK: We're going to make an earthquake.

CON: An earthquake? Are you now?

CUSACK: Followed by a tidal wave of such huge proportions that it will wash out the country from coast to coast. (*Pause.*) Isn't it on the tip of your tongue to ask us how we're going to do that? (*Pause.*) I thought it was. When the Pope jams himself into the cramped little cell at Clonmacnois where I first wrote down the stories of these heroes and made immortal the violence of an older Ireland there will obviously be a major disturbance. But that would not be quite enough to split the earth. So we're going to sacrifice those two terrible, ridiculous, discredited old bulls and project their tormented souls into the same supernatural forcefield as the Pope at the precise moment of his entry into my old cell at Clonmacnois. With Ireland more sensitive to reverberations today than any other for two thousand years, it cannot help but produce a convulsion of the beloved, suffering earth which will shake the Irish down to the back teeth, together. That's the thing. Together. (*Pause.*) I haven't got through to you, Miss Soames?

JANET: Yes, yes. The Irish must be shaken. I'm all for it, honestly.

MAEVE: Oooh, come on, let's get started. This waiting is itching my insides.

ALI: Now, you two disbelievers, best to keep out of the way while we do this. And don't interrupt. That's a blasphemy for which you could be made to suffer. (*Rattle of the bones. Low humming.*)

MAEVE: Clonmacnois!

> (*Fade sound effects of the abattoir. Fade in MAEVE's mind.*)

Can the earth hear my voice calling? It can.

> (*Fade out MAEVE's mind. Fade in the abattoir atmosphere.*)

Suffering Mother Earth, we have two great bulls to bring you peace. Accept them as the great druid and Pope stands on you at the place where we were written down to live for ever.

> (*Fade the abattoir atmosphere. Fade in MAEVE's mind.*)

Yes. The earth is listening. I know it.

> (*Fade out MAEVE's mind. Fade in the abattoir atmosphere. Rattle of the bones.*)

CUCKOO: (*Chanting.*) First will be the Brown Bull of Ulster! Dark, dire, devilish, handsome with health, horrible, hairy, furiously fierce, full of cunning, glowing with guile. Thirty grown men can stand on his back in a line! A beast enormous! A beast for breeding blood.

> (*Rattle of the bones.*)

MAEVE: (*Chanting.*) Then will come the White Bull of the South. Finnbennach, with his useless tits struck flat against his colossal belly of brawn. As he gambols, his weapon scythes the sweet grass, sharpened for slitting heifers and cows. Bellowing his pleasure he smells the future union.

> (*Rattle of the bones.*)

ALI: (*Chanting.*) I ask the air to take the souls of these two creatures, to ferry them through cloud and rain, over rivers, and hills crossing the green land to place them at the feet of Mother Earth at Clonmacnois!

> (*Rattle of the bones.*)

FERGUS: (*Chanting.*) Blood is sweet to the earth, the living wine of life. We are the sons and daughters of the mother of all men. Mother, these will be the greatest beasts of Ireland, slain for you. All we ask is that you tremble as you drink.

> (*The humming fades.*)

CUCKOO: It's the smell I can't stand, the smell of trees, pine trees, but no forest. Where's the forest? Who's taken the trees?

CON: Look, I'll give them a full day's pay, double-time, to leave us alone. I want to close up now. Sorry, Miss Soames, the shipment won't be made tomorrow.

CUSACK: You will have to stay until the bulls are slaughtered.

CON: Cusack, old son ...

JANET: We undertake to leave here and not go to the police. Agreed, Mr Sheehan?

CON: Absolutely. You can trust us.

CUCKOO: I can smell the forest but there are no trees!
I can smell the forest but there are no leaves!
I can smell the forest but there are no roots!

(*CUCKOO starts to snarl, yelp, growl and sigh. Then his breath goes into long, shuddering gasps and groans.*)

CON: Control the bastard, can't you? He's going off his rocker!

(*CUCKOO whimpers like a puppy, sniffs, growls.*)

JANET: He's getting ready to do it again. He's making himself do it, the animal! Oh God ...

(*CUCKOO bays, growls, snarls, spits in a furious convulsion. When his fury has spent itself he is left breathing deeply, whimpering, crying. Pause.*)

MAEVE: The power is still in him. That was a good warp-spasm, Cuckoo. The Hound of Ulster still lives in you.

CUSACK: What did you think of that, Miss Soames?

JANET: I presume it was some kind of fit.

CON: Ach, it's drying-out time. Sunday morning and the eight o'clock horrors.

CUSACK: You hear them, Maeve? Cuckoo put on his warp-spasm and it's a fit. Did I not tell you the truth when I said terror was dead?

MAEVE: In my own court I took the heads off people who deliberately blinded themselves. Self-mutilation is a sin. Now, you were here when Cuckoo was in the toils of his warp-spasm, weren't you?

CON: Yes, yes, of course.

ALI: Will you pardon me if I suggest that you might have overlooked the fact that he became a monstrous article, vile, terrible and shapeless?

CON: Yes, yes, I did notice ...

FERGUS: And did you notice how his shanks and his joints, every knuckle and knee-bone, every angle and artery and organ from top to bottom shook like a tree in the flood or a reed in the stream? Woman! You saw all that?

JANET: Yes. Of course.

MAEVE: Good. No doubt you were enthralled and entertained with the way his whole body made a tearing twist inside his skin so that all his flesh was loosened and wallowed around in him like a new-born pig in a bag. And did you see his feet, knees and shins switch round until they were facing the wrong way? The balled sinews of his calves flew round like big knots on a ship's rope. On his mighty head the veins of his temples writhed ... didn't they?

JANET: If you say so.

MAEVE: Oh, I do, I do. Just as I say that the sinews of his neck gathered into a knob the size of a month-old child's head and his face and features were thrust back until they became a deep, red bowl. You caught that?

JANET: Yes. Yes. If that's what you want, yes.

ALI: Did you see that special feature of his then? He sucked one eye so deep into his skull that a wild crane couldn't get at it with its long beak probing!

CON: Yes, we saw that too.

FERGUS: The other popped out of the socket and dangled there like a bell's clapper bumping against the cheek-bone. His mouth grew wider and wider in a terrible cave of distortion until all the skin was unrolled from the jaw and out heaved his liver and lungs from the gullet, flapping there like a great red flag while flakes of flaming blood flew all round his head. No doubt you captured these moments as well?

JANET: Yes, yes, yes.

MAEVE: This is truly a day of hope. Now I am sure tha[t] they must be capable of seeing the last and most terrible sign of the hero's warp-spasm.

MAEVE: Over Ireland, in the clear air, as high as a whale will throw the ocean, or a boy will throw a ball, from the very dead centre of his skull, will rise a fountain of blood.

(*A terrible cry from CUCKOO. The roar of a great gush of blood which rises to a crescendo, then fades away. Fade out the abattoir atmosphere.*)

CUSACK: Good people, never mind the hero's blood. There's plenty more where that came from. I'll give you something more worth your sympathy – me, in the old days at the monastery of Clonmacnois when I was still young – sixty at the most – collecting the stories of the heroes to put in my book of *The Cattle Raid of Cooley*.

(*Fade in the sound of a Gregorian chant at a distance. It is CUSACK's cell at Clonmacnois. The door is open.*)

CUSACK: Come in, come in all of you.

(*The sniffing, coughing and muttering of peasants. The door of the cell is slammed. The Gregorian chant is shut off. A very claustrophobic atmosphere. Every sound is audible – pen on sheepskin; breathing.*)

CUSACK: Right, snippets of the heroes. If you peasants have rested and cleaned up after your journeys here to Clonmacnois, let us start.

FERGUS: Will we have the money first?

CUSACK: You will not. Money comes after the information. Who's first?

FERGUS: That's me.

MAEVE: It is not! I got here long before you. Did you not see me sitting here getting my thoughts together?

CUSACK: Well then, young woman. What do you know of the story of the two bulls of Ireland?

MAEVE: I know a small portion.

CUSACK: What about?

MAEVE: Queen Maeve.

CUSACK: Let's hope you've got something good to say about her. All I've got so far is the most unmitigated filth.

MAEVE: Mine is a very simple and straightforward story illustrating the queen's essential humanity.

CUSACK: Well, that sounds very encouraging. Let's have it then.

MAEVE: It is soon told. Queen Maeve's son-in-law, Ferdia, was told to go out and fight the unbeatable Ulster hero, Cuckoo. Ferdia got himself ready and drove over in his chariot to say farewell. He did not think much of his chances of survival. At Maeve's tent he found her squatting in the darkness over something and saying, quite affectionately, 'Are you still asleep?'

CUSACK: 'Are you still asleep?'

MAEVE: My grandmother, from whom I learnt the story, thought that Maeve was pissing in the king's ear.

CUSACK: Why should she be doing that?

MAEVE: My grandmother said that it was the only way to talk to some men.

CUSACK: And that is your contribution?

MAEVE: I've walked fifty miles to tell it to you.

CUSACK: Here's your money. If you've got any more like that then leave them at home. Who's next?

FERGUS: That's me.

CUSACK: What story have you brought me?

FERGUS: The story of an encounter; a fight, if you like.

(*A heavy imperious knock at the door of the cell. CUSACK tuts. The door is opened. Gregorian chant is heard.*)

CUSACK: Your Grace!

CON: The holy sister here and myself would like to sit in on your work for a while.

JANET: Yes, I'm very interested in ancient Ireland.

CON: Please settle down again. Don't let us interrupt. Pretend that we're not here. Carry on now.

(*The door of cell is slammed shut. The Gregorian chant is cut off. CUSACK sighs.*)

CUSACK: Get on with your story then. (*In a whisper.*) I hope it's an improvement on the last one!

FERGUS: Much better, brother monk, much better. It is soon told.

CUSACK: Get on with it then.

FERGUS: An Ulsterman called Ilech came against the army of the south at a place called Ath Feidli. His chariot was highly decrepit and falling to bits and it was pulled by two old jaundiced horses, spavined and knock-kneed to the degree where they could only shamble. Ilech had his old chariot full of stones and clods of earth and he threw these at the people who came to stare at him, for the old warrior was fighting stark naked and his worn-out weapon and bollocks hung down through a hole in the chariot floor, banging on the ground.

CUSACK: Oh God!

FERGUS: The army of the south jeered at Ilech and told him to get out of the way or they would trample on him. Ilech pulled his old worn-out weapon up and whirled it round his head, then cast it at the army of the south, catching a hundred warriors in a noose from which he hanged them from a tree while battering their brains out with his bollocks.

CUSACK: Have you finished?

FERGUS: That's the only bit I can remember.

CUSACK: Here's your money, though you don't deserve it. Your Grace, apologise ...

CON: Think nothing of it ...

CUSACK: Your mistress' ... sorry, the holy sister's ears ... I wouldn't want to pollute them further ... Your Grace, couldn't I be taken off this job and put on something else ... breaking rocks, or digging ditches ... anything, anything.

CON: Remember, my son, this is a pre-Christian poem we're dealing with. We can't expect the same high standards of decency as we observe ourselves.

CUSACK: But they only remember the filth! Why?

CON: Oh, to tease us. You know the Irish. They're probably making it up as they go along. We will have the opportunity to take a second look at it later and make suitable revisions.

CUSACK: (*To JANET.*) Please forgive them sister. They are lowly people with no idea of what they're saying.

JANET: I think it is charming, charming.

CUSACK: That's enlightened of you, sister. I fear there may be worse to come.

JANET: Nothing can shock me, brother. Before I came over from England I was trained in the ways of the Irish.

CUSACK: I could do with some of that myself. What mysteries did they explain?

JANET: Their natural courtesy and hospitality. Their good humour. Their particular sensitivities.

CUSACK: Aha! Could you enumerate for the sake of this rabble? They might learn something about themselves.

JANET: The Irish, I was told, have a highly-developed sense of wonder about human affairs. They are full of admiration for the business of being alive but often regret the intensity of the experience. They are prone to boiling over and overstatement.

CUSACK: Let it never be said!

JANET: Tremendous respect for family ties and bonds. An almost supernatural addiction to the ceremonies of death ...

CUSACK: This is a course I must get on. Your Grace. Send me to England for a refresher.

CON: Your great work must not be disturbed, my son. England would only confuse you. As an Irishman born and bred you might find much in the life of such a highly civilised people which struck you as worthless, overpractical and mercenary. Stick with it.

CUSACK: All right, Your Grace, but I don't think it's fair. The last twenty years of my life I've spent writing down this appalling stuff. I'd rather wear a hair shirt and go in for flagellation. Next!

ALI: That's me, brother.

CUSACK: You have a story?

ALI: I do.

CUSACK: Is it in any way to do with bodily functions?

ALI: Mine is about healing.

CUSACK: Ah. That sounds more like it. Gentleness, mercy, understanding ...

ALI: It is soon told. An Ulsterman called Cethern arrived at Cuckoo's camp with his guts round his feet after a fight. 'Get me a doctor,' he said. There were no Ulster doctors so Cuckoo sent word to the enemy to send one of theirs, and he came. When he saw Cethern's guts round his feet he said, 'You won't survive this.' 'Neither will you,' Cethern cried and fisted the doctor until the healing-man's brains splashed over his feet. Then Cuckoo found fifty more doctors to come to Cethern and they were all killed in the same way ...

CUSACK: (*Interrupting.*) Fifty?

ALI: Fifty. I can see my great-grandfather saying it now, a cup at his knee. Fifty.

CUSACK: Cethern killed fifty doctors for saying he wouldn't survive. Go on, go on.

ALI: The fifty-first doctor only got a glancing blow and Cuckoo saved his life.

CUSACK: Decent of him.

ALI: So Cuckoo sent to Ulster for another doctor and one called Fintin came from the King's own court. He looked at Cethern's injuries and said: 'The blood is black here. You were speared at an angle, right through the heart. All your guts have been cut off from each other and lie in a heap like a ball of wool, rolling round your body. I can't promise to cure you ...

CUSACK: So he killed him as well, splashing his brains over his feet.

ALI: Not at all, at all. Just hold your horses, brother, then the doctor Fintin went on to say: 'I'll tell you no lie, but your case is plain to me. A whole army has left its mark in your tripes and one way or another your life is nearly over. Either your wounds will have to be treated for a year and you'll live, or I can do it in three days and three nights and give you enough strength for one last fight. Take your pick!' (*Pause.*) Which choice did the Ulster warrior take, do you think?

CUSACK: You're telling the story.

ALI: What does the bishop say? Or the English nun? What does anyone say who's here? Don't we know what the man's choice was? (*Pause.*) Give me the strength for one last fight.

CON: I think we'll be going now, Cusack, my son. That was all very interesting, wasn't it, sister?

JANET: Absolutely gripping. I can't wait for the book to come out.

CON: Keep up the good work. Pax vobiscum.

JANET: Good night, and joy be with you all.

(*The door opens. Gregorian chant is heard. The door slams. Laughter.*)

CUSACK: Wisht now. Don't be disrespectful. Well, I think that will be enough for tonight.

ALI: What about the boy here. He's not said a word since he came in.

CUSACK: That's up to him. I'm not forcing him if he's shy. Some people are like that. (*Pause.*) Tell me, all of you, are the sore feet worth it. All this way for what?

MAEVE: We know we're forgetting things more and more. The old world is dying on us.

CUSACK: But people will stay the same. You know what I've got so far, after years of work, tramping over the bogs, sitting here with all kinds from children to grandfathers? A poem in praise of thieves and liars and murderers. Why did you bother to remember it? Why did your fathers bother to pass it on?

MAEVE: How do you spend a dark night? There's the rain, the wind, the cows. Not much else ... Hey, boy, isn't that so? (*Pause.*) Come on, talk to us. Where are you from?

CUCKOO: The feat of the javelin and the rope, snapping
   mouth, hero's scream, spurt of speed, stroke of precision.

   (*The rattling of the bones. Fade Clonmacnois cell atmosphere.*)

CUSACK: Good people, if you're ever short of a job, don't
   take up monking for a living. In your solitude you will
   come hard up against the question: What does the
   natural animal mind of man love most? And it has an
   answer that will shake your bones. There's wisdom in
   that answer though, painful as the truth may be. What
   man loves most he has plenty of. Blood. No man is poor
   beside this item of his adoration. There is no imbalance
   in the possession of it. I have as much as you and the
   other way about.

   (*Fade in the Clonmacnois cell atmosphere.*)

CUCKOO: (*Screaming.*) Aaaaaaah! Wha ...

CUSACK: What is it, lad?

CUCKOO: Wham! Wham! Wham! Wham! My heart is
   going.

CUSACK: A dream. It was only a dream.

CUCKOO: It was real to me, lying here on the stones.
   My hands are sweating as if I had been fighting. For a
   moment I had forgotten where I was.

CUSACK: You remember me?

CUCKOO: The collector of truths.

CUSACK: The collector of lies.

CUCKOO: There is one I was keeping for another day.
   If I tell it to you now, will you give me my fee and ferry
   me across the Shannon so I can head for home? There
   should be a moon.

CUSACK: Why the hurry?

CUCKOO: I do not sleep easy in this monastery. The
   stones are too hard.

CUSACK: It is my bed every night.

CUCKOO: I have the best story of all but it is lying heavy
   on my brain. It would help me to discharge it, then I can
   think of God and his mercy.

CUSACK: Is it a tale of lechery? If so, you will have to wait until morning. I suffer enough in the night, alone, my hammer in my hand.

CUCKOO: It is not a story of that kind. Will you hear it?

CUSACK: As long as it is not a story of sleeping, birth or women.

CUCKOO: It is soon told. The men of Ulster saw a boy rowing over the sea towards the strand in a small boat. He had a pile of stones beside him and as he rowed with one hand, with the other he slung shots at the sea-birds, stunning but not killing them. When they had recovered he let them fly into the air again. The king, Conchobor, saw this and was impressed. He told the men of Ulster not to let the boy ashore as he was a worker of miracles. A warrior was sent out to stop the boy beaching his boat. 'Come no further,' the warrior said. 'What is your name?' ''I'll give my name to no man,' the boy replied. 'And you must get out of my way.' 'You can't land,' insisted the warrior. 'I'm going where I'm going,' said the boy. 'Even if you had the strength of a hundred men you would not stop me.' With that he flung a stone. It roared like thunder and knocked the warrior headlong. So King Conchobor sent his greatest hero, Cuckoo. 'Name yourself or die,' he demanded. 'So be it,' said the boy and cut Cuckoo bald-headed with a stroke of precision. 'The joking has come to an end,' Cuckoo said. 'Now we must wrestle.' 'I'm too small. I can't reach up to your belt,' the boy complained. So he climbed onto two standing stones and threw Cuckoo down three times. Then they went into the sea to drown each other and Cuckoo played foul by bringing to use his terrible barbed spear the *gael bolga* without the boy's agreement. He brought the bowels of the brave boy into a bunch around his ankles. 'You have hurt me badly,' the boy said. 'I have indeed,' Cuckoo said. He took the boy in his arms and carried him to where the men of Ulster were watching. 'I now recognise this as my own son', Cuckoo grieved. 'Here you are. I have killed him for you.' 'Thank you,' said the men of Ulster. And they went home.

CUSACK: Here's your money. Keep it safe.

CUCKOO: You will remember the ferry over the Shannon. I'm sure there is a moon big enough for rowing a boat.

CUSACK: Take the boat yourself and leave it on the other side. Someone will need it from that direction soon enough.

(*The door of the cell is opened and closed. Pause. A bell sounds.*)

ALI: (*Waking.*) Oh, what's that? What's that?

CUSACK: Quiet now. It's only the bell for vespers. (*Pause.*) When you get home, will you laugh at me, stuck here in this grave, outlining witless fantasies for the future generations?

ALI: Somebody has to do it. People won't always pass the truth from mouth to mouth. It will have to settle down, close its wings and be caught.

MAEVE: Brother monk, do you know what Maeve looked like? Has anyone ever described her to you?

CUSACK: Only half a picture has emerged, all her activities being concentrated below the waist.

MAEVE: Was she beautiful?

CUSACK: Well, here's what I've got about her so far. A tall, short, long-round-faced woman with soft-hard features and a head of yellow, black hair and two birds of gold upon her shoulder. She wore a cloak of purple folded about her body and five hands' breadth of gold across her back. She held an iron sword with a woman's grip over her head. A massive figure, so a little girl told me, something like her mother, no doubt. Probably a hunchback as well as a whore is my guess.

MAEVE: Many men loved her. That's good enough for me.

CUSACK: Go back to sleep now. You've a long walk home in the morning.

(*There is a knock on the door. It is opened.*)

CON: Cusack, my son, would you step out here for a moment? There is something I would like to discuss with you.

CUSACK: Yes, your Grace?

(The door closes behind him. Change to the monastery general atmosphere.)

CON: Are they all asleep in there?

CUSACK: Doing their best. Christian floors are hard.

CON: Cusack, my son, I have news. The exiled King of Leinster, Dermot McMurrough, has invited Henry the Second of England to invade Ireland to help him get back his throne. The English army has already landed.

CUSACK: And what do you expect me to do about it?

CON: Inform those people for me. I have a lot to do. We will have to adjust to the change.

CUSACK: With respect, they'll get mad.

CON: Not if it is properly explained to them. A papal bull has been issued supporting the English king's invasion.

CUSACK: Ah. They'll understand that.

CON: They will? Why so??

CUSACK: Because they'll find out that Pope Adrian the Fourth was once called Nicholas Breakspear, an Englishman.

(The sound of alarm bells. Fade out the Clonmacnois general atmosphere. Sounds of battle. Fade. Fade in special atmosphere.)

CUSACK: Good people, now you know how I have suffered – a man pickling fantasies like a grandma doing her onions. It was never my intention to get involved. All I wanted was a quiet life doing a simple job that I could understand.

(Fade in the sound of rumbling inside the earth.)

Instead, I had become amanuensis to Ireland's fighting heroes – head-hunters, cattle-farmers, violent dreamers, and, by writing them down, I had made them seethe and bubble under every age in Ireland like the earth's blood waiting to erupt and scald the sky!

(The roar of a gusher. A long scream from CUCKOO. Fade out special atmosphere. Fade in abattoir atmosphere.)

JANET: *(Crying.)* Horrible, horrible! Blood shooting out of the top of his head! Clean it off me! I'm covered in it!

CUCKOO: Where are these bulls?

JANET: Stop it! Stop it!

CUCKOO: I'll balance them both on the point of my
sword, skin them in mid-air, split them from nose to tail,
scatter their bowels!

JANET: Stop it!

CON: Steady, Janet, steady. It's only blood ... Just tell
yourself, it's only blood. (*Pause.*) I'd consider it a favour if
you'd let us wash the worst of this off.

MAEVE: Why? You look fine to me. Isn't red your colour?

JANET: This will never come out. My clothes are ruined.
(*She weeps.*)

CON: Never mind, never mind. Don't cry now. Everything
will be all right.

MAEVE: Do you know, I think these two are in love.
Remember, Fergus?

FERGUS: With all my heart. Isn't your wife a great woman
to love, Ali? What lucky men we've been.

ALI: Well, Fergus, you haven't had the pain with her that
I have: this argument over equality.

MAEVE: That's true. Fergus has never doubted that I'm
better than him. Which one of you meat-merchants is the
stronger? In Ireland it's always the woman.

CUSACK: True, Maeve. The system was even exported to
America.

(*The telephone rings.*)

CUSACK: That'll be news. It's all right, I'll get it.

MAEVE: When Ali and me were married we found that we
were level-pegging in everything – power, position,
possessions ... nearly. We were a fraction out, so there
was a furore. I'm a stickler for the final detail, you
know.

ALI: A man less wise than your suffering husband might
say that you were pedantic. We were equal down to our
thumb-rings, our wash-pails, the rams of our flocks, the
stallions for our horse-herds, but ... I had a bull bigger
and better than hers – Finnennbach, the white – and

Maeve did not have the equal of him running with her cattle. There was only one other such bull in Ireland, in Cooley, Ulster.

MAEVE: I offered the farmer who owned it treasure, land, chariots, anything, and my friendly thighs on top of that. The fool said no.

ALI: So we had to go to war to match a pair of bulls. Where else would you hear such nonsense? Who cares about old and overblown cattle? Who wants them? We sold Ireland short with that war.

MAEVE: Oh, go on with you, it was good fun. Thousands upon thousands dead, all for the love of balance in nature. What do you say?

CON: Nothing, nothing at all.

FERGUS: It would never have happened if I'd had the taming of her, Ali. If I'd had Maeve from the beginning, as a young girl, what a woman I would have made of her. But now it's too late.

MAEVE: Wouldn't you do as much to be sure that you're getting your proper respect in the world?

JANET: Some of us do have to go to extremes to obtain that.

MAEVE: Ach, no one's equal now. They're just all as bad as each other. Don't you think so? I don't feel at home here.

CON: I think people are very confused now, you know, disoriented.

JANET: Yes. One big mess, isn't it?

MAEVE: No room for Cuckoo now. The childhood of Man is over. Bulls, battles, bravado ... baloney. Nothing gets done for show any more.

JANET: Yes. No style left, no panache. It's all so mundane.

MAEVE: Is that so? So you think the world needs livening up a bit, do you? Why did you really come here this morning. Eh? We'll have the truth this time, if you don't mind.

CON: We were going out, together.

FERGUS: Into the fields. That was what I saw in the woman's black-ringed eyes. The fields. Flowers, birds. The good old fields.

CON: Yes ... a picnic ...

MAEVE: Ah, you were going to slip off and leave Cusack to it for the day? He said you had a habit of doing that.

ALI: Mr Sheehan, your clerk, of whom we have the highest opinion with the regard to the truth of his tongue, tells us that you often absent yourself for hours on end from your office, that your lunch takes from twelve till half-past three, in fact, that Cusack the clerk runs this place for you. Would that be a fair thing to say?

CON: No ... I don't think so ...

CUCKOO: So, you were going to feast in the fields?

CON: We were.

CUCKOO: After you'd eaten, there'd be some weapon play. Then you'd be at peace, lying in the grass, listening to the herds and flocks. She would be dreaming about children. He would be dreaming about cattle. If I was out there with you, I'd sit apart and dream of war. (*Pause.*) You're more of a warrior than he is, like Maeve. Set aside your shield. We'll have a little hand-to-hand.

JANET: Please, don't touch me.

CON: Could you see your way clear to stop doing that to her?

CUCKOO: I'd fight a thousand men at this ford. No one would cross. My feats of arms would amaze the armies. The river would run red. After that, we would lie in peace in the grass.

JANET: Don't touch me ... please don't touch me ...

CUCKOO: Once a woman and a fool were sent to trick me by Maeve. She thought that the man would not arouse my suspicions as he was idle, and the girl, Finnabair, would take my weapon. I cut off the woman's breasts and thrust a great stone pillar into her wound. The fool's few brains I knocked out then thrust another great stone pillar up his arse. These pillars still stand. They will always be remembered, Finnabair and the fool. Will you?

JANET: Why are you doing this to us?

MAEVE: There's nobody else around. Everyone is following the Pope.

JANET: We don't deserve it, you know. We've done nothing to upset you.

MAEVE: I don't know. You manage to get under my skin somehow.

JANET: We're ordinary people, for God's sake! Ordinary people! Aren't we, Con?

CON: Oh, yes. Very ordinary. Almost non-existent.

JANET: Can't you just do your sacrifice when the bulls come and leave us out of it? We'll just sit in the office or something until you've finished. We won't interfere, I promise.

CON: We'll keep out of the road, okay? You do as you like. Feel free. Make yourselves at home. Feel free.

(*The sound of running across the yard.*)

CUSACK: Would you believe it? Would you be able to throw your mind into such convulsions that you could find the angle to credit this I'm telling? In your greatest moment of faith and acceptance of the vicissitudes of life, would you be able to swallow this vicissitude? You take two points a hundred miles apart. One in Connaught, one in Ulster. You put a white bull in a lorry in Connaught and a brown bull in a lorry in Ulster, then you point them both towards Dublin. Are you with me? From entirely separate directions! A hundred miles apart. What are the chances that at a certain junction half-an-hour to the north-west of the appointed place, these two vehicles should take it into their heads to collide and the bulls to escape and go charging round the countryside?

FERGUS: Myself, I'd give that story no credence at all.

CUSACK: Right. Now struggle with the news that as I was talking on the telephone to the driver of one of these lorries I could hear the television going in the roadside cafe where the poor lunatic was licking his wounds and spending his hard-earned pennies on a call. The television programme was from Clonmacnois. I heard the commentator saying that the Pope was delayed, held up by all the heavy traffic in the sky. Every helicopter in Ireland is fluttering around him, getting in the way.

MAEVE: So we might still make it ...

ALI: If they can recapture the bulls and get them here on time.

FERGUS: More delays can be expected. As soon as the great druid descends on the monastery there'll be thousands of children to kiss, hundreds of sacred places which cannot be passed without a prayer or a reverence. He'll be hugging the sick, giving blessings till his arm aches ...

MAEVE: So, they're both late – the bulls and the Pope. He's held up in the sky. They're held up on the earth. Only destiny will bring them together at the right juncture, random fate. We're in the hands of Time itself.

CUCKOO: (*Thickly.*) Where ... are ... the ... bulls?

CUSACK: Any minute, Cuckoo ...

CUCKOO: I can't hold back much longer. I'll have to fight something. All breezing around in my blood ... battle-needs ... I'm at the ford with my weapon ... help me ...

FERGUS: Quick, he's ready to blow. Get him something!

ALI: What? What can he hit here?

MAEVE: What have we got? All right, let him have these two for lack of anything better. Cuckoo! Here's a loving couple for you.

CUCKOO: (*Chanting.*) Slaughter, exile, corpses, blood, ravens, wailing women, heads bumping at my belt, Bones smoking veins death sings the Warped One! Death! Beloved Death! Brother!

FERGUS: You don't mind helping out, do you? You're only going where thousands and thousands have been before.

CON: Look, I'd like to help, honestly ... No! No! He doesn't want me!

CUCKOO: Is this all? It's not enough! A neck like that is nothing but a barley-stalk to slash with a stick. I must have ... bulk! Bulk! Bulk!

CON: Don't hurt me ... I'll find something ... something he'll like ...

ALI: You'd better be quick. He's on the verge of a major distortion.

CON: I'll get it, I'll get it ... all right? He'll really enjoy this ... stand back ... where's my keys now ... won't be long, now Cuckoo, I'm getting you fixed up ... I've got something in the old fridge here.

(*A jangle of keys. The sound of locks and bolts as the doors of a freezer are opened.*)

ALI: Calm now, Cuckoo. They're getting you something to play with.

CUCKOO: Oooooh! Hurry up! I'm in terrible torment! Give me something to hack in mercy's name! Have you no pity? It's rising in me ... I can't hold on ... I can't ... Ha! I must hack and hew! Where ...? Where ...? A target! Wham!

CON: Gangway, there! Here it comes Cuckoo! Stand by! Solid meat.

(*The rattle and jangle of a beef carcass on a running rail. The clang of steel as CUCKOO hits it with his sword.*)

CUCKOO: Aaah! My hand! My hand!

ALI: What kind of trick was that to play on a man in torment? Giving him a stone to hack at!

CON: It's frozen meat. If he'll give it time to thaw he can mangle it as much as he likes ...

CUCKOO: My hand is sprained. My elbow is absolutely dislocated.

MAEVE: The thing's as cold as ice. See, it steams but with winter. What is it?

CON: It's a full carcase of beef.

MAEVE: Beef? What do you eat it with? A hammer?

CUCKOO: Is it Death? It's Death itself. Cold as the grave. Where's the blood? Where's the bits of hair and fat? This was never alive. It's a rock, a memorial pillar to some old hero I'm being taunted with because I was never as good as him. (*To CON.*) My wrist will remember that, when the sting's gone out of it ...

JANET: You'd have killed me without a thought, wouldn't you?

FERGUS: He was in great need. It had to be let out.

JANET: You useless, gormless, revolting, layabout bastard!

(*She kicks him in the crutch. His body drops.*)

CUCKOO: Aaaaaah!

FERGUS: That must have been a good pamphlet.

JANET: Dirty, stupid lout! Disgusting, bloody moron!

CON: Janet, you really shouldn't have done that ...

JANET: Oh shut up! I don't care now. Poking people about, they're going to do this, going to do that. I'm sick of them. Bastard!

CUCKOO: (*Chanting.*) Now, broken and despairing, brought low by a woman warrior, I wish to die. My arm broken by a dead bull, what hopes of killing a live one?

CON: I'd like to apologise on her behalf. She's got this temper. It doesn't often show itself ... only under pressure, you understand. She doesn't mean what she's saying.

CUSACK: The heroes find that hard to understand. Their lives were all about consequences, Mr Sheehan. You did what you did, then you stood up and took the racket, right on the jaw. You didn't lie, or duck, when the axe came down.

JANET: Don't give me that! As soon as this place is surrounded you'll start negotiating for your miserable lives, and blaming everyone else for what you've done. That's what I loathe about you most. You can't accept consequences. If you kill then it's anyone's fault but yours. You're children, bloody children! I'm going.

MAEVE: Cuckoo, your admirer is leaving, so she says.

JANET: Come on, Con. We'll just walk out of here.

CON: Is that all right, everybody? (*Pause.*) Will you be able to manage, Cusack, old son! Lock up after you when you've gone.

MAEVE: So, you're off for your picnic?

CON: If it's all right with you. We won't mention this to anyone.

MAEVE: A drive in the country, a green field, a freshly laundered cloth laid out on the grass ... Ah! You should have seen my armies at their picnics. Their dishes covered Ireland. (*Pause.*) If it weren't for the fact that you are about to offend against the holiest and most time-honoured law of all men, we might have let you go.

CON: What's that? Tell us and we'll sort it out.

MAEVE: Hospitality, Mr Sheehan, hospitality.

CON: Hospitality?

MAEVE: Look at us. We're starving. The last drink we had was hours ago. Our stomachs are rumbling. Our mouths are dry. You have no idea how far we've come.

CON: You want to share our picnic? Come on then, we'll all go.

MAEVE: No. We'll have it here. Janet, you go and get it. Mr Sheehan, Con to his friends, will wait with me.

JANET: What a vicious bitch you are.

MAEVE: Maybe, but I get even worse when I'm hungry.

JANET: What do you think, Con?

CON: Don't stand there making up your mind. Go and get it! Quick.

JANET: I think she's bluffing.

CON: Will you stop gabbing and do as they say?

JANET: Why should I feed them?

CUSACK: I thought it was your business to feed animals?

JANET: Not political animals.

MAEVE: Would you want we Irish to start eating each other? Surely not.

JANET: If I forget to say it when I come back – I hope it chokes you.

CUSACK: It doesn't look good for you, Mr Sheehan. Your woman has got impulsive and passionate about the state of her health.

CON: You won't forget to come back, will you, love?

JANET: Oh, stop snivelling, will you?

(The door in the gate opens and bangs shut. Pause.)

ALI: Do you have any doubts about her?

CON: None whatsoever.

ALI: Lucky man you are. Could I say the same, Maeve?

MAEVE: Oh, I'd come back for you, Ali.

FERGUS: And me, Maeve?

MAEVE: What have you got to offer, Fergus?

(A car door slams. Pause. The engine starts.)

CUSACK: Ah, perfidious Albion.

MAEVE: Well, it looks as though we've missed our picnic.
Not that it's going to be one for you, Mr Meat Merchant.
Where do you want it? Head or heart?

CON: She's forgotten ... don't ...

MAEVE: Cuckoo, what will you give me to let you have
the hacking off of this one's fat head?

CUCKOO: A chariot, a gold chain, two lengths of best
purple cloth.

MAEVE: He's all yours but I think I got the best of the
bargain.

CON: She thought the key to the ignition was the key to the
boot. They're easily mixed up ...

CUCKOO: Would you hold his head steady for me? He's
bobbing about a lot.

CON: Or she might have left the picnic at home. She's got
a head like a sieve ...

FERGUS: Will you keep yours still and stop talking?
There're certain forms to be observed in the taking of a
head. The victim isn't expected to talk his way through
the experience. Try a dignified and heroic silence.

CON: I'm sure Janet doesn't mean you to interpret what
she's done as a sign that she's escaping. I think the
woman is probably just turning the engine over to keep
it supple ...

CUCKOO: (*Chanting.*) What strength in his brains, what
power, in his blood, what magic in his marrow, make mine.

ALI: Stick your neck out, man. Make things easier on yourself! Ready, Cuckoo?

CUCKOO: Oh yes! Oh, yes! Aaaaah!

CON: Would you pass on a message to my mother?

CUCKOO: Death! Brother! Embrace him!

(*The car engine is cut. A car door slams. Pause. The door in the gate opens and closes. The sound of footsteps which then stop. Pause.*)

JANET: Picnic time!

CUCKOO: Shit!

JANET: Everything has changed. We're on your side now. We believe you in everything you've said, don't we, Con?

CON: Er ... yes ... most definitely we do.

MAEVE: Not before time. We're getting impatient for our courtesy to be repaid.

CON: If you'll pardon my asking, what courtesy is that?

MAEVE: Do you think that we have ever doubted that you are what you are?

(*The sound of the picnic being laid out.*)

JANET: I think there's plenty to go round. We're happy to share it with you, aren't we, Con?

CON: Any barley loaves and small fishes? (*Pause.*) Sorry. Forget it. Oh, yes. There's plenty enough here, all right.

JANET: This is going to be great fun. I love picnics, don't you? Food just seems to taste better in the fresh air, I find.

MAEVE: Does it now? You taste all this, now. Everything.

CON: With pleasure. You're the guests. The best of service. Here we have bread. Cheese, Celery.

(*The sound of the crunching of celery.*)

JANET: Potato crisps.

(*The sound of potato crisps being crunched.*)

CON: Apples.

(*The crunching of apples.*)

CUCKOO: (*Over the sound.*) Aaaah!

JANET: Roast beef. Mm. There. Is everything all right?

MAEVE: Some poisons take time to work.

CON: True. How do you feel, Janet?

JANET: Fine, never felt better. (*She burps.*) Ooops! Sorry.

MAEVE: If your food gives us the wind then the world will suffer for it. You know, don't you, Cusack? You've seen it yourself.

CUSACK: Hurricanes roar through the countryside and there's the noise of terrible thunder. Roofs get blown off houses. Whatever you do, Miss Soames, don't give them beans.

MAEVE: Have I got the head of the table?

JANET: Of course.

MAEVE: And I get served before anyone. Understand? I've had the legs of serving-men broken for forgetting that.

FERGUS: What's this?

JANET: A scotch egg.

FERGUS: It must be hard to be a hen over there.

CON: Tuck in. Would you be after having a gherkin, Cuckoo?

CUCKOO: Wha! Trophies from the small green giants.

ALI: And where were you going for your picnic, you two lovers?

JANET: We thought we'd go to Tara.

FERGUS: What does the likes of you want in Tara, the home of the high kings?

CON: Very into history, Fergus, old son. Fascinated. Not much is left there now but ... the old vibrations ... associations.

FERGUS: So this banquet was intended for Tara. The new high king and queen. Ireland ruled by meat merchants. This is good beef.

CUSACK: Prime quality, Fergus. The best. Know their meat do these two. Fresh, rare, succulent, young. Why shouldn't they take care of themselves?

MAEVE: I'm used to somebody singing my food down. If I don't have music with my dinner I get trouble. Who is it worth asking?

CUSACK: C'mon, Mr Sheehan. Give Maeve a song.

CON: I don't know any songs, honestly. If I did I'd sing them for you.

ALI: Janet here strikes me as a singer; straight, bright like a bird, her eyes clear as rushing water. Sing to us, my love. Make a heartsore husband happy.

JANET: Well, I don't know really ...

CUSACK: Now Miss Soames, isn't it true that you are an active member of the Anglo Irish Folksong Society?

JANET: How did you know that?

MAEVE: You have the look of a woman who can follow a tune.

JANET: Well, it's very difficult to just turn on a performance like a tap.

MAEVE: Cuckoo, in your experience, is it possible to torture a song from a human throat?

CUCKOO: Maeve, with these bare hands I have made a hundred heroes sing higher than larks and lower than moles.

CON: She'll sing, won't you, Janet? Come on now! We're waiting, dear. Give us a song, please.

JANET: Very well. I'll do my best. (*She sings.*)
>Of all the money that e'er I've spent
>I've spent it in good company
>And all the harm that I've ever done,
>Alas, it was to none but me:

>And all I've done
>Through lack of wit,
>To mem'ry now I can't recall,
>So fill to me the parting glass,
>Good night, and joy be with you all.
>
>(*The HEROES pick up the tune and harmonise with it, humming softly. CUCKOO whimpers tearfully. She sings.*)
>If I had money, enough to spend,
>And leisure time to sit awhile,
>There is a fair maiden in this town
>Who sorely does my heart beguile:

Her rosy cheeks,
And ruby lips,
I own she has my heart in thrall,
So fill to me the parting glass,
Good night, and joy be with you all.

(*The accompaniment gets stronger and sadder. CUCKOO cries. JANET's voice fades. Sings.*)

Of all the comrades that e're I had,
They were sorry for my going away,
And all the sweethearts that e're I had
Would wish me one more day to stay: door, Con, door

But since it falls
Unto my lot,
That I should rise and you will not, door!
I'll gently rise and softly call,
Good night and joy be with you all.

(*The door slams shut.*)

MAEVE: They're getting away, stop them!

(*A confusion of crockery. Rushing. Cries.*)

Poets and dreamers! Liars and minstrels!

(*Screams from JANET. The sound of running: a door is opened and crashes shut. Outside in the street, the sounds of pursuit with shouts and cries. Fade.*)

MAEVE: (*Laughing.*) What a pair! They never give up, do they?

CUSACK: (*Laughing.*) They're not the only ones. I'm awestruck, totally.

MAEVE: People have been magnificent. Heart and soul.

CUSACK: And all off the cuff. Where do they get it from? I'm very impressed, I can tell you.

MAEVE: I thought Cuckoo was going to explode.

CUSACK: He frightens me, never mind them. But you, Maeve? Gorgeous!

MAEVE: Ach, go on with you.

CUSACK: I'm teeming with admiration. You've exceeded my wildest dreams. If I was a little bit younger ...

MAEVE: Don't you mean older? I'm two thousand, remember?

(*Fade in uproar in the street. JANET screams. The HEROES laugh.*)

CUSACK: Well, I think it's time we moved into the ultimate phase, Maeve. Put them right on the spot.

MAEVE: There's nothing else for it, is there? Here we go.

(*The sound of uproar at the gate. The door opens.*)

CON: (*Over the wall.*) All right, all right, we were just checking the car ...

(*Shouting, screaming, and the sounds of kicking coming into the yard. The door slams shut.*)

JANET: Get off you lousy bastards! Leave me alone! Kick them, Con! Kick them in the face like me! Stop it! Help! Bastards! Christ!

CON: Look, the car is on a parking meter. Parking meter ...

MAEVE: Right. That's the last time we trust you two.

JANET: Oh, shut up, will you? Who cares? You're all bloody mad, all of you!

CON: Cusack, old son. You must help us. Early retirement, a reasonable pension, call in when you like for a cup of tea and a slab of sirloin big enough to cover the crossbar of your bicycle. I'm reading your mind now. The indignation of your friends about your treatment here ...

CUSACK: Maeve, these bulls are not going to arrive on time, I'm afraid.

MAEVE: I think you're right, Cusack. We'll have to use these two for the sacrifice. It's a second choice but I suppose it's better than nothing.

CUSACK: With you all the way. Beggars can't be choosers. But what's the style of the sacrifice going to be?

MAEVE: I'm a one for disembowelling. Plenty of show.

CUCKOO: Or I could make holes so big that birds could pass in flight through their bodies with them watching.

MAEVE: I'm almost solid on disembowelling, then beheading.

FERGUS: What about the Hedgehog?

ALI: Oh, not that. I'm bored with the Hedgehog.

FERGUS: It's a great feat if done well. I've done a Hedgehog with thirty-seven spears in one man strung up like this, and I threw every one from a distance of five miles with a mountain in between.

ALI: Five miles, Fergus: Five miles?

FERGUS: All right then. You've caught me out lying. It was ten.

CUCKOO: How about the Bladder? I could do the Bladder for both of them. With one breath of mine down the throat of each I'd have them inflated to the size of ... Ireland.

ALI: That's a great boast, Cuckoo. Do you mean each one to the size of Ireland, or both of them together to the size of Ireland?

CUCKOO: (*Pause.*) Both, I think.

MAEVE: That sounds the best to me. When we get the telephone call then you'll do the Bladder on both of them.

CUCKOO: (*Breathing deeply.*) I'd better start stretching my lungs for this one. It will need plenty of puff to get these two hard cases up that big. I'd better start practising with the woman, I think. A little mouth to mouth ...

JANET: Get off me!

CUCKOO: Ouch! She bit me!

ALI: You'd better try it first with the man, Cuckoo. He might go up easier.

JANET: If you kiss my Con I'll bite your balls off you thick mick bastard!

CON: Janet ... calmly now ... he can kiss me if he likes ... it's only fun ...

CUCKOO: You're doubting my strength, the truth of my boast. Now I've got a split lip I can't do the Bladder, so that's out, but there's the worst of the lot, Maeve.

ALI: Oh, no, not that ...

FERGUS: Cuckoo, what a thought ... not the ...

CUCKOO: Yes ...

MAEVE: The Sack of the Seven Entrances ...

ALI: Whew! Dare we try it?

FERGUS: Come on! We've got nothing to lose. I'm for it. It's ages since I've seen that one done. It's a slow thing so let's start.

CUCKOO: Wham! Wham! Wham! Wham!

CON: Excuse me ...

MAEVE: We've alighted on the right flower, us bees. That will be the kind of honey the gods will like licking. The Sack of the Seven Entrances.

CON: Excuse me ... would you kindly tell ... what exactly is the Sack of the Seven Entrances?

MAEVE: The Sack of the Seven Entrances? You don't know? And you up to your arse in folklore?

FERGUS: The human body is a sack with seven entrances. Count them. Nostrils. Ears. Mouth. Arsehole. Weapon or wound. Taking coin of the realm, the sack is filled to the brim with money from the seven entrances. I have seen it done only a couple of times. It takes so long that the skin of the victim goes green from the corrosion of the copper working in the bowels. The final pieces of silver tarnish grey in the nose and gold goes dull while blocking up the fundament, so to speak. Your man dies stiff with riches. (*Pause.*) Now, we'll be needing some coins.

CON: I've got plenty of change. Here.

(*A rattle of coins.*)

Come on Janet. Be helpful, dear. Swallowing coins, that's all.

(*The telephone rings.*)

CUSACK: That will be Clonmacnois. Everything's getting out of phase. Be with you in a minute.

(*Fade.*)

MAEVE: Where would you like us to start on the Sack of the Seven Entrances? The mouth I think, so they can't sing again.

FERGUS: I'll do the first one. A big silver coin. Is your mouth open, Con?

CON: You want me to swallow a coin? I'll swallow a coin.

CUCKOO: Fergus, the honour of the first stroke in this feat is mine. I claim it and I will not be crossed. Stand back before a better man.

FERGUS: The honour is mine! I claim it for myself!

CUCKOO: A death as ornate as this must belong to the higher hero. Me!

FERGUS: Let Maeve decide ...

MAEVE: Ach, fight it out, fight it out. Give us some sport and spectacle. But no codding about, eh? The man killed is the man cured of pride.

CUCKOO: Fergus, my foster-father, no warrior holds you higher than me. I swear by Ulster's gods I'll churn you up like foam in a pool! I'll stand over you like a cat's tail erect! I'll batter you as easily as a loving woman slaps her son.

FERGUS: Cuckoo, my boy, it is with shame that I view the prospect of killing you. Now you won't see the great Sack of the Seven Entrances, or the shudder of the birth-pangs of a New Ireland. As druid and death come together in a cleaning. I taught you all I knew, with a few things I kept to myself. Those few things will kill you.

MAEVE: Hurry up. Fergus, if you are dying at any time soon, remember my friendly thighs. Will you dream to be buried there?

CUCKOO: (*Chanting.*) Old man, you will fall at an heroic hand which honours death more than a son his father.

FERGUS: (*Chanting.*) The sun in a bold Ireland will not shine brighter than the blood of this boy.

CUCKOO: For the first coin, Fergus.

FERGUS: For the first coin, Cuckoo.

(*A crash of blades. Fade out abattoir atmosphere.*)

CUCKOO: (*Thinking.*) His arm is raised. The way to his heart is opened.

(*A crash of blades in the abattoir atmosphere. Fade out immediately.*)

FERGUS: (*Thinking.*) His leg is too far forward for his weight ... Thigh!

(*A crash of blades in the abattoir atmosphere.*)

CUCKOO: (*Thinking.*) His shield's too low. A glimpse of his neck!

(*A crash of sword on shield in the abattoir atmosphere. Fade out immediately.*)

FERGUS: (*Thinking.*) He's unbalanced. A shove with my shield, a downward stroke to the head!

(*A crash of shield on shield, then sword on sword, then sword on shield in abattoir atmosphere.*)

CUCKOO: Ha! Grrr!

(*A crash of sword on sword, sword on shield, sword on sword. Pause.*)

FERGUS: Well done, Cuckoo. I taught you well.

CUCKOO: You're not too old to learn, Fergus.

(*FERGUS laughs. Pause.*)

MAEVE: What are you waiting for?

FERGUS: Our quarrel is finished.

MAEVE: To the death, I said.

FERGUS: I could have killed Cuckoo several times already.

CUCKOO: Yaaaah!

MAEVE: You're fooling yourself, Fergus.

FERGUS: I helped to bring the boy up!

MAEVE: By all the suffering gods of Ireland, if you do not fight I will kill you myself! What's left of you that's so worth keeping?

FERGUS: Maeve, I put the freedom of Ulster below the freedom of your heart. But now you have said enough. I see how you would be satisfied.

(*A crash of swords. Fade out abattoir atmosphere.*)

CUCKOO: Hack!

FERGUS: Swing!

CUCKOO: Cut!

FERGUS: Slash!

CUCKOO: Rrrrrrrrrrrrrrip!

(*Fade in abattoir atmosphere.*)

FERGUS: (*Screaming.*) Aaaaaah! Blood.

(*Fade out.*)

CUCKOO: Guts.

FERGUS: Weak.

CUCKOO: Strangle.

FERGUS: Dying.

CUCKOO: Strangle!

FERGUS: Little knife.

(*Fade in abattoir atmosphere.*)

CUCKOO: (*Screaming.*) Aaaaaaah!

(*Fade out.*)

FERGUS: Thing I kept to myself. Dying. Wonder.

CUCKOO: My blood. Going. Lost. Death. Brother.

FERGUS: Brother.

(*Fade in abattoir atmosphere.*)

JANET: (*Screaming.*) Oh, God ... this is mad ... mad! Can't you help them?

MAEVE: They're both dead. With honour, at least.

(*The rumbling of an earthquake; the clanking of steel.*)

CON: What's that? Is it me? Are you hearing things?

JANET: I'm going mad! Everything is moving! Stop it!

MAEVE: Mother Earth is trembling as she drinks!

(*The full force of the earthquake. Screams from CON and JANET.*)

CUSACK: (*His voice fading in over the end of the earthquake.*) We did it! We did it! Pope John Paul is in my old cell! But how did we do it with no bulls?

MAEVE: Mother Earth wanted Cuckoo and Fergus. It was their deaths made the earthquake work.

ALI: At such a sacrifice, no wonder Ireland shook. (*Pause.*) It would never have worked with these two scrawny offerings.

CUSACK: Poor Cuckoo, poor Fergus. Well, Mr Sheehan, all we have to do now is wait for the tidal wave. Are you ready for it?

CON: How long have we got?

CUSACK: A matter of minutes.

(*Fade in the sound of lorries drawing up. The bawling of bulls.*)

JANET: What's that?

CUSACK: Would you credit it? It's the bulls arriving, I think.

(*The door opens.*)

CUSACK: Hold it, we'll get the gates open and then you can back in! Give the drivers a hand out there will you Maeve, Ali? Thanks.

(*The gates are opened.*)

JANET: But you don't need the bulls any more ...

CUSACK: We can't send them all the way back now, can we?

CON: These are the two bulls of Ireland?

CUSACK: That's right.

CON: Thirty grown men can stand on the back of one of them?

CUSACK: Probably forty.

(*The sound of lorries backing in.*)

JANET: Keep them out of here!

(*The lorry engines cut. The sound of the bulls stamping and bawling.*)

CUSACK: Well, here's your consignment, Miss Soames.

JANET: I don't want them!

CUSACK: A deal is a deal. If you don't take these two old monsters then what will the dogs and cats of England do for dinner? If we all pitch in we might get their carcases down to the docks before the tidal wave sweeps Ireland clean. What do you say?

CON: I'd rather drown than look those two bulls in the eye. Leave them where they are!

CUSACK: Wouldn't you grant these two old Irish monsters a peaceful and humane conclusion? Shame on you! And, for the first time in their miserable, lecherous existences, the chance to be useful? Come on the white! Come on the brown!

(*The tailgate crashes down on the concrete loading ramp. The bulls' bawling and stamping rises to a crescendo, then cuts out abruptly. Booted feet march quickly down the lowered tailgate.*)

ALI: Good morning, Mr Sheehan.

CON: Ali? Is that you?

CUSACK: Let me introduce you to some heroes of the present: an inspector in the Irish Fraud Squad.

CON: Aaaah!

CUSACK: Who has been working hand in glove with a representative of the British Consumers Association.

MAEVE: Hello.

JANET: Maeve! No!

CUSACK: Ah, there's worse to come, Miss Soames. A stiff case of acute resurrection, I'm afraid.

CON: Fergus! You're dead! Cut to ribbons!

CUSACK: Not at all, at all. He's an official of the World Bank Agriculture and Animal Husbandry Division.

CUCKOO: Aaah ... grrrr ...

JANET: Oh, no! Not him! Not Cuckoo! Don't bring him back to life, please!

CUSACK: Don't worry, Miss Soames, he's only a member of the European Economic Community's Meat Products Standards and Subsidies Inspectorate.

CUCKOO: Grrrr!

CUSACK: I think.

CON: So! We're discovered!

JANET: Deceived and beguiled.

CUSACK: Within the convoluted and serpentine wickedness of the human mind would you think there resided sufficient diabolical skill and energy to invent an electrical meat-tenderising machine? As a further extension of this appalling concept – now working full-blast in an innocent-looking industrial building in Birmingham, invented and designed by ...

CON: Me! I did it! Shame and humiliation! I want to be punished!

CUSACK: Would you further toss around in your reeling imaginations the improbable possibility that geriatric Irish cattle carcasses are being shipped from Dublin to Holyhead on Monday mornings to feed this infernal machine? Would you care to haphazard a guess as to what company and what agent arranges this?

JANET: Who else but me? I fix it. I forge, fiddle and fantasise the paperwork!

CUSACK: Now sink deeper into shock and horror as you torment your brain-cells with the thought that reconstituted flesh from these ancient Hibernian herbivores is then sold at centres of the British meat trade such as Smithfield, posing as top-grade Irish beef.

CON: I've never been so ashamed in my life. How about you, Janet?

JANET: I'm full of self-disgust and remorse. I'm hoping for a very long prison sentence.

CON: By your brilliant subterfuge you have broken us down. We are both psychological wrecks, reeling under the impact of your ingenuity. Well done.

ALI: Thank you sir. We put a tremendous amount of hard work into catching you. You've no idea of the cost of all that special effects work we had to use. Can you imagine the price of an earthquake these days?

JANET: An excellent ploy, a dazzling piece of ethnic reconstruction which had us fooled all the way. May I add my congratulations?

ALI: Three months of research and rehearsal, it took us. Have you ever tried to learn Old Irish? Incredibly difficult. But none of it would have been possible without the help of your clerk, Cusack here, working for us on the inside.

CON: Yes, thanks Cusack, old son, thanks. Thanks a lot.

CUSACK: Just doing my duty, Mr Sheehan. You were robbing Ireland of her future. Without beef we'd be buggered.

CON: Thank heavens you stopped us in time then, before we could do too much damage. We will, of course, make a full confession.

ALI: Oh, good. That puts the crown on the whole scheme. I'm delighted. Thank you. Thank you.

CON: Think nothing of it. You deserve our fullest co-operation.

CUCKOO: Oooooh ... aaah ... grrrr ...

ALI: Come on, snap out of it Cuckoo. Relax now. It's all over. The Black Maria won't be long.

CUCKOO: Is that it then? All over?

ALI: I'm afraid so.

CUCKOO: Grrr ... I can't let go ...

ALI: Look, you did a great job out there, but you must come back!

CUCKOO: No! I'm staying!

ALI: But they're expecting you in your office tomorrow.

CUCKOO: What office? What tomorrow? Help me, Cusack!

CUSACK: You're putting yourself in terrible danger, letting your mind be taken hostage by lies.

MAEVE: Open the book again!

CUSACK: Maeve! You as well? These lies are for the enjoyment of idiots, remember?

MAEVE: Start at the beginning.

CUSACK: What a terrible waste. All of you could have made something sensational out of your lives.
    (*A hum.*)

CUCKOO: Quick, give it to us, give it to us, ooh, blood, slaughter, madness.

CUSACK: All right, all right. (*The opening of a book, the turning of pages.*) Once upon a time King Ali and Queen Maeve were in bed together arguing about equality.
    (*Humming.*)

ALI: You were lucky to have married me.

MAEVE: Lucky enough was I on my own.

ALI: Think of the gifts I gave you.

MAEVE: Only three that mattered to me.

CON: And what might they be?

MAEVE: He swore never to be jealous, never to be mean and never to be afraid.

JANET: That's a tall order. Did he live up to it?

ALI: I didn't do too badly, did I, Fergus?

CUCKOO: Aaaa, that's better, that's better.

> (*Fade abattoir atmosphere. Fade in music and Celtic twilight atmosphere. The HEROES hum.*)

CUCKOO: All of Ireland to walk in. Life, death, blood, brother. Brother.

> (*Fade. Fade back Celtic twilight atmosphere. Maintain humming.*)

CUSACK: Good people, while they start at the beginning we'll have to make do with the end. One thought gives me comfort – you've got more sense than to be taken in by heroes of any kind. But I am actually eight hundred years old; so that when the police approached me to be their man on the inside and asked if I had any ideas as to how we might catch Con and Janet I was able to make a few suggestions which I thought might be appropriate to their transgressions. I can see from your ears that you believe every word I've said. With such a genial approval upon me, I'll take my leave. Good night.

> (*Fade out the humming of the HEROES.*)

The End.

PLOUGHBOY MONDAY

Giles Cooper Award 1985

For Fred and Marjorie

Ploughboy Monday was first broadcast on BBC Radio 4 on the 9th of November 1985. The cast was as follows:

HAROLD, Jason Littler

VERA/MAUD, Judith Barker

GEORGE, Geoffrey Hinsliff

GRUNNIDGE, Geoffrey Banks

STAN, Colin Meredith

PERKINS, Gabriel Paul Gawin

VALERIE/ROSE, Lesley Nicol

HAYWOOD/RICE, Malcolm Hebden

COOK/GLADYS/TILLY, Ruth Holden

YATES/FARMER, James Tomlinson

MATCH JUDGE/
MEGAPHONED VOICE, Randal Herley

BROUGH/MANLEY/OWNER, Paul Webster

DIRECTION, Alfred Bradley

The parlour of the Ransom home. In the background, popular early twenties music is crackling. VERA has been talking for several minutes before we hear her. GEORGE, her husband, is in the room.

VERA: It doesn't make any sense to me at all. What's light work? Doing the weighbridge? I could manage that. (*Pause.*) When you come home and go off doing gardening jobs you dig, don't you? That's not light work – digging. You want to talk to the under manager about getting taken off light work. And what happens if you get a bad back doing gardening? You won't get compensation, you know, not for casual work. There's never any overtime on the weighbridge, is there? (*Pause.*) You should show them that you can manage proper work. I know you don't like asking but we need the money. (*Pause.*) You could ask.

GEORGE: The doctor lays down what I can do. Nothing can move him. And keep your mouth shut about gardening.

HAROLD: Mum, I'm home.

VERA: There's a pie out for you and some pickles.

HAROLD: Did timbering this evening, Dad. Stresses and strains.

VERA: Who taught you tonight, Harold? Anyone we know?

HAROLD: No, he was from Warsop Main. Good though. He knows Alan Brough...

VERA: *Mr* Brough. If he's to be your deputy down the pit, Harold, you must treat him with proper respect.

HAROLD: He doesn't mind.

VERA: Well, he should. I've never heard of any deputy allowing an apprentice to call him by his Christian name. It's not right.

HAROLD: Yes, Mum.

VERA: Your father would never think of calling Mr Brough anything but Mr Brough.

HAROLD: No, Mum.

VERA: Eat your supper.

HAROLD: Is this a pie I made?

(*He sits down at the table.*)

VERA: I don't put labels on them, Harold.

HAROLD: But it could be?

VERA: Get on with it. You have to be up early for school.

HAROLD: Your pies are famous, Mum. That's how people know me. I'm the son of the woman who makes Mrs Ransom's pies, they say. She makes marvellous pies.

GEORGE: She's the cat's mother. And don't call your mother a woman.

VERA: He's only repeating what he's heard folk say.

HAROLD: Sorry, Mum. Can I grind the meat up tomorrow?

VERA: If you behave yourself. Now be quiet. Your father wants to listen to the news.

(*Radio news from June 1930 that will identify the period – industrial news of a general nature to do with the slump would fit. It fades. The parlour atmosphere fades. The kitchen of the Ransom home. The clattering of trays as VERA bakes pies. It is 5.30 in the morning, August 1930. Birdsong can be heard through open windows.*)

HAROLD: Thirty-four, thirty-five, thirty-six, thirty-seven, thirty-eight any more I haven't seen, Mum?

VERA: Did you count the batch in the oven?

HAROLD: I think so. They were the first I counted. It must be thirty-eight ...

VERA: Must be isn't *is,* is it? I must know exactly. Count them again and concentrate, Harold. I've got customers.

(*There is a knock on the door of the back kitchen.*)

HAROLD: How many's in the oven?

(*The door opens.*)

VERA: A dozen. Good morning.

HAROLD: That's twelve, thirteen, fourteen ...

(*He counts on behind the dialogue.*)

HAYWOOD: Morning, Mrs Ransom. Two pies, love – one hot, one cold.

VERA: That's tenpence, Mr Haywood.

HAYWOOD: Hello, young Harold. When d'you start work down t'pit?

HAROLD: Twenty-three ... twenty-three ... oh, don't let me forget the number ... twenty-three ... it's today, Mr Haywood. I'm off in a minute.

HAYWOOD: Are you walking in with your dad? You'll be able to go together.

HAROLD: Oh, hell. I'm lost now. I can't remember those I've counted and those I haven't. Yes, Mr Haywood. I'll be going in with my dad. I'm starting today with Mr Brough. He's my deputy.

HAYWOOD: He's all right is Brough. Work hard, young Harold. Make your mum and dad proud of you. Ta-ra.

(*The door closes.*)

HAROLD: I'm going to be late if I don't watch it. Where's me dad?

VERA: He's gone in early.

HAROLD: Oh. D'you mind if I go now, Mum? I still think it's thirty-eight, but only think.

VERA: Go on then. There's your break. You don't have to guess what it is.

HAROLD: Thanks, Mum. Wish me luck.

VERA: It's not luck you'll need down the mine, Harold. Stay away from bad types and troublemakers. Do your job as you're told to do it. No answering back.

HAROLD: Yes, Mum. Can I go now?

VERA: You can't wait, can you? Your first day at work and you can't wait.

HAROLD: No, I can't. I've been dreaming about this, Mum. I've got a mining job. It's a job for life, they say. That's how I want it. I'll come straight home and tell you all about it. Bye, Mum.

(*The door opens and HAROLD runs in his boots down a side entrance. A pause filled with birdsong. The door closes.*)

VERA: Twelve in there ... thirteen, fourteen, fifteen, sixteen ...

(*Her voice fades. The cap-lamp room. The sound of lamp batteries being put down on the counter, boots, the hum of talk. BROUGH's voice fades in.*)

BROUGH: ... while the cap-lamp is in your possession, Harold, it's your responsibility. I don't want to find you playing games with it, swinging it round your head, knocking it about. Any damage you'll pay for, understand?

HAROLD: Yes, Mr Brough.

BROUGH: When you get your cap-lamp you tie the belt and battery round your waist like this ... see, make it firm, and run the cable up your back and over your left shoulder if you're right-handed or your right shoulder if you're left-handed. It keeps it out of the road while you're working.

HAROLD: Yes, Mr Brough. I remember. We did it at night school.

BROUGH: Give this lad a lamp in there.

GEORGE: He'll get no lamp here.

BROUGH: George ... what are you doing in the cap-lamp room? I thought you were on the weighbridge.

GEORGE: No son of mine is going down the pit.

HAROLD: Oh, Dad ... no ...

BROUGH: God, George, the lad's been going to night classes for three years. He's got his certificate ... the lad's done well!

GEORGE: I've been in three rock falls. I'm a cripple, fit for nothing. The only job they'll give me is charity. My son isn't going to end up like that.

HAROLD: I want to be a miner, like you. What's the matter with that?

BROUGH: You could have spoken up before now. We'll all look fools, you most of all.

GEORGE: That doesn't worry me none. Go home, Harold. There's nothing for you here. It's my right as your father to stop you if I want.

HAROLD: Dad, please! I've got me heart set on it ...

GEORGE: Go home and do as you're told. I'll talk to you tonight.

HAROLD: Talk to me? You've never talked to me! You've never talked to anyone but yourself!

(*HAROLD runs out. Some laughter from the other MINERS in the queue.*)

BROUGH: You've done a lot of damage there, George. But then, you'll have thought of that, won't you? Get back on the weighbridge and keep out of my way for a few weeks.

GEORGE: He never asked my permission. You never asked my permission. My own bloody wife never asked my permission. I was taken for granted and see where it's got you.

BROUGH: You stupid, stupid man. God help you.

(*Sounds of the cap-lamp room fade. The parlour of the Ransom home. The only sound is the ticking of the clock. The back door opens and closes. Heavy boots come close, very slow. GEORGE sits down. The ticking of the clock gets louder.*)

GEORGE: Take my boots off for me.

VERA: That's a job I'll never do for you again.

GEORGE: Tell Harold I want to speak to him.

VERA: He's gone.

GEORGE: Where to?

VERA: I don't know.

GEORGE: Pie for tea, I suppose. That's taken for granted. (*Pause.*) It's for his own good.

(*The radio is on: dance music.*)

VERA: You've taken his only chance away. There's no other work in this place. My only child and you've driven him out of his own home. I know him, George. He's like you. He won't forgive. We've lost him. That's all there is to it.

GEORGE: He'll be back. He can help you with the pies. He likes playing with pastry, it strikes me. But the pit's not pastry. The pit's only pain.

(*The parlour atmosphere fades, with the ticking of the clock being asserted over the music.*)

HAROLD: (*In his head.*) Bloody old bastard doing that to me in front of everyone, leading me on deliberately, never saying a word. I'd never end up like him anyway. He's always been half-asleep, bloody accident-prone old sod ... God, I hate him, I hate him ...

(*The open road on a summer evening, birdsong, cattle being driven.*)

STAN: Hey up, watch yourself. You'll get trod on.

HAROLD: Where is this?

STAN: Laxton Common. I don't know your face. What are you doing round here?

HAROLD: Just out walking.

STAN: Late to be out walking.

HAROLD: I just kept going until I was lost. Didn't think about it.

STAN: Where are you going to sleep?

HAROLD: Oh, I don't know. Up a tree.

STAN: Why don't you go home?

HAROLD: I've left home.

STAN: Go back then. Or have they sold your bed?

HAROLD: I'll never go back – well, not for a long time. Not till I've shown him.

STAN: Oh, you're showing someone, are you?

HAROLD: Fallen out with me dad. He's a right old bugger.

STAN: Mine's a right old bugger an' all. But I've given up showing him. He never takes a blind bit of notice.

HAROLD: Got anything to eat?

STAN: No. Come up to the farm and I'll get you something. You can doss in the barn if you like.

HAROLD: Won't they mind?

STAN: Mind? They won't even see you. The farm is so big they don't know what they've got on it.

HAROLD: What's the money like?

STAN: Thirteen pounds a year with food and lodging – that's boy's rate. I was on that last year. It's not much but it's better than nowt.

(*Fade on cattle being driven and a dog barking. The foreman's office at the farm.*)

GRUNNIDGE: If you're from a pit village, son, why aren't you going down the pit? It's what you'd get used to. Farming is different from mining. Not the same thing at all.

HAROLD: Never fancied going down the pit, sir. I like the open air.

GRUNNIDGE: What does your father think?

HAROLD: He's dead, sir.

GRUNNIDGE: How old are you?

HAROLD: Fourteen. I know I'm small, but I'm fourteen. Honestly, sir, I can prove it.

GRUNNIDGE: I think you better had. We'll write to your mother.

HAROLD: That's fine, sir. She'll have my birth certificate.

GRUNNIDGE: You're lucky, turning up on the doorstep like this. The boy has gone down with meningitis and his family say it's working up here that's done it. You were in the right place at the right time. I should cultivate that if you want to get along with me. I can't stand latecomers or shirkers. You're an opportunist. You'll find it very useful up here. Know your place, do your work, and you'll get on. You can start tomorrow.

HAROLD: Thanks for giving me a chance, sir. I'll work hard and I won't let you down, I promise.

GRUNNIDGE: Don't stick your neck out. Now bugger off. I'm busy.

(*Fade. The farm dormitory.*)

HAROLD: They say you're Mr Perkins. I have to see you.

PERKINS: Are you Tommy's replacement?

HAROLD: Was Tommy the one with meningitis?

PERKINS: Aye. He said it was the wind always whistling in his ears that did it. I'm the fourth waggoner. All right. There's the third waggoner, the second waggoner and the first waggoner, he's *the* waggoner in charge.

HAROLD: Where do I sleep?

PERKINS: In here.

HAROLD: Do you always lie on other people's beds with your boots on?

PERKINS: It's my bed as well.

HAROLD: But I've always had my own bed.

PERKINS: Well, you'll have to get used to sharing. Once you get in, don't move, don't wriggle, don't snore and don't fart and we'll get on. With Tommy I said he could read for twenty minutes, or talk, once he was in bed – if I felt like talking. Remember, I'd like my own bed as well. And I'm the boss, here, and outside. You look up to me.

HAROLD: Who says?

PERKINS: I have to take care of you. There's some funny customers amongst the cowmen, the shepherds and the labourers, but you'll find the waggoners are mostly all right. But keep your eye open.

(*Fade. The sound of the WAGGONERS fast asleep. HAROLD is crying softly.*)

PERKINS: There's nothing to worry about, Harold. Have a good cry tonight and get up in the morning having cleared your mind. This is your home now and you do things our way.

(*Fade. Fade in the stable and PERKINS.*)

PERKINS: You'll be on boy's jobs, locking up the chickens, helping with the milking, mucking out, thistle-spudding, anything that's got no skill. One day they could put you on the plough. We plough all year on this farm. Never stop. There're eighteen horses. We look after them as well as ourselves. What do you know about horses?

HAROLD: Nothing.

PERKINS: Everybody knows something about horses.

HAROLD: I mean nothing useful.

PERKINS: Horses have power and strength, but they're a bit thick, like some people. I'm going to be head waggoner before I've finished and I'll do it through knowing horses. There's no other way. D'you want to learn?

HAROLD: Yes, I do. I have to.

PERKINS: Plenty don't these days. We only have three kinds of horses here – Shires, Suffolks and one hunter for the trap and riding. Show me an entire in this lot.

HAROLD: An entire what?

PERKINS: An entire horse, stupid.

HAROLD: They're all entire horses as far as I can see.

PERKINS. That's where you're wrong, Harold mate. An entire is a stallion that's entire, not a gelding, a complete horse. All right? It's a new language you're having to learn so think on – keep your ears pricked – and remember, even carting muck has a craft to it.

HAROLD: Same as mining is then. They even taught us how to use a shovel at night school.

PERKINS: You went to night school for mining? What the hell are you doing here then?

HAROLD: I changed me mind. Let's say I didn't like the idea of being in the dark.

(*Fade. An open field. The sound of ploughing with three horses. Gulls.*)

PERKINS: Bodkin. We're ploughing bodkin, Harold.

HAROLD: Right. Bodkin.

PERKINS: Ploughing with three horses, two in the furrow and one on the land is bodkin. What type of ground are we ploughing, Harold?

HAROLD: Clay.

PERKINS: Strong clay. Why are we ploughing it?

HAROLD: Break it up, kill the weeds, aerate the soil, prepare ...

PERKINS: Show me the cross-aim. (*Pause.*) Show me the swindle-trees. (*Pause.*) Take the ayles.

HAROLD: What's the ayles?

PERKINS: The handles, stupid. Come on. Have a try.

HAROLD: I won't get it right ... hey, it's not such a strain, is it?

PERKINS: The two horses on the land are pulling sideways, you have to counter that. My ploughing's not so good today. Over my shoulder I'm aware of running out, dog's hind-legs and pencil-lines on my seams. Don't be confused. Setting your rig is everything, Harold. I didn't set my share at the proper distance from my

coulter and my wadsticks are all over the place.
Drinking, Harold, beware of drinking. Doesn't go with
ploughing. This field has had sheep on it so I shouldn't
be ploughing deeper than one and a half inches. One and
a half inches for sheep, Harold. Keep the dung in the top
level. Better than night school, eh?

HAROLD: You're a torment, Mr Perkins.

PERKINS: I love to see a lad learning something.

(*Fade. The foreman's office.*)

GRUNNIDGE: You'd better sit down, young man.

HAROLD: What is it, Mr Grunnidge?

GRUNNIDGE: I wrote to your mother, as I said I had to.
That was two months ago and I hadn't had a reply so
I did some checking up through a friend. Did you know
that your mum and dad weren't in that house any more?

HAROLD: Not in our house? Who says they're not?

GRUNNIDGE: Someone went round. There's a different
family altogether living there now. Nobody ever
mentioned to you that they might be moving away?

HAROLD: No.

GRUNNIDGE: So you don't know where they are?

HAROLD: No.

GRUNNIDGE: But you do know that your dad's not dead
like you told me he was. (*Pause.*) Why did you tell me a
lie like that?

HAROLD: I'm sorry.

GRUNNIDGE: Puts me in a spot. It's nothing to do with
me if you don't get on with your family, is it? But we'll
have to find them, or you'll have to.

HAROLD: Yes, Mr Grunnidge.

GRUNNIDGE: Of course, it might take a while. There's a
lot of ploughing work. Can't spare anyone. You'll have to
wait until next May before you get a break. When's your
birthday?

HAROLD: December. But I'm already fourteen, like I said.

GRUNNIDGE: Well, maybe. Don't you need your mother
though? I thought every lad needed his mother.

HAROLD: I'll catch up with her one day.

GRUNNIDGE: Well, only you will know if that's enough. We're pleased with you, Harold. Work first, worries second. Go on, hop it.

HAROLD: Thank you, Mr Grunnidge.

(*Fade. The dormitory. The sounds of men and boys asleep and HAROLD whimpering.*)

PERKINS: (*Whispering.*) Come on, Harold. Cut that out. Everyone can hear you. (*Pause.*) What's up?

HAROLD: Nothing.

PERKINS: Nobody cries about nothing. What did Grunnidge want?

HAROLD: To say I'm doing all right.

PERKINS: That's enough to make anyone cry, I suppose. Hey, tell us what's up or stop snivelling. (*Pause.*) I'm supposed to help you, you know. I can't if you don't tell me anything.

HAROLD: I don't have a home any more. Me mum and dad have left our house. I don't know where they've gone.

PERKINS: They'll turn up one day. Think on the bright side, Harold. If you haven't got a home you can't be homesick. A man's job is his home, anyway.

HAROLD: They don't care about me.

PERKINS: They don't have to. You're supposed to be taking care of yourself.

HAROLD: That doesn't mean they should just forget about me.

PERKINS: Maybe they just got fed up living there.

HAROLD: No, they liked it. They've moved away so I can't find them. And I won't. I won't even look. They can rot for all I care. (*Pause.*) Well, me dad can rot. Me mum's all right.

PERKINS: It's all right you saying that. Both my parents are dead. I miss having someone. In fact I think you shouldn't say things like that about your father, no matter how hard he is. It's bad luck apart from anything else.

HAROLD: I can't help it, Mr Perkins.

PERKINS: You can call me Joe from now on.

HAROLD: Thanks, Joe.

PERKINS: You can look on me like a father if you like.

HAROLD: But you're only nineteen ... Joe.

PERKINS: It's old enough to be your father.

(*Fade. An open field. The sound of four horses harrowing.*)

PERKINS: Harrowing this clay after the frost has been at it is like crumbling sugar. It's the easiest job you'll get.

HAROLD: Except for shutting up the chickens. I can't stand doing that. It makes me feel like no one at all.

PERKINS: I had to do it. It's a farm boy's job.

HAROLD: If Grunnidge wants the chickens shut up he should do it himself.

PERKINS: I can see that happening. After thirty years in farming he'll want to spend his time chasing hens around a field.

HAROLD: It's not a job at all. They should train a dog to do it. They herd up sheep and cows, why not chickens?

PERKINS: You want to tell that idea to Grunnidge. He'd like to hear it. Chickens can't abide dogs, Harold. To them there's no difference between a farm dog and a fox. And a chicken is always in a panic. It doesn't trust anyone.

HAROLD: It's about time I got some proper jobs to do, that's all.

PERKINS: You've only been here five minutes.

(*The sound of an approaching lorry.*)

HAROLD: If Grunnidge tells me to lock up the chickens tonight, I'm going to say no.

PERKINS: Let me be around when you do it. I don't think he knows that he's got such a Bolshie on the property.

(*The lorry stops close by.*)

Here's your chance. Go on, tell old Grunnidge he can chase his own chickens. I want to hear you.

GRUNNIDGE: Harold! Come over here.

PERKINS: Hope it's not trouble you're in.

HAROLD: Shouldn't be. I haven't done anything wrong.

GRUNNIDGE: Hurry up, I haven't got all day.

(*HAROLD runs over to GRUNNIDGE. Away from the harrow that keeps moving.*)

HAROLD: (*Fade in.*) What is it, Mr Grunnidge?

GRUNNIDGE: Get in the lorry.

(*The sounds of the open fields fade. Fade in the lorry cab atmosphere and its noise as it drives off.*)

HAROLD: Where are we going?

GRUNNIDGE: We have to pick up something near your home. I thought you could go along and see what you can find out about your parents.

HAROLD: What, like this? I don't want to go back all dirty...

GRUNNIDGE: I brought your clean clothes. They're under the seat.

HAROLD: But I don't need to find out ...

GRUNNIDGE: You're a cold-hearted little tyke. If you don't go and find out, I will. By heck, they must have done something to upset you. What was it? Did they cut off your toffee ration?

HAROLD: I've left home. I'm taking care of mysen now ...

GRUNNIDGE: And they don't matter anymore? They bring you up, feed you, clothe you, protect you – and then it means nothing. I wouldn't like a son like that.

HAROLD: There's plenty of time for me to find them later on.

GRUNNIDGE: If you know what's happening. And you don't.

(*Fade. Fade in the exterior of the Ransom house. A knock on the door. It is opened.*)

YATES: What d'you want?

HAROLD: I used to live here.

YATES: Well, you don't live here now.

HAROLD: My mum and dad lived here last.

YATES: Was the name Ransom?

HAROLD: That's right.

YATES: So, you're one of them Ransoms, are you? You didn't take care of this house much.

HAROLD: Yes, we did. It was always kept spotless.

YATES: Threw you out, did they? Or have you been to Borstal?

HAROLD: I'm working. The post hasn't been arriving ... I just wondered if they'd left an address ...

YATES: No, they haven't.

HAROLD: Oh.

YATES: There's been a few people looking for your parents.

HAROLD: It's a mix-up of some sort.

YATES: That's what I thought. What were they running away from? You?

HAROLD: It had nothing to do with me. I'm working now.

YATES: You don't know anything about them moving?

HAROLD: As I said, I've been working ... far away. (*Pause.*) You haven't heard anything?

YATES: Your dad left the mine so he had to leave the house. Somebody said he'd taken up gardening, working on an estate somewhere. Where your mother went, I don't know.

HAROLD: She'll have gone with him.

YATES: Oh, no. She left before that.

HAROLD: Where did she go?

YATES: Your dad didn't even know that. (*Pause.*) Someone should at least have told you that. I heard she'd done a bunk.

HAROLD: She'll have gone to stay at my gran's ... both of them will have.

YATES: That's what's happened. Perhaps your gran's been poorly. Now, I'm in the middle of me tea ... I'll have to close the door.

HAROLD: If you hear anything, will you write to me?

YATES: Yes, yes. I'll keep you up to date.

HAROLD: I'll send you the address.

YATES: All right. Good luck. Off you go.

(*The door closes.*)

HAROLD: (*In his head.*) I can't remember me granny's address ... would I ever find it? I'll ask Mum's friends ...

TILLY: No, Harold, she just went, overnight. No with or by your leave ...

ROSE: Well, you know your father, Harold, after your mum had gone he said even less than he usually did, which was never much. Then he packed up and left. Didn't say goodbye to anyone ...

MAUD: My own opinion, Harold, is that she left because of you. It just wasn't worth her living with him after you'd gone ...

GLADYS: She said to me once – he's flown the nest, and the nest is no longer any use to me.

HAROLD: (*In his head.*) Mum! Where are you?

(*Fade in the lorry cab.*)

GRUNNIDGE: So, how d'you get on, Harold?

HAROLD: Me mum's gone to me granny's near Rotherham. Me dad's doing gardening work and looking for a house.

GRUNNIDGE: Oh, plenty of information then.

HAROLD: I asked the neighbours.

GRUNNIDGE: I'll be able to write to your mum ... at your granny's then.

HAROLD: Yes. I'll get the address.

GRUNNIDGE: Ah. You haven't got it on you?

HAROLD: I'll have it somewhere. What have we got in the back?

GRUNNIDGE: Seed-corn, Harold. For planting, you know.

(*The lorry cab fades. Fade in the open field. The sound of ploughing in the rain. Fade in PERKINS.*)

PERKINS: Oh, God, I'll be glad when this's finished. The horses are paddling in mud. Run up and bring the new horse round, Harold.

HAROLD: Gee again, come on ... gee again.

PERKINS: Gee again, you great idiot! God, he's a numbskull this one.

HAROLD: Stupid lump! You'd think he'd have learnt by now.

(*Sounds of the turning plough. Thunder. The horses crash and shake in the traces.*)

PERKINS: Hold his head! Hold his head! Grab hold of his ears if you can!

HAROLD: I've got him. Stand still you gormless thing. It's only thunder ... (*More soothing.*) Only thunder ... you'll be all right ... there we are.

PERKINS: Hold him until the storm passes. I don't think we can do much more on this. The mud's just getting thicker and thicker.

(*More thunder.*)

HAROLD: Steady now. Nothing will hurt thee ... we'll go home soon ... get in the dry and I'll rub you down ...

PERKINS: Grunnidge says your parents are in Rotherham.

HAROLD: He should mind his own business for a change.

PERKINS: Oh, I shouldn't say that. He's taken a shine to you.

HAROLD: Gently now. He's trembling all over ... there, you're safe with me ...

PERKINS: Gardening, he said. That's the same line as you, really. You're in gardening on a big scale. Farming's gardening, isn't it?

HAROLD: How long are we going to stand out here in this rain?

PERKINS: It'll pass. There's no point in us arriving back before time with the sun starting to shine. We'll wait.

(*A tremendous clap of thunder. The horses lunge in the traces. The plough is pulled over.*)

Don't let go of that horse's head, Harold! Christ, that was close. Did you feel it? Bloody lightning nearly hit the plough.

(*Fade. Fade in a large horse team with a roller moving quickly.*)

PERKINS: Four horses in hand now, Harold. In Canada they have twenty and they plough for twenty-four hours in one line, then turn and plough twenty-four hours in the opposite direction. So don't feel hard done by. At least you don't have to sleep out.

HAROLD: They can get up a fair speed, can't they?

PERKINS: With the Cambridge roller they can. It's only a big wheel, after all. We're bloody charioteers, Romans!

HAROLD: Ploughing is plodding ... I like plodding.

PERKINS: And paddling. You can race with the roller. Giddiup!

(*The roller goes faster. The sound of PERKINS laughing.*)

Move, you great lumps. Shift yourselves! Tanks going into battle. Charge!

(*Fade. Fade in the open field. Ploughing sounds with two horses working. Birdsong.*)

PERKINS: Gee again! Bring 'em round. Lovely. Lovely. Loveleeeee.

HAROLD: They really know what they're doing these two. They just do it without being asked.

PERKINS: They know when it's time for a break, when it's time to go home. They know when you like them and when you don't like them.

HAROLD: Not a bad job, ploughing.

PERKINS: On a day like this, it's not. Try it in January with an east wind and you'll think different.

HAROLD: But they do it all, don't they? The horses do all the work.

PERKINS: You have to guide them. They have to do what you want them to do.

HAROLD: Would they work for me?

PERKINS: If they trusted you.

HAROLD: How would they know that?

PERKINS: They have a knack of telling.

HAROLD: They can trust me. I'll get that through to them. It's not like working, is it – being with horses – these horses. The only horses I had anything to do with were those down the pit. They had hooves covered with green slime and they brought them out once a year. My dad

took me to see them come out. When they let them loose
in the field these big horses rolled on their backs and
kicked their legs in the air like babies. Next week they
went back down again for another year.

PERKINS: That's cruel. Mining's cruel.

HAROLD: (*In his head.*) Not a word. Two horses side by side
and not a word to each other. They just ... do it. Do it.
Do it. That's how I'd like to be. Just do it, and be done.
(*Fade. Fade in the stable, and GRUNNIDGE.*)

GRUNNIDGE: I'm going to try you on your own. Choose
your team.

HAROLD: I like this one and that one. I've come to know
them.

GRUNNIDGE: That's a mare and a stallion. After April
I wouldn't let you mix them. You know their names.
Bonny's the mare, Fred's the ...

HAROLD: (*In his head.*) I know their names. I've always
known their names. Well, you two, I'm master now.
You'll have to do what I say, when I say it.

GRUNNIDGE: You won't find a more docile pair of horses
in all Nottinghamshire. They have natures sweeter than
thine, Harold.
(*The sound of gulls, rooks and crows following the plough in the open
field. The jangle of the plough, and labouring of two horses.*)

GRUNNIDGE: (*Fade in.*) Hey, hold on, hold on ...

HAROLD: Arve again, Dad, arve again Mum. Come round!

GRUNNIDGE. (*Running.*) Harold, stop! What d'you think
you're doing?

HAROLD: Faster! Come on Dad, lift your feet up! Mum's
out-running you!

GRUNNIDGE: Harold! Stop those horses, you're driving
them too hard!

HAROLD: Whoa!
(*The plough stops. GRUNNIDGE and the horses are breathing hard.*)
What is it, Mr Grunnidge?

GRUNNIDGE: Get off that plough.

HAROLD: I haven't finished yet.

GRUNNIDGE: You've finished all right. Listen to those horses. You're a nutcase, son. Perkins never taught you to try and plough at that speed. It's a wonder you didn't smash the rig up.

HAROLD: Well, it's light ground and it's dry, I thought I could get it done quicker and start the next field.

GRUNNIDGE: Not with two dead horses, you wouldn't. Go back to the farm and report to me after your dinner. I'll walk your horses home.

HAROLD: You'll not walk my horses home!

GRUNNIDGE: Won't I now? Don't you answer me back, lad.

HAROLD: I brought 'em out and I'll take 'em back. I'm not having everyone laughing at me.

GRUNNIDGE: You should have thought of that before you wrecked this field. It looks like I've let the pigs loose in it. Go on, get away from here before I'm tempted to belt you.

HAROLD: You raise your hand to me and I'll tell. I'll have the Law onto you. I know my rights ...

GRUNNIDGE: There's a law against cruelty to animals as well, Harold. We'll have to talk about that if you're to stay on. Your job's in danger, son. Don't say anymore. Just bugger off back like I told you and we'll sort this out later. Come on Bonny, come on, Fred ... you're all right now. Go on, you little savage! Get back to the farm!

HAROLD: (*In his head.*) I'll be back, Mum and Dad. Now you're lathered up I can love you. I'll plait your manes, I'll plait your tails, I'll wax your hooves and rub you down with whisky till you shine like two great big stars.
(*Fade in the foreman's office.*)

GRUNNIDGE: What's got into him, Perkins? The lad's not right.

PERKINS: I think he got carried away with himself.

GRUNNIDGE: And my horses.

PERKINS: It's his first time, Mr Grunnidge. He was on his own out there, miles away ...

GRUNNIDGE: He was screaming at those horses, Perkins.

If he'd had a whip he'd have used it. Did you tell him
there's no accelerator pedal on Bonny and Fred? They
have two speeds. Dead slow and stop.

PERKINS: He knows that. He knows all the horses, the
time he spends in the stable.

GRUNNIDGE: There's something up with our Harold.
I know what it is and I should think you do as well. But
he mustn't take it out on the beasts. That's not on.
I won't have it.

PERKINS: He knows that now, Mr Grunnidge. I don't think
it will happen again. Things haven't been easy for him.

GRUNNIDGE: Some parents need shooting.

(*Fade. Fade in the stable.*)

HAROLD: I have to apologise, Mum and Dad.

(*The sound of a restless horse.*)

Don't be fright. Let me come near. It will never happen
again, my word on it ... that's all over now ...

PERKINS: Hello, Harold.

HAROLD: They don't like me now. All I get is the whites
of their eyes.

PERKINS: Can't blame them, can you?

HAROLD: It was only a joke.

PERKINS: I have to go and plough that field all over again
tomorrow.

(*A blow. The horses shy away, frightened. HAROLD falls.*)

You've messed up my chances, Harold. Put me back a
year in Grunnidge's books, you little shit! I'll beat the
daylights out of you.

HAROLD: Don't fight near the horses! They'll trample me!

PERKINS: I've been working on this bloody farm for three
years and things had just started to go my way when you
come along and ruin everything.

(*A kick. The horses shy away.*)

HAROLD: Don't! They'll start fly-hacking!

PERKINS: I couldn't care less if they trample you to death,
you stupid, selfish little sod! Who do you think you are?
Something special? You're not.

HAROLD: All right, all right.

PERKINS: Come out of there. I want another swing at you.

HAROLD: You taught me, Joe. If a horse is going to start kicking, get close to it. I'm staying between these two. You're out of control.

PERKINS: Don't you come anywhere near our bed tonight. You can sleep in the midden for all I care. It's where you belong, pit-boy.

HAROLD: Better than being a bloody yokel!

PERKINS: Why don't you get back there where you belong? Go and eat bloody coal.

HAROLD: Because I can plough better than you, and I could mine better than you. I'm not thick, you see, not thick at all! (*He weeps.*)

PERKINS: I've never known such a lad for crying.

HAROLD: (*Furiously.*) I can't help it! D'you think I want to weep in front of the likes of you?

PERKINS: You deserved it. I don't regret hitting you.

HAROLD: That didn't hurt.

PERKINS: I'll remember that next time you need a beating, Harold. (*Pause.*) I'll leave you to sort yourself out. And don't be too long about it.

(*Footsteps going out of the stable. HAROLD's renewed crying, at first in anger and frustration, then in a flood of released self-pity. The horses snicker and whinny softly on either side of him. Out of the horse-sounds emerge the voices of his mother and father.*)

VERA: Gently, now, son, gently. Don't cry anymore.

GEORGE: They brought us out of the darkness once a year ... green slime.

HAROLD: I didn't mean to push you too hard.

VERA: Don't lie anymore. Make us proud of you.

GEORGE: They broke my back, crushed my ribs and smashed my hip-bone, Harold. But I can still work. Treat me right, and I can still work.

VERA: Gently, Harold, gently.

HAROLD: Don't grip the ayles too tight, don't force the furrow. Bring your big wheel up for deeper down, Dad.

The breast of thy plough, the hymn says, glitters like an angel's wing. We'll stay together, won't we? Say we'll always stay together. You'll never leave me.

VERA: Gently, son, gently. Only beasts of burden.

GEORGE: Don't expect too much from labouring folk.

(*The voices of his mother and father merge back into the whinnying and snickering of the two horses. Fade. Fade in the foreman's office, and GRUNNIDGE.*)

GRUNNIDGE: ... I'm not asking you, Perkins, I'm telling you. I want him out on field seven tomorrow with a two-horse hitch.

PERKINS: He's not ready yet. He's such a moody little bugger, Mr Grunnidge. You don't know when you've got him. It would go to his head.

GRUNNIDGE: I've got to get as much ploughing done as I can before the rain comes. Have you heard the weather forecast? Storms, and more storms. By the end of next week field seven will be a bog.

PERKINS: Well, God help the poor horses, I say.

GRUNNIDGE: Give people credit for learning, Perkins. Aren't you two hitting it off anymore?

PERKINS: He's not with the rest of us. Lives in his own world, day-dreaming. Talks in his sleep, thrashes about. (*Pause.*) I've been thinking of asking to share with someone else.

GRUNNIDGE: I'd take that as an admission of failure if I were you. Perseverance conquers, Perkins, not grumbling and grinding when things get difficult. I'm putting you up to third waggoner as from Monday.

PERKINS: Because of him? I don't want to get a leg up because of him. I want it on my own merit. You're bribing me, Mr Grunnidge. My pride won't let me take it.

GRUNNIDGE: It's not such a big, big thing, being third waggoner. Take the money, Perkins, and stop being such a twerp.

PERKINS: If he ever found out that you'd bribed me to stick it out with him I'd go mad.

GRUNNIDGE: We all have a soft spot for something. With some it's drink. With others it's women. With me, it's the orphans of the plough. Spend your money wisely.

(*Fade. Fade in the stable. The sound of brushing and rubbing down of horses.*)

PERKINS: (*Fade in.*) Good news for you, Harold.

HAROLD: What's that?

PERKINS: Promotion.

HAROLD: Don't be daft.

PERKINS: A friend of yours has been made third waggoner. How about that?

HAROLD: Oh, so *you've* been promoted. You don't deserve it.

PERKINS: Merit, Grunnidge said, pure merit. Doing well. Even with you round my neck.

HAROLD: You deserve a medal for that I've no doubt.

PERKINS: You're to take a two-horse hitch, and plough field seven tomorrow to a depth of ten inches. Get all the muck under. Left to right from the gate. Take Robin and Duster.

HAROLD: He's letting me out on my own? I thought it would be six months before I'd have another chance. Can't I take M ... Bonny and Fred?

PERKINS: I told you which horses you could have. Robin and Duster. I'm using your favourites tomorrow if there's anything left after you've finished rubbing them down.

HAROLD: You're doing that to spite me.

PERKINS: That's right. Don't get too close to dumb animals, Harold. They don't understand.

HAROLD: They do.

PERKINS: See where you've got yourself? Go to church, Harold. Ask someone for some help.

HAROLD: If I say so – they won't work for you. All I've got to do is whisper it in their ears – don't pull for Joe Perkins – and they won't.

PERKINS: You're going mad, Harold.

HAROLD: I'll give you five shillings to let me take Bonny and Fred out tomorrow.

PERKINS: You haven't got five shillings.

HAROLD: I will have come next May. When I get paid out I'll give it to you.

PERKINS: That's more than a week's wages to you.

HAROLD: Take it.

PERKINS: I couldn't. Have the bloody horses. What's the difference to me?

(*Fade. Fade in the open field. The wind blowing. The horses are standing, metal tinkling.*)

HAROLD: Now, I've got to get this perfect, Mum and Dad: straight furrows, every inch turned, no muck left on the surface. No wandering to one side now. Help me. I've got to show Grunnidge what I can do. Gee up.

(*The horses pull and the ploughing starts.*)

(*In his head.*) Cutting, not ripping and tearing. No great stones in this field, please God. I'm the man who makes the grass disappear, folding it in, tucking up the turf. Steady. Keep to the pattern. Leave no part of the land untouched. All the green has to go, Mum and Dad. All the green has to go.

(*Fade. Fade in the foreman's office, and GRUNNIDGE.*)

GRUNNIDGE: ... they were all at some dinner or other, Harold, you know, a few brandies afterwards, a bit of bragging about his farm and his horses and his turnover. Then they got onto ploughing and our owner, bless his heart, spoke up and said he had the best ploughboy in the district and he'd back him to beat anyone under the age of eighteen in a match. Drunk as he was, he bet five guineas on you.

HAROLD: He should have made it ten.

GRUNNIDGE: Harold, you're only sixteen, son. There're lads on the other farms who've had two more years ploughing than you have for an under-eighteen match. Be circumspect in your boasting. Be humble, even.

HAROLD: When's the match?

GRUNNIDGE: Saturday morning.

HAROLD: Whose land?

GRUNNIDGE: Johnson's. I reckon I know which one he'll choose. It's on a fair slope and the clay is thicker at the bottom than the top. His ploughboy will have worked on it before.

HAROLD: Have we got a field anything like it I could practice on?

GRUNNIDGE: Near enough.

HAROLD: Does it need ploughing before Saturday?

GRUNNIDGE: Strange you should mention that. Bonny and Fred?

HAROLD: They'd do it blindfold. All I do is hang onto the back.

(*Fade. Fade in a pub, and the MATCH JUDGE.*)

MATCH JUDGE: Gentlemen, I won't keep you waiting. My decision, after looking at that field and the various bits of ploughing by your boys, is that plot four was by far superior. I don't know who did plot four but all I can say is I wish he was working for me.

(*Applause. Fade. A corridor nearby. Still the pub atmosphere.*)

GRUNNIDGE: That's thirty guineas the owner's won on you, Harold. He's very pleased.

HAROLD: So he should be.

GRUNNIDGE: They want to see you in there. Don't be too bold, son. The owner will give a guinea or even two. Take it with a smile and thank him.

HAROLD: He should be thanking me.

GRUNNIDGE: That's not how it works, Harold.

(*Fade. The pub. The main bar, now noisier. Fade in the OWNER.*)

OWNER: I'm very proud of you. Terrific display. Here's a guinea for you, boy. What's your name again?

HAROLD: Harold, sir. Thank you for the one guinea, sir.

OWNER: Harold is my champion! Watch out for him at the big show.

GRUNNIDGE: Would you like that: a crack at Southwell Ploughing Match?

HAROLD: If it's worth my while.

GRUNNIDGE: It is, if you win.

HAROLD: How much would I get?

GRUNNIDGE: Five pounds for first prize. Another couple from the owner if you remember your manners. That's half a year's wages at one hit. And then, Harold, there's the glory. Now you'd better get out and walk those horses home before the bobby catches you drinking.

HAROLD: There's nothing to beer. It has no effect on me at all.

GRUNNIDGE: Well, the rest of us are only human. It makes me quite cheerful after a dozen pints or so. Get out of here, you big-headed brat. The men are going to celebrate your victory.

(*Fade. Fade in the atmosphere of country road. Two horses walking on a metalled surface.*)

HAROLD: I told you we'd win, Mum and Dad. It was no contest really. We're a good team and no one can beat that.

(*The sound of a bicycle bell and an approaching cycle.*)

PERKINS: (*Approaching.*) You did it, Harold! What d'you say to the man who taught you everything you know? I had to work so I couldn't watch you. But they told me how great you were. Wiped the floor with them all.

HAROLD: Boss gave me a guinea, the mean old bugger.

PERKINS: That's not bad.

HAROLD: When I'd won him thirty!

PERKINS: There's a letter for you. I've left it on the bed.

HAROLD: A letter?

PERKINS: Yes, a real letter. On paper. With a stamp.

HAROLD: Do us a favour, Joe. Walk Mum and Dad home for me and lend us your bike.

PERKINS: Walk who home?

HAROLD: Come on, please! I want to read me letter.

PERKINS: (*Laughing.*) Mum and Dad, is it? I get you. All right, Harold. Here, pedal off. But I'll expect you to treat me for this.

HAROLD: I will. I will.

> (*HAROLD pedals off, leaving the horses. The sound of wind in the hedgerows and the whirring of the wheels.*)

HAROLD: (*In his head.*) It'll be me mum's tracked me down. I knew she would. Wait till I tell her about today. And it will be one in the eye for Dad. Jesus, he'll look stupid when he finds out I'm winning ...

> (*Fade. Fade in the dormitory and the sound of HAROLD running, picking up the letter.*)

HAROLD: (*In his head.*) Is that me mum's handwriting? I'd forgotten what it ever looked like ...

> (*The sound of the letter being torn open. Fade the dormitory.*)

YATES: (*Voice over.*) Dear Harold Ransom, As I promised to let you know if I heard anything that could help you find your mother and father, I'm writing to say that Mr Ransom is working at Egmanton for a man called Rice who employs him as a gardener at his private home. This is reliable information as I got it from the pit office who had to follow him through because of his insurance stamps. I hope this is useful. There is no news of your mother. Yours sincerely, Thomas Yates.

HAROLD: (*In his head.*) Egmanton. That's only a couple of miles from here. But what's he done with me mum?

> (*Fade. Fade in the stable. The horses are being groomed.*)

PERKINS: So who was your letter from?

HAROLD: A girl I used to go round with.

PERKINS: You must have started early. Love letters from women at your age. What did you do that they remember you so kindly?

HAROLD: Childhood sweetheart.

PERKINS: Childhood. That's ages ago with you, Harold. I sometimes think you've overtaken me in years. I've never had a letter from a woman. Had a man's hand, that girl who wrote to you. But then people in a pit village can't tell the difference between men and women, can they? Everyone's covered in coal-dust.

HAROLD: They're entering me for the Southwell Ploughing Match.

PERKINS: I expect they'll ask me to go in as well – in the senior class, of course.

HAROLD: I wouldn't mind taking on the over-eighteens. I wouldn't mind taking anyone on.

PERKINS: You won't get the blue rosette for modesty, Harold, that's for sure. Bonny needs a shoe.

HAROLD: I'll tell the waggoner.

PERKINS: Or is it Mum needs a shoe? (*Pause.*) It's all right, Harold. I won't tell on you.

HAROLD: If you want any ploughing lessons let me know.

PERKINS: Cheeky little beggar.

(*Fade. Fade in a garden atmosphere. The sound of a gravel drive being raked. Birdsong. The crunching of boots on gravel. The raking continues. The boots stop.*)

HAROLD: Hello, Dad.

(*The raking stops.*)

GEORGE: What are you doing here?

HAROLD: I work at Laxton, not far away.

GEORGE: You've grown. How did you get over here?

HAROLD: I walked over.

GEORGE: Some have the time to walk.

(*The raking starts again.*)

HAROLD: Why did you leave the pit?

GEORGE: Mr Rice doesn't like gossiping. If I'm working, I'm working.

HAROLD: I went back to the house.

GEORGE: Still standing, is it?

HAROLD: There's someone called Yates living there now.

GEORGE: Keeping fit, are you? You seem all right.

HAROLD: What happened after I'd left? I'm sorry I went like that.

GEORGE: You'd had enough. You flew the nest, that's all.

HAROLD: But you and Mum ... I didn't know you'd break up.

GEORGE: That's nothing to do with you.

HAROLD: I'm your child! Both of yours' child ...

GEORGE: Are you still a child? Is that what's standing in front of me? It doesn't look like one.

HAROLD: I didn't want to lose touch.

GEORGE: Did you walk all that way to watch me raking gravel in a rich man's drive? Was that worth it?

HAROLD: I've missed you both.

GEORGE: That won't help any of us now. You'll just have to manage as best you can. (*Pause.*) Nobody should expect too much from their parents.

HAROLD: I only wanted to see you.

GEORGE: Well, here I am. Got what you wanted?

HAROLD: I haven't seen you for over two years.

GEORGE: Is that something to complain about?

HAROLD: Where's Mum? Where's she got to?

GEORGE: Mr Rice is watching us through the window. That's all he's got to do with himself.

HAROLD: I'll wait for you when you've finished.

GEORGE: You'll have a long wait.

HAROLD: There's a lot to talk about.

GEORGE: There's nothing to talk about. I don't know where your mother is.

(*The sound of a window opening nearby.*)

RICE: (*Calling.*) Ransom! Who's that with you? Is he looking for work? Come here, boy!

GEORGE: Get off with you. You're getting me into bother.

HAROLD: I'll wait in the road.

GEORGE: You won't. Wait behind the last cottage on the left as you go out towards Kirton. But don't go in.

(*The garden atmosphere fades on the raking of gravel. Fade in a field.*)

VALERIE: Hey, what are you doing hanging around here, young man?

HAROLD: I'm waiting for someone.

VALERIE: Who are you waiting for?

HAROLD: For my dad.

VALERIE: (*More tentatively.*) What's his name?

HAROLD: The same as mine.

VALERIE: Is your name Ransom?

HAROLD: How did you guess?

VALERIE: Your manners are like his. You might as well come inside.

(*Fade. Fade in a cottage parlour.*)

VALERIE: You must know him, what he's like. Why should it surprise you? He never talks about people if he can help it.

HAROLD: He's never mentioned me? Never said he has a son?

VALERIE: No. Don't feel put out. He never mentions anybody.

HAROLD: I bet he mentions me mum.

VALERIE: Her least of all. Which you might expect, under the circumstances.

HAROLD: What d'you live with him for?

VALERIE: He's someone to have around.

HAROLD: But he's married to me mum.

VALERIE: She walked out, not him. If I thought he had a heart I'd say she broke it for him.

HAROLD: How did you meet him?

VALERIE: He was doing part-time gardening at the house where I was the cook. I had to feed him. He came into the kitchen every day he was there. I suppose I got used to looking after him.

HAROLD: Do you like living with him?

VALERIE: It's better than being on my own.

HAROLD: Does he know where me mum is? I've asked him and he says he doesn't, but he could be lying.

VALERIE: Your father speaks so seldom that he'd never bother to waste words on a lie.

(*The door opens and closes. The sound of footsteps entering the parlour.*)

GEORGE: I told you to wait outside and not come in here.

VALERIE: He was waiting round the back. I invited him in when I found out who he was. Do you want your tea?

GEORGE: He's my son. His name is Harold.

VALERIE: I didn't know his name was Harold.

GEORGE: He's over at Laxton. Can you give him some tea as well?

VALERIE: Yes. I'll get it now.

GEORGE: What are you doing over at Laxton?

HAROLD: Ploughing.

GEORGE: Ploughing. I sometimes wondered what you'd get up to.

HAROLD: I just won a ploughing match. I was competing with five others.

GEORGE: How far is it to walk?

HAROLD: If you plough an acre you have to walk eleven miles altogether.

GEORGE: I mean how far from Laxton?

HAROLD: I don't know. An hour or so on foot. I'm being entered for the Southwell Ploughing Match. The foreman says I might get sponsors interested if I win. I could go on, get big money.

GEORGE: Do they treat you right?

HAROLD: I could make seven pounds at one match if I win.

GEORGE: I said – do they treat you right? Do you get paid decent wages? Is it a good job where you work?

HAROLD: Not bad.

VALERIE: Do you like meat pie, Harold?

(*GEORGE laughs wryly.*)

HAROLD: I won't stay for tea. It's a long walk back and I have to shut up the chickens.

VALERIE: Don't go. It'll be on the table in a minute.

HAROLD: I must. Dad, do you know me granny's address in Rotherham?

GEORGE: Your mother's not there. I tried.

(*The door opens and closes quickly.*)

VALERIE: What was all that about?

GEORGE: A bit of history. If he comes again, don't serve him pie.

VALERIE: I thought we were getting on all right. I'd like to see him again. He looks like you.

GEORGE: That's something for him to worry about, not us.

VALERIE: I'd often wondered why we had to move up here ...

GEORGE: I'll have me tea now, if that's all right.

VALERIE: Why don't you tell the lad that you care about him? Tell me, and all, while you're at it. Do you have to be so secretive?

GEORGE: Don't interfere, Valerie. He's my son, nor thine.

VALERIE: Who needs telling? Being with you two in the same room is like watching a couple of goldfish in a bowl.

(*Fade.*)

VERA: (*Voice over.*) 14 Anderson Street, Dundee. 25th April 1931. Dear Harold, I am very sorry that it has taken me so long to write to you but I did not know where you were until your father sent a letter to your gran for her to forward to me. I have been up here in Scotland for over two years now working in a commercial hotel. It is not a bad job except that the hours are long and I spend a lot of time on my feet. One day I will come down for a visit and you can show me round the farm. I never expected you to end up in that line, I must say ...

(*Fade. Fade in the country road. Footsteps.*)

HAROLD: Hello Dad. I've been waiting for you.

(*The footsteps continue, joined by HAROLD's, and the ticking over of a bicycle being pushed.*)

I kept out of Mr Rice's way. He didn't see me. I've had a letter from Mum.

(*The footsteps quicken. HAROLD's follow.*)

She says she's coming down for a visit.

GEORGE: Is that your bike?

HAROLD: No, I borrowed it.

GEORGE: See you take good care of it then.

HAROLD: Mum's in Scotland. Why did she go up there?

GEORGE: I don't want to know.

(*The footsteps stop.*)

HAROLD: But you wrote to her.

GEORGE: But I didn't know where she was. I just reckoned your granny would. I don't want to know where your mother is, and she doesn't want me to know. So, now I've been told it's Scotland. We'll leave it at Scotland. It's a big enough place.

HAROLD: If she comes down ...

GEORGE: Don't bring her over here.

(*The footsteps and the bicycle resume.*)

HAROLD: I've been entered officially for the Southwell Ploughing Match. Perhaps you'll come and watch me.

GEORGE: There's no fun in watching other men work.

HAROLD: Mr Grunnidge thinks I'm in with a chance. All the big firms will be there looking for people to sponsor – Cooks of Lincoln Ransom Sims and Jefferies of Ipswich, best ploughs you can get. Same name as us, Ransoms. Isn't that strange? Our owner's given me two days off, he's putting me up in a boarding-house, all paid ... say you'll come ...

GEORGE: What for?

HAROLD: So you'll see how I'm getting on ... that I'm good at something.

GEORGE: You're bloody good at talking, I'll say that for you.

(*Pause. The footsteps and bicycle sounds continue.*)

HAROLD: Can I come back home with you? Or will your ... friend mind?

GEORGE: I'd rather you didn't.

HAROLD: Why?

GEORGE: That's none of your business.

HAROLD: I've done a day's work then got myself over to see you ...

GEORGE: Without being asked.

HAROLD: I can see my own father if I want, can't I?

GEORGE: Well, now you've seen me. What do you find? I'm tired, Harold. I want to be quiet. So, don't torment me. (*Pause.*) Get on your bike and go back to Laxton. Come over next Sunday for your dinner if you like.

HAROLD: Thanks, Dad. I will, I will. The ploughing match is in two weeks.

(*The sound of the bicycle being mounted and ridden off, the bell being rung.*)

GEORGE: (*To himself.*) Scotland, eh. About as far as she could get.

(*Fade. Fade in the stable. The sound of brushing of horses.*)

HAROLD: Got to make you beautiful for tomorrow, Mum and Dad. Everyone will be looking at you ...

GRUNNIDGE: How are you doing, Harold?

HAROLD: Just bedding them down, Mr Grunnidge.

GRUNNIDGE: We're running that stallion close, you know.

HAROLD: He's all right.

GRUNNIDGE: We're into the season. I shouldn't have let you take him with the mare. It could ruin your chances if he starts to play up.

HAROLD: He won't. He's as firm as a rock.

GRUNNIDGE: You won't stop him if he gets the idea into his head. I don't want us looking fools in front of all Southwell and district.

HAROLD: I feel lucky, Mr Grunnidge. I don't think I'll have any trouble.

GRUNNIDGE: Get a good night's sleep. No sloping off to the alehouse. Come to think of it, I'll get you some whisky to do their coats with in the morning. Makes them shine, Harold. I love that. Two shining horses, and a shining plough. Is your father coming to watch?

HAROLD: He said he'd try ... it's the bloke he works for, Mr Rice ... he's not likely to give him time off.

GRUNNIDGE: That's a pity. You should have mentioned it to me. I know Mr Rice. He's only an old solicitor from Newark. I've done business with him before he retired.

HAROLD: He's a hard task-master, my dad says. On his back all the time. Wants his pound of flesh.

GRUNNIDGE: Doesn't sound like the man I know, but I'll take your word for it. Don't be long out of bed now. Goodnight.

HAROLD: Goodnight. (*Pause.*) You won't let me down tomorrow, will you, Dad. No nonsense, no being carried away, or biting, or kicking ... just side by side, with Mum, together.

(*Fade. Fade in an open field: the ploughing match. A MEGAPHONED VOICE.*)

VOICE: ... and on plot nine, Harold Ransom of Laxton Common with a pair of Shires, Bonny and Fred ...

(*The MEGAPHONED VOICE fades.*)

HAROLD: (*In his head.*) Small wheel set for forty-five degrees. Coulter and share a penny's-width apart. No slack in the reins. Everything is firm. We're ready, Mum and Dad. (*In the atmosphere.*) Gee up!

(*The horses pull the plough. The share cuts into the ground and sends up the first seam of earth off the breast.*)

(*In his head.*) We're well set in. Open the rig out, turn, close the rig, keeping the line, always keeping the line ...

(*Ploughing sound effects at a greater distance. Fade in GRUNNIDGE.*)

GRUNNIDGE: ... don't ask me how he does it. He's a bad-tempered, awkward little beggar is our Harold, very stiff-necked, Mr Manley, but if you want to sell ploughs for your company, take Harold on to sponsor him.

MANLEY: Will he win today?

GRUNNIDGE: Watch him. He's only been up and down the plot four times and it looks as though he's drawn those furrows with a ruler. When he's finished it will look like a geometry exercise. I've never seen such regular, even ploughing.

MANLEY: He must have been well taught by someone.

GRUNNIDGE: No. The man he spent most of his time with will struggle all his life to get halfway to Harold's standard.

MANLEY: What's he got then? Is it temperament? Doesn't sound like it. Strong wrists? Or does he just like staring at horses' backsides?

GRUNNIDGE: It's the place where he loses himself.

HAROLD: (*In his head.*) Don't keep looking at her, Dad. I should have put the blinkers on you both. Put your head down, Dad!

MANLEY: Your stallion is starting to act up. Left it a bit late to have him hitched to a mare, haven't you?

GRUNNIDGE: That's Harold's team. Defying nature is natural to him.

MANLEY: They'll run away with him if he's not careful.

GRUNNIDGE: I don't think so. The plough is what matters and it's cutting perfect seams in perfect shapes, no matter what's going on ahead of it. Harold has his hand on all the vibrations.

(*Fade.*)

HAROLD: (*In his head.*) Don't keep banging into her with your shoulder you stupid, bloody brute! If you bite her I'll whip you with these reins until you bleed!

(*Special atmosphere.*)

GEORGE: Hit me, son, go on, hit me. But it won't stop me doing anything I want to.

VERA: ... I have to spend a lot of time on my feet.

VALERIE: Don't go. It'll be on the table in a minute.

GEORGE: It's time for me to hurt her, Harold. You can't do anything about it.

VERA: ... so long to write to you. So long to write to you.

(*Fade the special atmosphere. Fade in the ploughing sounds.*)

GRUNNIDGE: Keep it up, Harold! You've got it like lines in an exercise book! Watch out for Fred though. He's getting nasty.

HAROLD: I've got him well in hand, Mr Grunnidge. He won't get away from me.

(*Fade. Fade in the stable. Restless horses clattering and snorting.*)

GRUNNIDGE: I want to introduce you to Mr Manley who's the chief salesman for Ransom, Sims and Jefferies of Ipswich. He'd like a word with you.

MANLEY: Congratulations, Harold. That's as good as I've seen for a long time. You came out a worthy winner.

GRUNNIDGE: Harold, straighten up now and talk to the gentleman.

HAROLD: We must get the horses separated, Mr Grunnidge. He's going to kick the stable down.

GRUNNIDGE: Don't you worry. I'll deal with the horses. Have a talk to Mr Manley and remember, he's offering you some help you could do with.

HAROLD: Those two have nearly yanked my arms out of their sockets. I'm aching all over. He'd have bitten her in half if I'd let him, the sod.

MANLEY: Don't know how you controlled them. Come on, we'll have a drink somewhere. Mr Grunnidge can catch up with us later.

GRUNNIDGE: Lemonade only for him. He's under eighteen, remember.

MANLEY: It's the All England under-eighteen Ploughing Championship I want to discuss with him – so, lemonade it will be.

(*Fade. Fade in a kitchen atmosphere, the sound of many people working.*)

HAROLD: Mrs Ransom.

COOK: What's her first name?

HAROLD: Vera.

COOK: What d'you want her for?

HAROLD: I'm her son.

COOK: We're in the middle of doing lunch at the moment. She can't be spared.

HAROLD: I've come up all the way from Newark on the train to see her.

COOK: Go and amuse yourself till half-past four when she gets a break. You'll find her out the back with the rest getting a breath of fresh air.

HAROLD: Don't tell her I'm here, I want it to be a surprise.

COOK: Oh, she'll be ready for a surprise by then. Go on, you're in the way ...

(*Fade. Fade in rear of hotel open atmosphere. A group of HOTEL WORKERS chatting.*)

HAROLD: (*Whispering.*) Mum.

VERA: Harold! How did you get here?

HAROLD: I came on the train.

VERA: This is my son, Harold.

COOK: We've met.

HAROLD: You're smoking, Mum. You didn't used to.

VERA: Come on, we'll go for a walk.

COOK: Back here for five, Vera.

VERA: (*Under her breath.*) Oh, shut up, will you.

HAROLD: I hardly recognised you. You've lost a lot of weight.

VERA: It's the Scottish way of working, Harold. You run everyone into the ground.

HAROLD: D'you mind me coming?

VERA: I was coming down to see you in a month or so, when I'd got some money together.

HAROLD: I can give you some money if you like.

VERA: Well-off now, are you? How did you get rich?

HAROLD: I'm not rich but I save. And I've won a couple of ploughing competitions. I got seven pounds for the last one.

VERA: Ploughing competitions. What are you doing in ploughing competitions? Doesn't sound like my Harold. Baking pies, perhaps. You got my letter, then.

HAROLD: Yes. I didn't write back because I couldn't sort out what to say.

VERA: That's a bit too like your father for comfort.

HAROLD: I look like him, don't I?

VERA: More and more.

HAROLD: A man should look more like his dad than his mum, surely?

VERA: Oh, aye.

HAROLD: When are you coming down to see us then?

VERA: I'm seeing you now, aren't I?

HAROLD: You can see Dad as well. He lives only a couple of miles away from the farm where I work.

VERA: How is he?

HAROLD: He has a job as a gardener.

VERA: At least that's something he can do. Better than hanging around the pit doing half-jobs.

HAROLD: When are you coming down, then?

VERA: Well, I'll have to think about that.

HAROLD: Can you make it in September?

VERA: Why September?

HAROLD: I'm competing in the All-England Ploughing Match at Lincoln. You could come and watch me win.

VERA: Oh, so you're going to win, are you? You know that already.

HAROLD: Only the under-eighteen section. They won't let me take on the seniors.

VERA: I bet they're relieved to hear that. You're very cocky these days.

HAROLD: You could come and live near Laxton. I could stay with you and give you my wages for the housekeeping. There're lots of cottages vacant.

VERA: But you're on your own now, Harold. You don't want to be living with your mother at your age.

HAROLD: We could meet Dad now and then.

VERA: I'll try and come down for a week in September. Do you know the date of this ploughing thing?

HAROLD: The tenth. But come down on the ninth so we can travel to Lincoln together. They'll put you up, if I ask them.

VERA: Who's they?

HAROLD: My sponsors. They're big farming machinery manufacturers. Ransom, Sims and Jefferies. They'd do anything for me.

(*Fade. Fade in the parlour of the Egmanton cottage.*)

HAROLD: September the tenth, at Lincoln. If you ask Mr Rice now, give him some notice, he'd let you have a couple of days off.

GEORGE: Would he now? You seem to know a lot about the way his mind works.

HAROLD: Our foreman knows him. He says he's not a bad sort.

GEORGE: Your foreman doesn't work for him.

VALERIE: Ask the old misery if you can go. It'll do you good. We can have a holiday. I'd like to go to Lincoln.

HAROLD: Oh ... I was meaning that Dad could come with me ... stay in the boarding house ... my sponsors would gladly pay for him but I don't think they'd run to two of you ...

VALERIE: I could pay for myself.

HAROLD: If they knew who you were ... that you weren't my mother ...

VALERIE: I see.

HAROLD: It'll be my big day, Dad.

GEORGE: Sounds like it. Have you heard from your mother?

HAROLD: No. I'll write to her some time.

(*Fade. Fade in the dormitory.*)

PERKINS: You can have the bed to yourself now, Harold. If they take on a new boy now you're fourth waggoner and I'm leaving, I'd suggest you tell Grunnidge that you've got some terrible skin disease so you can sleep by yourself. Since you and I have shared that bed I've never had more than three hours proper sleep in a night.

HAROLD: What are you going to do with yourself, Joe?

PERKINS: Won't be farming. I thought about joining the army.

HAROLD: Doing what?

PERKINS: Anything, so long as it's nothing to do with horses. Ride a motorbike, drive a lorry, I don't care. I'm fed up with this kind of life. This place is behind the times.

HAROLD: Grunnidge is getting a tractor next year.

PERKINS: He's been saying that ever since I came to Laxton. He's not a tractor man. Too old, Harold, too old. Tractors are part of the future. That's why you're wasting your time with these ploughing competitions. It's from a bygone age, all that stuff. You're playing games.

HAROLD: You'd have been interested if you'd have been good enough.

PERKINS: What? Put all that time and energy into something as simple as ploughing? Talking to horses? Listen, Harold, the daftest bloke alive can plough. Anyone can plough. It's simple.

HAROLD: Why couldn't you do it as well as I could, then?

PERKINS: Wasn't worth it. Mum and Dad. What was all that about? Calling a couple of stupid horses your mum and dad.

HAROLD: I don't do that anymore. I was just playing ... because ... well, I was young. You never told anyone, did you?

PERKINS: I said I wouldn't, didn't I?

HAROLD: Do you want to know if I win or not in September?

PERKINS: Oh, it will be all over the papers, I expect. Front page headlines. 'Our Harold Does It Again.' (*Pause.*) Send me a postcard.

HAROLD: Where to?

PERKINS: Care of the dole office. Ta-ra.

(*Fade. Fade in the open field at the All-England Match, Lincoln.*)

GRUNNIDGE: This is it then, Harold. There's your plot, you've set your plough, all you have to do is win. Second nature to you now, I should think, isn't it?

HAROLD: I thought me mum and dad would be here to watch me.

GRUNNIDGE: I know, son. You must be disappointed. But I expect they're busy. I'm here, aren't I?

HAROLD: You're not family.

GRUNNIDGE: Near enough.

HAROLD: I wanted them to be here. I don't know who I'm doing this for, Mr Grunnidge.

GRUNNIDGE: I could say, the pride and the glory: I could say Ransom, Sims and Jefferies: I could say our farm, our owner, bless him: I could say me – but ... it must be for thee, son. You've mastered something. Show them.

HAROLD: I'll never forgive them for this. Even if I win, and I will, by God, I will, I'll not speak to those two again as long as I live. Gee up!

(*The plough starts moving. Fade. Fade in the dormitory.*)

GRUNNIDGE: What standard of production have we got for Plough Monday then? Have you got your lines learnt?

STAN: We're struggling with them, Mr Grunnidge. Harold keeps forgetting.

GRUNNIDGE: Which part are you playing, Harold?

HAROLD: I wanted to do Saint George but they've got me on the Doctor.

GRUNNIDGE: Old Et Essum Squocum. I did him a few times. Doctor, doctor, five pound for a doctor. I'll give you ten to stay away.

HAROLD: You can do it if you like.

GRUNNIDGE: I'm too old to go pulling a plough around. There's snow on the way according to the feller on the weather forecast. Where are you going to go with your play?

STAN: All round here. Harold says we might try Egmanton. Depends how well we do. If no one lets us in to do it we might get fed up and go down the pub.

GRUNNIDGE: No, you must take your play out on Plough Monday. It's always been done. New Year wouldn't be the same without it. Plenty of folk will let you in, and be open-handed.

(*Fade. Fade in the farm house. A small crowd of people in a good mood. Fade in the PLOUGHBOYS.*)

PLOUGHBOYS: Good master, and good mist-er-ess,
　　As you sit by the fire,
　　Pray think of us poor plough lads
　　That plough through mud and mire.
　　We're not the London actors
　　That act upon the stage,
　　We're just the country plough lads,
　　That plough for little wage.
　　We've done our best that best can do
　　And best can do no more,
　　We wish you all good night, good luck,
　　And another happy year.

(*Applause.*)

FARMER: Well spoken, lads. Brandy is the only reward for such artistry. I've never heard that play done better – even by Henry Irving.

(*Laughter; the clink of glasses. Fade. Fade in a country road. The sound of horses pulling a cart containing the PLOUGHBOYS and the plough.*)

STAN: But this is a private house, Harold, not a farm. We're only supposed to go round the farms.

HAROLD: (*Quite drunk.*) It's a big enough house, isn't it? There's farms all around. Get the plough out of the cart and I'll knock the old bugger up.

STAN: I don't think we should. If he's not a farmer he won't know what we're doing.

HAROLD: The rule is, if anyone turns us down and won't let us perform in their house, and won't give us a few bob, a bit to eat and a beer ... he pays a forfeit.

Anybody. Not just farmers. Anybody. Mr Rice, who lives here, has people tilling his land. I know that. I'll sort him out.

(*Fade. Knocking.*)

HAROLD: (*To himself.*) Come on, Rice. Open the bloody door.

(*The door is unbolted and opened.*)

RICE: Yes? What do you want?

HAROLD: We've come to do our play. Let us in.

RICE: Who is 'we', may I ask?

HAROLD: We're ploughboys from Laxton. It's Plough Monday, today, in case you hadn't noticed.

RICE: No, I hadn't. And, I must say, I don't like your tone.

HAROLD: I couldn't care less. You're a tight-arsed old bastard.

RICE: I think you'd better go. You're drunk.

HAROLD: You're turning us down. You won't let us in to do our play?

RICE: Certainly not. Now get off my property.

HAROLD: Right. Thank you very much indeed.

(*Fade.*)

STAN: Aw, come on, Harold. We don't need to make him pay a forfeit. He's not one of us ...

HAROLD: He threw me out. He broke the rule. Get everyone in those traces. You lot are going to be my horses.

STAN: What are you going to do?

HAROLD: Plough up his bloody lawn.

STAN: He'll see us.

HAROLD: Not in snow this thick, he won't. And I don't make a lot of noise when I plough. That's one thing you learn when you're an All-England champion. You don't make much noise. You just do it.

(*Fade. The slight tinkling of the plough. The heavy breathing of boys pulling the plough. The sound of share cutting the turf.*)

STAN: (*Breathless – whispering.*) How are we getting on, Harold?

HAROLD: A yard or so left, that's all.

STAN: You've made a neat job of it.

HAROLD: It's coming over like roast beef off a knife.
(*Fade.*)

HAROLD: We'll stack all the turfs against his front door so when he opens it in the morning, he'll get the lot fall in on him.

STAN: Hell, Harold, that's going too far. He'll have the bobby onto us.

HAROLD: Ploughboys never get done for Plough Monday forfeits round here. And Rice is an offcomer anyway. No one will listen to him.

STAN: When did you dream this up?

HAROLD: It just came into my head. Get working.
(*Fade. Knocking.*)

HAROLD: Come on, Rice. Shift yourself. I'm freezing out here. Ooooh, what a night, what a night.
(*The door opens.*)
Hell, Mr Rice! What are you doing in your house?

RICE: I told you to go away.

HAROLD: Well, I thought as I'd tried the front door first time I'd better come round the back and see if I had better luck. It's a good play we've got for you. The best actors for miles. All we want is ten pounds, a bottle of brandy, no, make that two ...

RICE: I'm going to call the police.

HAROLD: I'm your gardener's son.

RICE: I thought I'd seen you before.

HAROLD: Harold Ransom, son of George Ransom, not so you'd notice. I expect you'll have to fire him now, won't you?

RICE: Step inside for a moment.

HAROLD: Not likely.

RICE: Have you seen your father lately?

HAROLD: No. I never see him. He's lost his job now, hasn't he? I've stopped him ... like he stopped me ... I hate him, Mr Rice.

RICE: Your father doesn't work here anymore. He left my employment at the end of September to go to Scotland.

HAROLD: Scotland.

RICE: We'll forget all about tonight. I can see you're upset. I think you should get back home now. This is becoming quite a blizzard. Good night.

(*The door closes.*)

HAROLD: Scotland.

PLOUGHBOYS: In comes I, the ploughman,
    Don't you see my whip in hand,
    As I go forth to plough the land
    To turn it downside up?
    Straight I go from end to end,
    I scarcely make a bulk or bend,
    Then to my horses I attend,
    With Gee, whoa, back and arve.

HAROLD: It wasn't all that bad ... Scotland ... I could go mining now, of my own accord ... live close by, not too close but ... close enough to call in. They'll be glad to see me. Yes, I'll go to Scotland ...

The End.

FLOS

BBC entry for Prix Italia 1983

Flos was first broadcast on BBC Radio 3 on 10th October 1982. The cast was as follows:

TURSTIN, Mike Gwilym

KING JOHN, Peter Vaughan

PRIOR ALEC, Michael Williams

ST THOMAS, Robert Eddison

ALNOTH/ALAN/BASS, Anthony Newlands

HARPER/MURPHY/HAMISH, Jim Reid

ALICE, Frances Jeater

BOY, Elizabeth Lindsay

PERSE/TENOR/MONK 2, Nigel Graham

SCARLET/ALEXANDER/ALBERT, Henry Stamper

LIL, Anne Jameson

LITTLE JOHN/ABBOT, Crawford Logan

ROBIN HOOD/MONK 3, James Kerry

HAMMERHEAD, Jill Lidstone

FELIX/MONK 1/TREBLE, Stephen Boxer

DIRECTION, Ronald Mason

Small, claustrophobic atmosphere, full of men. Hammering on tabletop.

ALNOTH: I call this company to its discipline. All matters
discussed here or performed fall under your oaths of
secrecy. The hymn we bought from Felix the fallen priest
has been rehearsed and will be sung in parts. Brothers
are reminded of the perils of discovery in this case. The
church would not approve anything but a straight line
through. (*Pause.*) Let the Church go where it will. We
look upwards. One. Two. Three.

ALL: (*Sing.*) God built Jerusalem on high,
our lads built that below,
the temple of lord Solomon,
we raised with skilful show.

Hosanna, the temple grows!
Each day the earth retreats!
Each stone laid by a mason's hand
The Devil's cause defeats!

We set the cornerstone of Christ,
make shelter for the poor,
king, abbot, emperor and pope
beg, mason, build us more!

Hosanna, the temple grows!
Each day the earth retreats !
Each stone laid by a mason's hand
The Devil's cause defeats!

(*Hammering.*)

ALNOTH: Quiet for the case of Turstin Stacey. What do
you ask of your brother masons?

TURSTIN: I ask advice from this company of good men,
some of whom are longer in the craft than I, some better
in skill, or so I'm told.

ALNOTH: What do you need?

TURSTIN: I have an outstanding debt owed to me for work
completed two years ago. Bearing the absence of payment
has become impossible. I demand help.

ALNOTH: Call in the debt. We will back you up, even talk
to this customer if you like: we will visit him, we will
persuade him. But is the debt worth it? Are we talking
about chickens or feathers?

TURSTIN: The debt is two hundred and seventy-two silver
marks.

(*Buzz of amazement.*)

ALNOTH: Your craft must be doing you good if you've
born a debt so large for that long. It is shameful. The
lodge will make an approach in law. We will get it out
of him. Who is your debtor?

TURSTIN: The King.

(*Another buzz in an equivocating tone.*)

ALNOTH: Ah. Then you're better on your own.

TURSTIN: I thought I might be. You haven't the courage
to stand by me. What is the use of my membership of
this lodge?

ALNOTH: King John is a reasonable man, though
harassed by this speculative French invasion. London
keeps him at arms length because he has betrayed the
charter, with the Pope's blessing. The King is beyond
our reach until the matter is settled. There is no point
in talking to the barons about it. One thing they are
indifferent to is anyone else's royal owings but their
own.

HARPER: Turstin, I have collected debts from this King,
from his brother, Richard, and even that tightarse their
father, Henry. What I did was woo the money out of them.
To me they were women, girls, tarts full of promises but
no performance.

ALNOTH: Turstin is a straightforward man, Harper. He
hasn't got your charm, or your eloquence.

HARPER: First, I recommend that this meeting of the
lodge pray for the intercession of Saint Thomas on your
brother's behalf.

(*Small bell is rung. The prayer is chanted by all. It has the note of a
well-worn ritual.*)

ALL: Saint Thomas Didymus, disciple, doubter, friend of all stone masons, entreat Our Lord to move the mind of King John of England that he make good his debt to our brother, Turstin Stacey for work dutifully and decently performed. This prayer dated the twenty eighth day of August, this year of Our Lord twelve hundred and sixteen. Set in the saint's ledger. Amen.

ALNOTH: Entered. And listened to, I'm sure.

TURSTIN: Follow the King. Get out and track him down. Then hang on. Slide in when he's not looking. We'll look after your wife. And Turstin, buy yourself some flattery.

(Fades. Fade in TURSTIN's house atmosphere.)

TURSTIN: *(Fade in.)* Flattery! To get what I'm owed. Do you think the King doesn't know when a plain man is crawling to him? I can't do it.

ALICE: You'll have to try. If the debt isn't paid, husband, we're ruined. This house, this garden, all the furniture, the horses, everything. Even your tools.

TURSTIN: I won't do it! It's not right! I'd rather die than grovel for my proper due. I'll start again, build up my business.

ALICE: Husband, you're thirty-eight. There is no time to start from the beginning. I hear King John loves music.

TURSTIN: As well as he loves lies?

ALICE: A man called today. He was going from door to door asking if anyone needed a song written for a special occasion.

TURSTIN: There's a business man for you. That would be Felix the fallen priest. He is everywhere these days.

ALICE: That's because the church is so dull with its tunes. Get this man to help you.

TURSTIN: And pay out more? Then will someone start paying me for a change?

ALICE: David sang for King Saul and sweetened his nature. And if you know this man Felix he might give you good terms.

(Fades. Sound of KING JOHN coughing.)

(Cross fade from TURSTIN''s house atmosphere to Swineshead Abbey atmosphere. The Abbey Church. It is empty except for KING JOHN, the ABBOT and two MONKS.)

ABBOT: Sire, we should let the others in now.

JOHN: No. I am happy here, sweating, smelling myself.

ABBOT: We must carry out our offices at the prescribed time. We need the church. Wouldn't you be better off in bed? You are sick with fever, Your Majesty.

JOHN: I'll sit where I like. With these two fat monks on either side I could sleep for a hundred years. You're comfortable, you portly Cistercians. Your breath doesn't smell too bad. How about mine?

ABBOT: We have a room ready for you, sire.

JOHN: I think I might die tonight. After the life I've had it would be wise for me to die in church.

ABBOT: Then we will work around you. Stay with us while we worship.

JOHN: No. I've heard all that music. It doesn't register with me anymore. I just want to be quiet and look at the light. Tell these oafs to stop fidgetting about! If you're going to support the King, support the King! Keep me upright! I'm tired. Where am I?

ABBOT: Swineshead, sire.

JOHN: Somewhere in the east. I hate the flat country. Once you've seen it once you've seen it for ever. Nothing develops. It makes the eye a useless organ.

ABBOT: Sire, that is not true. It is the receiving instrument for light. And it can shine itself.

JOHN: Quite correct. You do well to lord and lecture me. And light is the most holy substance. Did I tell you that Pope Innocent the Third is dead?

ABBOT: You have been celebrating the fact for a month, sire.

JOHN: A great persecutor. Did you know that evil creature was ordained priest one day and consecrated pope the next? He was a lawyer. Any wonder I had to pay him a thousand marks a year? He raised crusades against our truth, abbot. I would like to believe in the fires of Hell for him.

ABBOT: Fire is a good principle, sire. It gives off light.

JOHN: Ah, light. Console me.

ABBOT: It is not the time. Matter and darkness still have you in their hands. There is life in you yet.

JOHN: Are they waiting for me at Worcester? There is someone who can give me consolation?

ABBOT: Anywhere you go, sire, there will be one of us waiting. We will not let you down.

JOHN: I gave my kingdom to a lawyer who pretended to be a Christian. I gave my kingdom to Christians who pretended to be lawyers. There is only the brotherhood. Even they condemn me. I failed the light. (*Pause.*) Death, come on.

ABBOT: Sire, the whole fraternity is waiting outside to sing mass. We cannot disturb the regularity of their devotional timetable. That is the Rule in this house. Even the King – pardon sire – cannot vary it. (*Pause.*) And it is raining on them.

JOHN: Good. Now they know how it feels to be me. Why am I shivering? Who is causing my teeth to chatter?

ABBOT: You have the fen fever, sire.

JOHN: Everything I eat turns to water. Another sign of authority. I bet you held mass when my country lay under the Pope's Interdict. Innocent forbad mass, baptism or burial, but I bet you had mass here. You went through your motions, eh? No matter. I envy your secret life. I am the Pope's friend now. Perhaps that is why I'm shaking. Ah! Help me you fat men. Hold me close. Stop me rattling to bits. Jesus!

ABBOT: Embrace him! (*Pause.*) Has he fainted?

MONK 1: He's very still, father. I can't hear his heart.

MONK 2: And burning! God save us. He's in Hell already!

JOHN: Hail! It's me! Abbot, have you a copy of the charter here? The one I made at Runnymede.

ABBOT: Yes, sire. We copied it from one at Beverley.

JOHN: I need something to wipe my arse on. Bring it to me. I despair of every drop of French blood in my veins. I should have been pure English to have ruined England so. That is my dream. To be an English monk in an English garden saying English prayers to an English God. France has slaughtered me, made me suicidal. Did I make your liberties safe, abbot?

ABBOT: For peace of mind, sire, put it from consideration.

TURSTIN: (*Fade in.*) Who is the King here? Show me where to kneel.

ABBOT: Get out! Out!

TURSTIN: I have followed him from Reading to Cambridge, from Cambridge to Stamford, from Stamford to Lincoln, from Lincoln to Lynn and from Lynn to here. I have waited long enough to see him.

JOHN: Look your fill. Won't be long. It's me, knucklehead.

ABBOT: Who let you in?

TURSTIN: A shilling at the door. Sire, you owe me money.

JOHN: Ding dong.

TURSTIN: Turstin Stacey, master mason. Two years ago I did work on your behalf at Northampton and at Bedford. Invoices were submitted but never paid.

JOHN: Northampton held. Bedford fell. I owe you money. I owe everybody money. Who is this boy with you?

TURSTIN: He is a singer.

JOHN: Poor child. He's shivering. Don't come near me, boy. I'm oozing poison all over this seat. Yes, I never pay. The French King's son has entered my lands but I never pay. What is this place called?

ABBOT: Swineshead, sire. You are at the Abbey of Swineshead.

TURSTIN: Sire, I need the money you owe me for the work on your fortifications. On the strength of it I borrowed to build a house for myself in Nottingham.

JOHN: Why have you brought in a singer? This place has hundreds. Big monks with big mouths bellowing.

TURSTIN: When I requested money in advance for that building work to buy materials, your clerks said yes but they meant no. I laid out my own funds for stone and timber to finish before the campaigning season began. I paid craftsmen and labourers from my own pocket.

ABBOT: You think that the King hasn't more important issues on his mind than your finances? He is sick, and at war.

JOHN: Nothing is more important than one's debts. I want mine carved on my tomb. I always favoured very large tombs, very, very large tombs. Boy!

BOY: Sire?

JOHN: Did he bring you here to sing to me?

BOY: Yes, sire.

JOHN: I like you professional men. You will do anything to get your money. You've dragged this poor lad all over these stinking bogs to winkle a few shillings out of a dying king. What a man you are, mason.

TURSTIN: It is not a matter of a few shillings. The debt is two hundred and seventy-two silver marks.

JOHN: Has he maltreated you, boy?

BOY: No. Will you hear the song? He had it written for him by Felix the fallen priest. When I've sung it I can go home to my mam.

JOHN: Where is home, boy?

BOY: Lightwater, sire, near Hook, near Bagshot.

JOHN: Never heard of it. Do what you have to, mason. There is no money, but should you not pay this poor boy I'll have you whipped till your backbone shows. I'm dying. I've been dying for a year. Maybe I'll die for another year. But I am dying. Perfectly natural.

ABBOT: Can't you see the king is distracted? He cannot pay debts in the worst of a fever. Leave him be.

TURSTIN: Then I'm ruined. My house will be taken from me. My wife will be turned out into the street. But I will pay the boy. You broke our contract. Is it any wonder the land is desolated? Your word has gone.

JOHN: No wonder at all. Get work with honest men. I know your name. I will find you something. I have influence you know. Oh, yes. Sit me up you Cistercians! Put your hands under my chin so I can listen to this fine English lad looking alert at least. Sing, then, sing.

TURSTIN: A word of explanation sire. It says in the gospel of John that there was one disciple whom Christ loved specially – above all the rest. He is never named. We masons say that it was Thomas Didymus, Thomas, our patron saint.

JOHN: What inspired self-interest. Do you masons also remember that Thomas was the disciple who would not believe that Jesus – poor suffering man, God help him! – had risen from the dead until he, Thomas, had put his finger into a nail-hole?

TURSTIN: He was also, sire, the only one of the disciples who wanted to die with his Lord on the Cross.

JOHN: I know the feeling. As one who God has loved specially and peculiarly, and as one who has doubted, I will forbear pulling out your tongue for trying to teach me scripture.

TURSTIN: A plain song, Saint Thomas. Sing, boy! Don't stand there scratching your head! And no grace-notes in front of the abbot. Keep it simple. Sire, this song is for your eternal glory. May you live for ever, amen.

JOHN: Rats, rats, and overrun with rats. Rats everywhere.

BOY: (*In Plainsong.*)
Didymus, O light of doubt
brother of debt and charity,
craftsmen of our lord's sweet love
build a shining soul for me,
Were you best loved for honesty
or friendship in His time of trial?
Thomas, give me your great strength
to doubt and die in glory.
We have to put our dirty hands
into the earth's wide wound
to build our hopes and spirits up.

On steps of chopped and chiselled stone,
we walk towards your city fair.
Our prayer is to be crucified
by Time, like Him, but live for
ever, far beyond the carved tomb.
Dear Tom, implore this earthly king
to pay his debt.
'Twill buy him more than Turstin's thanks,
a piece of Heaven's land, perhaps,
where he may hear a bird sing angel-song
better than me, in light eternal.

JOHN: Good lad, good lad. Well done. (*Laughs.*) Don't look
so downcast. You're free. You've sung your song. I wish
I were you, son. I'd sing my song and fly over the
horizon, back to my mam.

(*JOHN laughs again – then has a coughing fit.*)

BOY: If it works, sire, and you pay the mason, I get my
wages doubled.

JOHN: I'll double your shilling, son. But him? He's another
question. Men who've taught themselves a special
cunning have to be carefully answered. Even from empty
coffers.

(*Fades. Fade out Swineshead Abbey atmosphere. Fade in special
atmosphere. Music of the spheres.*)

ST THOMAS: I, Thomas Didymus, apostle, lover of our
Lord, Thomas Didymus, disciple, doubter, martyr,
patron saint of masons, heard your song, sweet boy. But
I cannot intercede. Nothing can be done with John. He's
beaten, tired and broke. The King will not pay because
the King cannot pay. Yet John will find something for
this debt. Turstin, the mason, will get work. It may test
him, faith and self. But will it bring him cash. We'll see.
Meanwhile, my martyr's crown needs to be refurbished
down on earth. The old and famous pain must be
repeated. No one better to travel with to find this
bloody workshop for my soul, than this determined
mason.

Ho-s-an-aaaaaaaaah!

(*Fade special atmosphere. Fade in journey on wind.*)

(*Fade in outside Swineshead atmosphere. Rain beating down. Murmuring of damp Religious.*)

MONK 1: (*Fade in.*) There's room for all of us in the rotten church! Old King John is doing this to us deliberately!

JOHN: (*Voice over.*) Cool their libertarian ardour. As prayer-houses I find most English monasteries excellent alehouses.

MONK 1: How long are those miserable bastards going to keep us here?

(*Muttering of wet MONKS. Sound of church doors opening and closing. Murmurs of anticipation.*)

ABBOT: The King has fallen asleep. He has given me an order that I could question were he in better health. He orders that the mass be sung out here in the rain.

(*Murmurs from the MONKS.*)

ABBOT: We will do it for him. Not only that, we will include him in our prayers. England lies at the mercy of invaders, rebels, thieves and ignorant, benighted men. It is not the time to be frightened of a little of God's rain. Take it as a hail of blessings.

(*Uproar of wet MONKS. Fade in abbey interior atmosphere.*)

JOHN: If you click with Alec, the Prior of Carlisle he could commission you to work on his greystone church. Remember that a cathedral is as much a king's bed as it is God's wardrobe. When I die I am going to Worcester to sleep. The masons will dress me, for all time. I like Worcester. Never mind your Saint Thomas Didymus. Saint Wulfstan's your man. Worcester and Saint Wulfstan for me. Pure English. Pure humility. We'll do a letter for you. Watch Alec at work. He's a creative man with many friends.

TURSTIN: Does it have to be so far away. The border with the Scots! Isn't there any building going on nearer home?

JOHN: Not in these times. War up there is part of everyday life. They're used to it. You will build between the bolts of fire. That's the best way.

(*Sound of the Kyrie Eleison being sung from outside. A thunder storm has started.*)

Yes, by the feet of God, I will be buried at Worcester wearing a monk's habit, free, at last, from all evil forces.

TURSTIN: Sire, I do not wish to sound ungrateful, but there is a technical point.

JOHN: You're asking the right man. What I know about architecture would fill a thimble. But I know what I like. Big, round things!

TURSTIN: The Prior. Has he authority over the fabric of this church?

JOHN: Oh, yes, yes.

TURSTIN: And it has the status of a cathedral?

JOHN: Good God, yes. It's huge!

TURSTIN: Who is the bishop?

JOHN: Ah. Ah. You saw it coming. No bishop. They don't want a bishop. They hate bishops up there. You know the trouble I've had with dumping unwanted bishops on loyal towns. Bastards! I hate them! It is my right to appoint bishops ... but Alec doesn't want one. He can manage. Do you know King Alexander of the Scots? From what I hear, Alec can twist his nose whenever he likes. Good old Alec. You'll work well together. Would you like to be a secret bishop, infiltrate Alec's ménage then rear up and reveal yourself? Learn to speak Scots. I fear it may be useful.

TURSTIN: Sire, has he the authority of the crown and the archbishops or his order to build, or rebuild, or extend? And has he the money to pay me?

JOHN: He has all that. And his freedom. Enough now. Ah. A mass amidst the raindrops. The wrath and the tears of God.

(*The mass increases in volume. Thunderclaps.*)

Listen to that. Just as it should be. God and Man singing together. Mason, do people say that I worked with the Almighty or against him?

TURSTIN: They are quiet on the subject. What kind of work will it be up there? Tell me about this greystone church.

JOHN: Don't do it in the French style. If I hear that you
have done it in the French style there will be ructions.
I don't get along with the French style at all. Do you like
the French style, boy?

BOY: The French style of what, sire?

JOHN: They point everything: their shoes, their questions,
their fingers, their swords, and now their churches. If
you were God, boy, would you want the French to be
pointing churches at you?

BOY: Whatever you say will do me, sire. I just want me mam.

JOHN: Mason, I require a contract with you – forget my
welshing on the last one, who cares? – a contract that
should my friend the Prior commission you for his
rebuilding work on his cathedral you will definitely not
point it. By then, you see, I will be in Heaven, and it will
be pointing at me! That I couldn't stand. Kiss me, boy.
I enjoyed your singing. You're a good lad. I wish I had
something to give you. Make it English, mason. I repent
of my brotherly blasphemy.

TURSTIN: And what style is that, sire?

JOHN: Aha!! Now you're asking. Dare you stand there and say,
poor John Lackland, poor John Softsword, what is English?

TURSTIN: If the King doesn't know, who does?

JOHN: The English style is of the eye. Study the eye of this
Lightwater boy with its glittering arches. Reproduce
them. Let in light. It is a vastly commodious substance
in which everything can be seen: every spot and flaw,
every wrinkle. Do you know why God came down to
earth, mason? To see what it was like. The point about
eternity is this – everyone is blind, dazzled by too much
light. (*Pause.*) Pray for me as you build. Boy, kiss your
King. I hope your voice never breaks.

(*Fade out Swineshead atmosphere. Fade in special atmosphere, then
music of a journey with a rushing wind. A sense of falling but under
control.*)

ST THOMAS: The mason has had his prayer answered
from the depths of a king's guilty despair. That is a

stronger force than summer promises, or any
interference from me. Without wishing to show he is
pleased, the mason feels the swell of success and
ambition. They may let him build a cathedral! To him
that means a chance to re-shape the earth, to outdo the
original, to challenge the architect of chaos, Nature and
life to a drawing-match. In a dark corner of his mind he
says – I will show my God his error of earthcraft.

(*Fade out journey atmosphere and wind and music. Fade in outside
Swineshead atmosphere.*)

ST THOMAS: Sir, a moment of your time. Is the King of
England inside the abbey? And is he alive?

TURSTIN: What's left of him. He lives through his clerks.

ST THOMAS: Is it worth waiting to see him?

TURSTIN: Not if your suit is a long one.

ST THOMAS: What are you saying? I should wait for the
next king? I have no suit. I only wanted to look at him.

(*Horse being mounted.*)

Where are you headed?

TURSTIN: What's it to you?

ST THOMAS: I'm going northwards, keeping to the
King's safe territories. From here up the valley of the
Aire to the Lancaster lands, up the Eden valley to the
border of Carlisle.

TURSTIN: What's your business?

ST THOMAS: Looking for work.

TURSTIN: And listening. Whoever built these walls made
a bad job of it. Move aside.

ST THOMAS: Let me be your man.

TURSTIN: What skills have you got?

ST THOMAS: Listening. It will be a hard journey alone. Let
me walk by your stirrup and lead your pack horse. The
poor beast is going at the knees. A mason's tools are heavy.

TURSTIN: You can travel with me for one day, and then
I'll decide. Don't expect much from me. I have a heavy
loss to contemplate. Come on if you're coming.

(*Horses moving off. Jangle of steel. Music. Ends with a rudimentary portable organ. Fade in Carlisle cathedral atmosphere.*)

PRIOR ALEC: Well, you have the King's recommendation. So do many weak instruments in England. And this, your precious letter from him, is the weakest of all.

TURSTIN: It was written at his side. I saw him sign it.

PRIOR ALEC: The King is dead. The news got here three days ago. It will be in the ear of the Scottish King by now. I had a mason for this work. When he heard the news he left. Who can blame him? The Scots will be here as soon as they can. All we can do is pray for hard weather. Are you still interested?

TURSTIN: I have to have it.

PRIOR ALEC: I need more than that. Or do I? If you want it for beauty's sake the first crack and you'll run off. Yes, why not? You need the money. Do you have the time to spend?

TURSTIN: How long will it take?

PRIOR ALEC: The rest of your life, at least.

TURSTIN: I got the impression that it was just some re-building work.

PRIOR ALEC: So it is. I want to rebuild two-thirds of the cathedral. I need a new nave. I have to extend the choir from two to seven bays and I fancy a short chancel sans aisles. The idea is to let in more light and give me room for more altars.

TURSTIN: Your Grace, you are a much older man than I am.

PRIOR ALEC: Oh yes. I will have to supervise most of it from beyond death. But that's a place I know.

TURSTIN: You're pulling my leg. I've had a long journey to get here. I'm far from home. God knows what my family is suffering. I'm as good a man as you are and I understand common sense. So don't play with me.

PRIOR ALEC: My dear son, perish the thought. I am absolutely serious. My life has been blameless. I have followed the gospels. My achievement in remaining

chaste for my entire life is one to be marvelled at.
Expectations of paradise come easily to *me*. Where have
I gone wrong?

TURSTIN: I did not mean to suggest that you were
unworthy, only that it has nothing to do with the job in
hand.

PRIOR ALEC: Nonsense. How could I make such long
term plans without being part of them? Do you think I'm
going to all this trouble and expense on the part of some
ambitious upstart who comes after me? (*Pause.*) Why is it
that men of your trade cannot take religion seriously?

TURSTIN: We do.

PRIOR ALEC: Not so. Whenever you masons get together
you huddle in a corner and do things your own way.
I see you. Even at mass you're looking at the roof to see
if it's leaking. Tell me, what is your private faith?

TURSTIN: I am a Christian.

PRIOR ALEC: Pooh. You might just as well be a Saracen.
We will argue, you and I, but I don't mind that. You have
one good eye and one evil. Same with hands. Sit down
with me and look at this terrible old place. Built for
monsters, it was. Do you know what I think? The
Normans built their churches as blinkers. To me a church
is a singing-house in crystal. I hate this thick choir.

TURSTIN: It's strongly built. It will be a useful fortress,
song or no. Music does not deflect.

PRIOR ALEC: Oh, we've used it for war many times.
Everyone comes hurrying here when the Scots are on the
rampage. They've tried everything. We've broken the
hearts of their siege captains many times. The stones
from their machines just bounce off. But, for our
purposes, mason, we might hope that this time they have
better equipment. Have you ever seen a trebuchet in
action?

TURSTIN: I have seen what it's done. It's a weapon of great
destruction, throwing huge stones high.

PRIOR ALEC: I hope the Scots have trebuchets this time.

TURSTIN: Tom!

ST THOMAS: (*Fade in.*) Master?

TURSTIN: Saddle our horses. Pack the gear.

ST THOMAS: But we've only just arrived.

TURSTIN: I'll not be mocked. Sir, you are an old man,
probably venerable to some, but to me you sound like
a fool.

PRIOR ALEC: The Scots come at us every year, my son.
Each spring we wait for the weather to break then, here
they come. If we held on to build our new cathedral in
a peaceful time we would never get anywhere. All they
want are cattle, goods, coin, a few token deaths. Let
them break this old, thick church down for us and do
something useful for a change.

TURSTIN: I am leaving. I have to put a price on my own
sanity.

(*Fades.*)

PRIOR ALEC: What a pity. And we were getting along
well together. Strange men, the masons. Very secretive.
Don't you find that?

ST THOMAS: No. He's a transparent man. But you?
I stood at the back there and listened. Has the material
world left you behind? Are you already a spirit?

PRIOR ALEC: No, I'm still here. You're impudent. Talk to
him for me. Keep him here until I can get some sense
into him. This work will keep him and his family for the
rest of his life.

ST THOMAS: If he lives. Do you want to bless me? Your
fingers are twitching.

PRIOR ALEC: That's old age. I like the look in your eye.
You stick up for yourself and that is what a great church
has to do as well. It must be a holy place where men can
stick up for themselves, not a dungeon.

(*Fade out cathedral atmosphere and organ. Fade in horse sounds.
A busy street. Sounds of loading gear into saddle bags.*)

TURSTIN: (*Fade in.*) Where have you been, you loon? I told
you to load up!

ST THOMAS: The old man wanted a word in my ear.

TURSTIN: He'll talk to anyone. He's mad. He's been up here too long. All this way and nothing at the end of it.

ST THOMAS: Perhaps you should listen to him again?

TURSTIN: No.

ST THOMAS: I think he has the money. He wants the job done. Who are you to doubt his politics?

TURSTIN: He's out of his wits. I tell you, most churchmen are like that. Every man of religion I have had to deal with has been warped. This earth isn't cockeyed enough for them but they have to make it worse.

(*Horse being led off.*)

ST THOMAS: So where will we go?

TURSTIN: Down to London. If King John is dead – which I give leave to doubt – we can check that – then the rebels may have talked peace to the King's brother. Everything might be changing down there. And I'd like to see my wife at Nottingham on the way.

ST THOMAS: Empty handed?

TURSTIN: She'll understand. She'll have to.

(*Fades. Horses moving on road.*)

ST THOMAS: Ssssh! Wait! Can you hear that?

(*Horses halt.*)

TURSTIN: I can't hear a thing. Come on. We've no time to waste.

ST THOMAS: No. I'm better at listening than you. Stand still.

(*Distant sound of skirling bagpipes.*)

TURSTIN: The Scots will come down from the north. This is the south road. What are they doing here?

ST THOMAS: Cutting off treasure that is running away. Today that includes us, the dribs and drabs.

TURSTIN: We'll have to go back! Yah! Hurry! God damn the King for dying! God damn all lunatics and Scots! God damn!

(*Horses galloping, clanking of tools, bells start ringing in distance. Sounds merge into pacey song.*)

SCOTS: (*Sing.*) By the gates of Carlisle
  lies a smiling, newborn child,
  'go in, go out, go round about',
  it cries, 'tame and wild,
  go your own way home
  through the streets of Carlisle
  before I close the town!'

  By the gates of Carlisle,
  squats a bony beggar bare,
  'go in, go out, go round about',
  he cries, 'stand and stare,
  go your own way home
  through the streets of Carlisle
  before I close the town.'

  By the gates of Carlisle
  stands a prisoner in chains,
  'go in, go out, go round about',
  he cries, 'pleasure and pains,
  go your own way home
  through the streets of Carlisle
  before I close the town.'

  By the gates of Carlisle
  sits a holy nun in tears,
  'go in, go out, go round about',
  she cries, 'hopes and fears,
  go your own way home
  through the streets of Carlisle,
  before I close the town.'

  By the gates of Carlisle
  lies a corpse in linen shroud,
  'go in, go out, go round about',
  it cries, 'humble and proud,
  go your own way home
  through the streets of Carlisle
  before I close the town.'

  By the gates of Carlisle
  stands Jesus Christ our Lord,

'go in, go out, go round about',
he cries, 'power and sword
go your own way home
before I close the town.'

(*Sounds and song music fade, followed by the crashing together of great gates in open atmosphere, then followed by crashing of great door of cathedral. The sound reverberates. Many murmurs, squeaks, mutterings.*)

PRIOR ALEC: Ah, you're back. I thought you might be. King Alexander likes to vary his tactics. Sometimes he swings round west from north, sometimes east, sometimes right round, for a change. When we capture him and kill him I am going to put his head on the roof. With the wind in his hairy ears he should make a wonderful weathercock.

TURSTIN: Under the circumstances I must put myself under your care and protection.

PRIOR ALEC: Of course. You must join all these poor creatures who have scuttled in here. We have the idiot, the sick, the runaways, the drink-damned, the unworthy, fallen women, bastards, and now you two. What heading shall I put you under?

TURSTIN: Strangers exposed to death. It was to you that I came here. By custom you must protect me in this case.

PRIOR ALEC: You will have to work. We always put up resistance. King Alexander sharpens his sword on us before his excursions into England. Have you ever seen a warrior break his own, favourite sharpening stone? Can you comfort madmen? Heal the sick?

TURSTIN: No. I am clumsy that way. Give me something else to do.

PRIOR ALEC: Your man there can help me out. He knows how to comfort folk in fear. You? Yes, I have a task you can perform. I presume fighting does not interest you?

TURSTIN: And what if I should injure my hand, my arm? My skill is in my body as much as my brain. Let me work on the town's defences.

PRIOR ALEC: No, no, it is too makeshift a business for a true craftsman. Too hurried. Let lower mortals shovel rocks. You, my son, must only build beauty, even in war. Wait for me by the refectory. Go on. I want to talk to your man about how to handle the dregs of Carlisle.

TURSTIN: He should help me, carry my tools ...

PRIOR ALEC: Get out before I throw you out, you proud pig!

(*Commotion rises from the crowd.*)

TURSTIN: Because I need your help, I will not answer. But I take it badly and it is being remembered. I will wait until waiting tires me, then I will do what I think is useful. (*Fades.*)

PRIOR ALEC: I like him more and more. He is the man for me. If I can teach him to read my mind, we will be friends. This town is an island. Its life is governed by the spirit of war and the west wind, not London. Heal the sick. Cast out demons from those who foam at the mouth or bite their tongues. Can you do all that?

ST THOMAS: I can try.

PRIOR ALEC: I thought you could. I'm a good judge of souls. Time to deal with your master – our master, as he would have it. I leave these poor people in your care.

(*The sound of the crowd rises as PRIOR ALEC leaves.*)

(*From a distance, in the echo of the place.*) I'll be back. This fine fellow will take care of you. Trust him. Listen to what he says. I'll be back. (*Fades.*)

PERSE: Ma mother. Ma mother is coming with the King. She wants me dead. Ma mother is a whore.

ST THOMAS: Is she now?

PERSE: I don't want to see her. She'll skin me alive.

ST THOMAS: Gather round me. Sit on the floor in a ring. There are many walls between you and the war. Forget the evil outside. You are safe here. Now, what are you doing? That's a font not a pissing bowl! Climb down off that cross! The next one to finger the angel's legs will answer to me! Settle down. Listen.

(*Sounds of war, thud of battering ram on gates.*)

ST THOMAS: Do you recognise that sound?

PERSE: It's the ram at the gates! Ma mother's on the end of it. She's got it between her legs, the whore!

ST THOMAS: Listen again!

(*The thud of the battering ram gets louder.*)

That is not the ram at the gates of Carlisle. That is the knocking of Christ Our Lord to be let in.

PERSE: I'll open the door. I'll open my heart. Is my mother with Him?

ST THOMAS: That is not the ram at the gates of Carlisle. It is the knocking of Christ to be let in. Say it after me! All of you!

ALL: That is not the ram at the gates of Carlisle. It is the knocking of Christ to be let in.

(*The thudding gets more powerful.*)

ST THOMAS: Again! Believe it. Even though it is not true, believe it!

ALL: That is not the ram at the gates of Carlisle. It is the knocking of Christ to be let in.

ST THOMAS: Repeat it. Keep repeating it. When you hear the gates break, when you hear doors burst open, when you hear the wind of the sword that will release you from this bondage, believe it is Christ's breath not some drunken Scot. That is not the ram at the gates of Carlisle. It is the knocking of Christ to be let in!

(*Sound of the gates giving way. Charge of warriors. Screaming. Bagpipes skirling.*)

Hold steady. It is Christ who is wearing a kilt today. The Prior has left the door unlocked.

(*Doors crash open. Rush of feet, clank of steel. Horses are ridden into the cathedral. Shouts and whistles. Pause.*)

ALEXANDER: Kill them. Do as you like.

ST THOMAS: When you hear the wind of the sword that will release you from this bondage, believe it is Christ's breath. These people are blessed and quiet, King Alexander. Enjoy your animal hour.

ALEXANDER: I will, especially the taking of your fast-talking head, Father Bunloaf!

(*Wind of a sword striking. A blow. Then a host of sword-winds and blows. But no groans or screams. Suddenly the sword sounds stop. Pause.*)

ALEXANDER: Listen lads. Can you hear them all ascending?

(*Roar of laughter. Blast on the bagpipes. Thunder of drums.*)

ALL SCOTS: (*Sing.*) Great Alexander wasnae Macedonian,
Great Alexander wasnae Greek,
Great Alexander's canny, canny, Caledonian
And strong where Aristotle's weak!
Come, great Alexander, show your leg,
Make the Persian princes beg!

HAMISH: One of Felix the fallen priest's best in a long time.

(*Fade out cathedral atmosphere. Fade in outside atmosphere. Sounds of looting in the background, some screams, horses neighing.*)

PRIOR ALEC: (*Fade in.*) Here we are, my mad mason. Not a very wholesome dwelling. The tenants have been complaining.

TURSTIN: You bring me to a pigsty?

PRIOR ALEC: The beasts have rooted right under the wooden walls. The whole thing is rotten.

TURSTIN: Your town is being sacked and you bring me to a pigsty?

PRIOR ALEC: I want it all done in stone. That will bruise their snouts. Will you do that for me?

TURSTIN: Why are you choosing to insult me at a time like this? Your people need you and you stand here yapping about pigsties. How did they make a savage like you into a prior?

PRIOR ALEC: Because I attend to all details. I leave nothing and no one out. My people are being cared for.

(*Terrible screams from nearby.*)

TURSTIN: You won't make a move to help them, will you?

PRIOR ALEC: That is only the sound of the meek inheriting the earth. In my teaching, the grave is a good place.

HAMISH: Stay! Don't move a muscle. What are you doing, skulking here? Are there any pigs in there with you?

PRIOR ALEC: Captain, it is me, the Prior.

HAMISH: So it is. King Alexander is looking for you. Who's this?

PRIOR ALEC: He's my pig-man.

HAMISH: D'you want him done for? Is he incompetent? Would you have him gone like those cretins in the cathedral?

PRIOR ALEC: No, no. He's perfectly sound. Take me to Alexander.

(*Fade out atmosphere. Fade in cathedral atmosphere. Sound of bucket of water sluicing over flagstones.*)

(*Fade in.*) Well, my dear King Alexander? Now do you feel better?

ALEXANDER: My old enemy, John, is dead. I had to do something to show how pleased I am. He should never have done me over so cruelly at Berwick last year. That made me resentful. I'm afraid my lads boiled over again. Understandable frustration. No booty after a hundred mile march through rough country.

PRIOR ALEC: Understandable disappointment, Your Majesty. I think they have been most lenient, considering the circumstances.

TURSTIN: Where's my man? I had a servant here. He was left in the church with the others.

PRIOR ALEC: This is a great Christian king you're talking to! Show more respect! Ignore him sire. He's an ignorant fool.

ALEXANDER: Was he all there, your man? Did he drool, gibber, scratch? There was only one whole man in the church. And he was evil.

TURSTIN: You can call him evil? You?

ALEXANDER: He persuaded the whole lot of them to bow their necks to our swords in silence. If some had pleaded, begged, run away, fought us, one or two might have survived in the sport. Your man is more of a murderer than I am. Who is this indignant creature?

PRIOR ALEC: A man who is too proud to be Christian, too ignorant to be pagan and too greedy to be respectable.

TURSTIN: If this is your Christian world, and my poor man was a murderer, I'll go back to that rotten sty at the back of the slaughterhouse and live in it, be a pig, and wait for Christ to come and cut my throat for Christmas!

(*Fade in special atmosphere. Music of the spheres.*)

ST THOMAS: Nothing is as bad as it's painted, especially the second time round. My first martyrdom was in Myapore, India, off the beaten track. So strange. I remember hearing my own head hit the floor. So little has changed except that my head crashed to a Christian floor this time, not a walking-place for wild unbelievers but one flagged for the feet of the faithful. Everything is getting very late. After twelve hundred years Christ has not come again so each Christian must try to know Him in his imagination. It is a struggle. Many do not have the mental means. But one group of men are hard at it. They are pondering a proud boast that Christ made but never carried out. Our Lord claimed that if the temple of Solomon had been destroyed He could have rebuilt it in three days. The masons would like to see Him try. Just so they could observe His technique. And join His lodge if he succeeded.

(*The music rolls on.*)

Music, they know, is the sound of God's mind working. But masons are half-deaf with the hammering of apple-wood mallets and picks. The only music they really understand is the screech of crane-ropes and the caterwauling of pressured timber. So they render music into stone through harmonious measurable numbers.

(*Fade music of the spheres. Fade in outside atmosphere at Carlisle cathedral.*)

PRIOR ALEC: (*Fade in.*) Come on, Turstin. Come out of the pigsty. This isn't doing any good. Everything is back to normal. The Scots have gone. The dead are buried. It's a beautiful day. We have business to talk over.

TURSTIN: Go away.

PRIOR ALEC: What would you have done in my place? Let Alexander have the healthy and hopeful citizens? Most of those poor folk were suffering beyond the limits we should ask ourselves to endure.

TURSTIN: I am trying to find the strength to kill myself.

PRIOR ALEC: Man, life is brief enough. Don't make a sweat out of shortening it. We have a great church to build.

TURSTIN: No. I will never put stone on stone again as long as I live. If I cannot die then I am going to become a hermit. I will live here, in this pigsty, and praise God. All pride and vanity I abjure!

PRIOR ALEC: Turstin, would you believe me if I told you that it is the people of this town who want this new church? With all the destruction and murder they have seen they want to tear down this old fortress of a church and build something more vulnerable, more admitting of light. After everything they have suffered year in, year out; with all their poverty and isolation here on this wild, bleak border; they want to move with the times. Yes, even these times. You must do it for them.

TURSTIN: Oink! Oink!

PRIOR ALEC: Dream something up for them. Put them in touch with what is going on. Make everything new.

TURSTIN: I don't believe a word you say. You don't even make a credible swineherd. And you have taken holy vows, you! Oink, shit and damn you! Oink, indeed!

PRIOR ALEC: I'll leave you to brood upon it. The nights are getting colder. It will probably rain soon. Think hard, mason. A hermit's life is not happy unless he has the spirit for it, and a good roof.
(*Fade.*)

TURSTIN: Everything I can touch, everything I can taste, everything I can smell, everything I can see, is evil. The soil, stones, flesh! Ah! I will eat dung. Dear God, I make a bargain with you. Keep your cruel world from me and I will spend my miserable life in praising your name, but not your creation.

LIL: (*Fade in.*) Oi, move over. What are you doing here?

TURSTIN: Go away, woman! Leave me in peace.

LIL: These are Prior Alec's pigsties, aren't they? Then get out yourself. This is my spot. Shift yourself. Or would you rather stay, sweetheart?

TURSTIN: Get back where you belong. There's no trade for you here. Try the alehouse.

LIL: So, I'm a whore, am I? I've got a written licence to be religious. Here, signed by old Alec himself. The ink is still drying. Licence to live as a hermit for one woman, Carlisle Lil, that's me. So out you go.

(*Sound of rain on the roof.*)

TURSTIN: Oh, God. (*Cries.*)

LIL: Old Alec didn't tell me there was anyone here already.

TURSTIN: He is persecuting me.

LIL: Do you think he meant us to think about living together? No. It's supposed to be done alone. That's the point, isn't it? Well, what's one night after all the life I've had and the repentance I've got to work through – a mountainside of it, I can tell you, what's one night? This place could do with cleaning out.

TURSTIN: No. I want it filthy.

LIL: Doesn't matter what you want any more, does it? I'm the one with the licence. Forty-five years of fornication I've got to rub off. Can you imagine it? Forty-five years on the game. In Carlisle that's a record, I'm told. But I'm not well. So here I am, ready to do my stuff. Here, come under my shawl.

TURSTIN: Don't touch me. I've rejected the material world.

LIL: That's me all right. What's happened to you? Life's given you a hard time. Well, I'm the same. Thank God those Scots have gone. That's what made me decide. They abuse me every time they take the town. You're cold.

TURSTIN: I don't want to talk.

LIL: Oh, you don't have to talk to me. Most men I spend
the night with won't give me a word. What's the matter
then? Come on, you can tell old Lil. You won't turn my
hair white. I've heard it all before.

TURSTIN: Holy Mary, Mother of God! (*Cries.*)

LIL: There, there, hold on to me. We'll make you feel better.
Yes. Go on, son, have a nuzzle. I tell you something. I'm
glad you don't think I'm part of the material world. That
would be a bad start for my new life as a hermit.
Wouldn't give me a chance, would it?

TURSTIN: This world is a wicked place. How I miss my wife!

LIL: You want me to be wife for you? Far away from home.
Carlisle Lil is your woman, is she? Well, you pretend old
Carlisle Lil is your lovely wife and be comfortable.

TURSTIN: I will never taste pleasure again. Never! Ah, help.

LIL: Quiet, boy. You don't know Felix the fallen priest,
I bet. He's a devil, and, I'm afraid he's very much a part
of the material world. He has this little song he sings at
times like this. He seems to find it soothing.

TURSTIN: Oh, no! Not him again! Not this far north! Well,
I suppose I should be glad that someone is prospering.

LIL: (*Sings.*) Frustra fundatur falsi fideles
quai funditus finietur fiducia
fenerantis et fumo inferni ficti
ferintur et omnes utique umbra
honoris operti ut appareant in
aulis avaris.

Fervebunt fetentes formidine futura
formosus et fortis in feno fallantur
et idio imbuti impio instinctu
fervore felici nunquam fruentur
quai federati fuerunt in factis
falsorum ut fixi in
fervore finiendi favoris feruntur
cum furibis facibus frementes.
(*Fades.*)

(The rain lashes down, the song dies away into sleep then snoring as deep and glottal as a pig's grunt. Fade in special atmosphere. Music of the spheres.)

ST THOMAS: They affect me, these two. Both of them are giving up their laboriously learnt skills in order to punish themselves for the state of the world. He will not be a mason any more, she will not be a whore. In fact, of course, it is God they are punishing, not themselves. Deep in their hearts they believe that the Almighty will mourn the waste of their intricate and passionate professions. And that is how they spent the winter, living in a tumbledown pigsty behind the old grey church, locked in each other's arms for warmth, listening to the wind.

(Fade out special atmosphere. Fade in Carlisle cathedral atmosphere.)

PRIOR ALEC: Now, listen choir. You're all I've got left to brighten up this heavy old hulk, this dark dungeon.
I can't start any building work till spring. The people are impatient. They want light and colour in their lives *now*, not in fifty years time. I can't start knocking the old place down in this weather, so all I've got is your singing to do the job for me. You will try hard to enliven this old tomb, won't you?

(Confused murmur from the CHOIR of men and boys.)

I knew you would. Now I have to start wooing this mason, Turstin, the one round the back with old Carlisle Lil. He's my only hope for spring. I've got to bring tears to his eyes with this new carol I bought from Felix the fallen priest. Turstin is being brought here at the moment. He's going to be wheeled in, held down and forced to listen. You've got to get it right first time. Now don't let me down. Bring him in!

(Doors being opened.)

TURSTIN: Let go of me! I'm not going in there again, not into that butcher's shop!

PRIOR ALEC: Cold Christmas, Turstin, venerated holy man.

TURSTIN: Murderer!

PRIOR ALEC: Not at all, dear fellow, not at all. Don't get
upset all over again. You've got it wrong about me.
Anyone will tell you, I saved the town. I always do.
(*Door crashing shut.*)

TURSTIN: O, hateful woooooorld!

CHOIR: (*Sing.*) Lile children born this yesternight
who died for Herod's fear,
your blood protected Christ, Our Lord,
you must have held him dear,
in innocence, in innocence, in innocence.
you must have held Him dear.

Search not for our Saviour
in the houses of the poor,
soldier, look you lower,
behind the beastly door.

Lile children born this yesternight,
brief, brief the lives you live;
your deaths were caused by Christ, Our Lord,
Him you must all forgive,
in innocence, in innocence, in innocence,
Him you must all forgive.

Search not for our Saviour
in the houses of the rich,
soldier, look you lower
in the bottom of the ditch.

Lile children born this yesternight,
the Church will not account
the price you paid to Christ, Our Lord,
in the correct amount,
in ignorance, in ignorance, in ignorance,
in the correct amount.

Search not for our Saviour
in the house of Mother Church,
soldier, look you lower,
where good and evil lurch.

PRIOR ALEC: Excellent. What do you think of that, holy
man? The Slaying of the Innocents makes excellent

sense. Have you ever heard of the work of Felix the
fallen priest? What do you say? Give us a chance, sir.
Judge our work!

TURSTIN: Let me go back to my pigsty. I prefer it to here.
I don't blame you people in the choir. Only this evil
man who leads you.

PRIOR ALEC: You're harsh, Turstin. Can't you see that there
is a pattern to all your experiences here? They can be
explained, with thought and a little philosophy. I have here
the contract for the rebuilding of the cathedral church of
the Holy and Undivided Trinity. Will you sign it?

TURSTIN: I will not.

PRIOR ALEC: I have all the latest equipment for you. For
the demolition I have borrowed one of King Alexander's
trebuchet siege engines. They are tremendously effective.
On my schedule here I plan for the first rock to be thrown
against the walls of this arsehole of an apse, this buttock of
cold, grey stone on May-day! Great celebration! I plan to
fire that missile myself. I want you by my side.

TURSTIN: Tell your bullies to release me. I have no
interests here.

PRIOR ALEC: Aren't you cold and miserable, even with
warm old Lil?

TURSTIN: My body is, but not as cold as my soul gets when I
listen to your blasphemy. You pollute all Christian thought.

PRIOR ALEC: Said in my own church, to a man like
myself, a prior of black Augustinian canons, servant of
a great thinker. Saint Augustine himself thought, in his
youth, that the church had a stupid attitude to evil. He
was all for recognising it as a power of God. As he grew
older he became less outspoken. You should listen
closely to the lyrics of Felix the fallen priest. He still has
his courage.

TURSTIN: He is a heretic!

PRIOR ALEC: Pooh. So was every great doctor of the
church at one time. Perhaps you think that Felix seeks to
subvert the state? Can you subvert a state of chaos?

TURSTIN: You people here should know that this man is a
    murderer and a heretic! He should be cast out of his
    high office and put in prison by the King's servants! He
    is not above the law.

BASS: We have no law in Carlisle except his. He takes care
    of us. The King never bothers.

TENOR: Don't abuse Prior Alec in our presence. Without
    him this town would have been levelled to the ground
    and everyone massacred by the Scots – or the English,
    damn them. We're on our own up here. Everyone just
    uses us.

TURSTIN: Including Prior Alec. You're fools! Idiots!

BASS: If we're fools, what are you? A skilled craftsman with
    his own trade living in a pigsty with the worst whore in
    the town?

    (*Laughter – it echoes in the CHOIR.*)

TREBLE: At home my mam and dad say that Prior Alec will
    be a saint one day. They've got a pair of his cast-off gloves
    put aside to sell if they need money in their old age.

TURSTIN: And what will you steal of his, boy? His
    honesty? You would find it hard to find.

TREBLE: I'd lick the dust from the soles of his feet and never
    swallow again, that's how much I love this holy man.

PRIOR ALEC: That was a little extreme, boy. How would
    you eat and drink? I know, I know. You would die for
    me. Such loyalty. (*Pause.*) My poor, troubled, mad mason
    – do you know that we now have a new king?

TURSTIN: That is nothing to me.

PRIOR ALEC: He is a child of nine years! The third Henry,
    as if the other two had not been enough. It is a very
    sentimental time, Christmas. The Pope, the mercenaries,
    the thieves, murderers, barons, even the guild of England's
    hangmen are on their knees worshipping Christ in one
    crib and young Henry in another. (*Pause.*) And I have
    chosen a new stone for my church. Grey, I hate. It is the
    colour of old age. All the work will be done in red
    sandstone. There is plenty of it about. Let him go.

TURSTIN: Curse you! You corrupt the air you breathe!

PRIOR ALEC: This contract will be nailed to the door of
your squalid home. Until you sign it you will have no
food or drink. The pigs who lived there before you will
have had a better time of it.

TURSTIN: I welcome these measures. It will mean I get
out of this filthy life faster. But let the woman go.

PRIOR ALEC: Let Carlisle Lil go? Never. She is my
guarantee that you will stay alive long enough to sign.
She will persuade you, and keep your heart going. Take
him back!

TURSTIN: May God damn you to the most horrible pain!
May you suffer Hell deeper than the mind knows.

PRIOR ALEC: There is no Hell that goes beyond what my
mind suffers, mason. But I build out of it!

CHOIR: (*Sing.*) Search – not for our Saviour
in the house of Mother Church,
soldier, look you lower,
where good and evil lurch.

(*Fade cathedral atmosphere. Howling wind. A snowstorm. Wood
rattling.*)

PRIOR ALEC: How are you, mason? February is a wicked
month.

LIL: Come to mock again, Alec?

PRIOR ALEC: The contract is still flapping about like a
wounded bird. How is the poor man?

LIL: He's alive. Your guards are as corruptible as you are.

PRIOR ALEC: Of course. They were hand-picked to be
corruptible in exactly the right amount – subsistence
only. And you pay them in the only way you know how.
Admirable.

LIL: He'll never sign. You'll have to work out a design for
yourself. And, if you do, I hope the whole thing falls
down on your head.

PRIOR ALEC: Lil, Lil, why so vehement? This is your old
protector here. Mason! I hear that the west front of the
royal monastery of Saint Denis in Paris has four great

windows in a two to three proportion of area. Saint Augustine's ideal of architecture has the proportions of musical consonances. In harmony he sees the stability of the cosmos. We might discuss this when you've finished sucking at Lil's tit.

LIL: The man is nearly dead of cold and hunger. This is the milk that his own child will be having by the month of May. Alec, if the child lives, I will teach it to cut your throat at your own altar, and smile.

PRIOR ALEC. At my *new* altar, Lil. I know that in your man's mind there lies a great church that will give me an eternity I understand. By hook or by crook I will have it out in the open air. Suck on Turstin. You're balanced on the bones of your existence. From there you can think of nothing but the true forms of God's beauty. That is what we're looking for. (*Fade.*)

(*Fade storm and outside atmosphere. Fade in special atmosphere. Music of the spheres.*)

ST THOMAS: It is the hardest winter in Carlisle for fifty years. I, Thomas Didymus, disciple, doubter and divine intercessor watch the great storms circling the seas and they always seem to head for that broken-down pigsty. Turstin is suffering from exposure, guilt, inner confusion but he will not sign that contract. It flutters on the nail, torn to tatters by the west wind, the shreds beating on the rotten door, frail fists demanding entry. But in his head, alas, his natural self has started to build a church. It makes his brain bulge as his body withers. He cannot help it. It grows inside him as fast as his child grows in the womb of Carlisle Lil. And it kicks him as the child kicks her.

(*Fade in and out Carlisle pigsty atmosphere for line.*)

TURSTIN: (*In a nightmare.*) Aaaah! Tear it down! The foundations are cracked!

ST THOMAS: I hear him, but I can do nothing to ease his pain. The poor man is cursed with a creative soul. No matter what he says he'll do, churches, halls and houses will sprout out of his mind like mushrooms in August.

(Fade music of the spheres. Fade special atmosphere. Fade in pigsty atmosphere.)

TURSTIN: *(Fade in on scream.)* Aaaah! Not that rock. Take it away, you and your samples. I don't want stone with shells in it.

LIL: Wake up! Hey! Wake up! You're having a nightmare.

TURSTIN: Who put the shells in the stone? Who put the fishbones in the stone? Who put the leaves in the stone? Who put the perfect spirals, the faultless circles, the pure earthcraft in the stone? An evil, artist god?

LIL: Turstin, you're all right, love. You're here with me.

TURSTIN: I must get away from here.

LIL: Yes, yes. We'll do all that. Shush now.

TURSTIN: I'm going to escape.

LIL: We'll go away when the child is born.

TURSTIN: No, I must go today, or go mad. Lil, I am designing that devil his church in my mind in spite of myself. He's winning.

LIL: It's not me you're running away from, is it? Plenty have, especially when I got up the spout.

TURSTIN: No, it's not you. It's him, it's this place and what's growing in my head. I can't wait here or he'll have it out of me, I know.

LIL: You're not going back to Nottingham and your wife, are you? Not that I'd blame you much.

TURSTIN: Lil, I should never have come here. It was greed, pride, the worst part of myself brought me.

LIL: And the child?

TURSTIN: I want nothing to do with the child. You must give it away, get it cared for. I don't want to be reminded of this place. *(Pause.)* It will be my first child.

LIL: You don't want it? Your own child? All right. It's not the first time but I've never had one before when I was sure of who the father was. I'll get rid of it, give it to someone to make a beggar out of. Poor child. What has it done to you?

TURSTIN: If a child is like its father I can hold out no
hope for it. Since I came to Carlisle I have seen nothing
but death, deception and destruction. The child will be
born out of that, not you.

LIL: No, Turstin. It may be an ordinary babe. But if you're
frightened of it and it makes you sick, then get away.
(*Pause.*) I don't think you will ever send for me, nor will
you ever come back. But the child and I will stand that,
I suppose. (*Fade.*)

(*Fade pigsty atmosphere. Fade in special atmosphere.*)

ST THOMAS: Two weeks later, as a fog rolls in from the sea
on an April morning, Turstin slips away while his guards
share the favours of his patient, generous paramour and
fellow hermit, Carlisle Lil, under the Prior's pear trees –
which were in full white blossom. Carlisle Lil smiles as
those rough, simple-minded churls play see-saw on the
fulcrum of her enormous womb. Tomorrow will be
another day and she will make peace with it. Turstin heads
for the forests and hills, the church growing, growing in
his head.

(*Music.*)

Down the Eden valley to Appleby. Across the wastes of
the Lune Forest to Teesdale, then south to Aysgarth,
south again to Ripon, always skirting the towns, moving
by night which keeps away the worst of the nightmares.
York. Doncaster. The forests thicken as he heads further
south into the fat part of England, keeping his eye on the
road to Nottingham from little woodland tracks that keep
him hidden from any pursuit. In a leafy glade he pauses,
his church-filled head in his hands.

(*Twang of a bowstring. Thwack of an arrow striking a tree. Laughter.
Winding of a horn.*)

(*Voice over.*) Some outlaws have caught him unawares.
They put a poacher's sack over his head and march him
through the forest. Inside the stinking blood-soaked
sack his tormented brain is building that terrible church
of guilt up to roof-height in red stone. He cries out and

stumbles. The outlaws laugh and whip him with their unstrung bows. I want to lean down and whisper in his ear – evil, as such, does not exist. It is only good gone wrong – but his hearing is already full of the tumbling bells as his skull-bones become vaults, arcades and aisles.

(*Music, starting sweetly, then distorting.*)

(*Sings.*) His eyes, two rose windows.
His nose, a copper-plated steeple.
His jaw a joist for a cold crypt entrance.
His tongue the fine red carpet for a
prior's softshod foot.

(*Bells ringing in distortion. Moans from TURSTIN.*)

I want to comfort him, but I can't. I have a grudge against these men, the masons. As a stone falls, pulled down by a terrible power, so once an angel fell, in punishment. The identity of that dark angel defines the force he flew on. Gravity is gravely evil. It is the upward thrust of good gone wrong. And what is gravity but the mason's building frame? Moreover it keeps Mankind earthbound in its killing pride.

TURSTIN: (*From inside the sack.*) Help me! Help me!

ST THOMAS: Stay in your sack a little while. It's May.
A seed has sprouted in Carlisle.

(*Fade in cathedral at Carlisle atmosphere. Cry of child.*)

PRIOR ALEC: Good. It's perfect! Better than all the others! Let's hope this one lives. It seems strong enough. Well, Lil, what are we going to call it?

LIL: God knows.

PRIOR ALEC: It is a problem. We cannot even determine its sex. It must have hurt you to have it. Poor Lil.

LIL: Perhaps I should smother it.

PRIOR ALEC: Oh, no. You must give it to me. I am the one who it was intended for. Lil, here's ten shillings. There is a ship on the coast leaving for Ireland in the morning. Take it. You'll feel at home over there. Ah! Don't snatch, Lil. First you have to tell me where

my mason was going? Ten shillings, Lil. A fortune
to you. A new life in Ireland?

LIL: That I should breed a monster. What a wicked life
I must have led. I wouldn't settle down in Nottingham
would I?

PRIOR ALEC: Never. It's not the town for you. Full of
whores already, my dear Lil. If you meet more priests,
keep your knees together and only ask for reading
lessons. Forget the child. I will see he leads a useful life.

(*Fade out cathedral atmosphere. Fade in forest atmosphere.*)

LITTLE JOHN: (*Fade in.*) Nearly there now. Won't be long.
How are you doing in there?

TURSTIN: (*Inside sack.*) When you take this sack off my
head stand well back.

SCARLET: Why? Are you going to thrash us?

TURSTIN: And cover your eyes! Don't look at me. For the
sake of your souls, don't look at me.

ALAN: Why not? What's going on in there?

TURSTIN: Remember the Gorgon! Think of Lot's wife!

LITTLE JOHN: Come here. Let's have a look. Take the
sack off, Alan.

TURSTIN: Turn away!

(*Sack is pulled off.*)

Don't look at me!

(*Pause.*)

LITTLE JOHN: What's supposed to be the matter?

TURSTIN: Can't you see? Look at me. My head's a church!

SCARLET: You look all right to us.

TURSTIN: You're blind. My head comes to a French point.

LITTLE JOHN: We're here, anyway. Here's a simpleton we
found, Robin.

ROBIN HOOD: Greetings, mad mason. Your reputation
has travelled before you.

TURSTIN: Cut off my head!

ROBIN HOOD: I can't do that. Prior Alec would never
forgive me. Come into the glade.

(Murmuring of a large crowd.)

TURSTIN: Prior Alec is back in Carlisle. Don't let him see my head! He'll copy it down and have it built in red sandstone, a blood church. Give me that bag back. Would you like to see your head rising in the centre of a city?

(Fade out greenwood atmosphere. Fade in ship at sea atmosphere. Sails flapping, timbers creaking. Gulls.)

MURPHY: *(Fade in.)* I'm sure that a fine, big, woman like you will have no trouble in finding a spot to settle down in Ireland. They'll be forming a queue at the jetty when they hear that Carlisle Lil is sailing into town. You won't have a minute's peace, I can tell you.

LIL: I'm a changed person. My old life means nothing to me.

MURPHY: Don't say that. You're the best thing to come over these cold waters since Saint Patrick.

LIL: No, all I want is a quiet life of contemplation on a mountain somewhere. I've got a lot to think about.

MURPHY: Here's me importing a nun to Ireland.

LIL: Captain, I have decided that I must be a wicked woman. Something awful happened to me. I was in receipt of a child. I won't shock you with the details.

MURPHY: I was after locking my eye on the magnitude of your fair and freckled breasts, thinking you'd make a figurehead that a nautical man would he proud of. Now you've told me the cause I hope it's not too temporary. I was thinking of asking you to be my wife.

LIL: Your wife? You'd marry me? Carlisle Lil? With my reputation?

MURPHY: You're held in high respect the entire length of the Hibernian seaboard I can tell you. What do you say?

LIL: Do you want children?

MURPHY: That was a confession that I'd hoped you wouldn't wring from me. I have not the power to generate children, much as I've tried for these sixty years, and will keep trying, even though I know it's futile, as it were.

LIL: (*In her mind.*) I am going to say yes. In the arms of this
seafaring man I may find the peace I need. Also, I suspect,
from my close knowledge of sailors, he'll be hell to live
with, full of drink and endless gabbing and this will keep
from my mind the memory of that monster child I bore in
Prior Alec's pigsty.

(*Fade sounds of the sea and ship atmosphere. Fade in forest
atmosphere. Murmuring of a great crowd. Winding of horn.*)

ROBIN HOOD: Brothers in the true faith of the
Albigenses, I bring before you a novice for initiation.
Turstin Stacey, freemason, freeholder of Nottingham who
asks for admission to our faith.

ST THOMAS: (*Voice over.*) In the greenwood glade Turstin
found gathered a great and gorgeous company. They
glittered with gold and green – magnates, abbots, barons,
merchants. Of the outlaws, only a few he found, acting as
ushers. He recognised men of power and wealth from
court, from London, from the highest places in the land:
lawyers, doctors, princes of the realm.

ROBIN HOOD: We await only Prior Alec with the child.
He has been sighted on the fringes of the forest on a fast
horse, the child strapped to his back like a sword. They
fly towards us. Welcome him with music, Felix the fallen
priest!

FELIX: I have a newly-minted hymn to the martyrs of
Carcassonne. Will you hear it?

ROBIN HOOD: Let us listen and remember.

FELIX: I have written a song out of their agony. It does not
reflect pain, only faith. We know they died like true
spirits. My music was made to perpetuate their sacrifice.
Seven years ago, on the orders of that vile, foul demon of
Rome, Pope Innocent the Third, Louis of France – may
he suffer eternal pain in the form of toad, worm or
salamander – sent Simon de Monfort against Carcassonne.
There he massacred the flower of our faith. Thousands
upon thousands perished and were immediately swept in
light to God's feet like dust from a broom. Since then the
Vatican has sent its Dominicans, its Franciscans and its

Inquisitions, but we have not been broken. For we live out our faith in secret. We dissemble because truth is worth dissembling if that is what must be done so it can survive.

(*Horse at a fast gallop. Crying of a CHILD.*)

PRIOR ALEC: (*Shouting exultantly.*) I have it here, the symbol of the future of the faith! The mason's child!

ROBIN HOOD: Welcome him with music! Welcome him with song!

(*Galloping of horse, halting, jangle of bridle. Crying of child. Horns winding in the greenwood.*)

PRIOR ALEC: Wonder at the shape of this child!

(*Dark murmur of surprise and horror. Music.*)

FELIX: (*Sings.*) O bright lord above me,
O dark lord below me,
ever show thy battle-wounds
to thy marvelling servant.

Gabriel ascending,
Lucifer descending,
all Man's laws a-bending
like the longbows of the lords.

Hell was harrowed slowly,
Adam brought down lowly,
let us travel slowly
through lead and silver mountains.

Light and dark in battle,
good and evil tattle,
sin was baby's rattle
in the crib at Bethlehem.

See the city falling,
hear the children calling,
plunder wagons hauling
gold and grief over the land.

Walls and towers are tumbling,
gates and ramparts crumbling,
godly war is humbling
all but those who know the law.

In between great forces,
poor men run their courses,
oceans find their sources
in the tears of Carcassonne.

O bright lord above me,
O dark lord below me,
ever show thy battle-wounds
to thy marvelling servant.

(*Cry of CHILD. A collective sigh of amazement.*)

PRIOR ALEC: The child is alive, even within this form!

(*Fade greenwood atmosphere. Fade in ship at sea atmosphere.*)

LIL: (*Fade in.*) Before you pledge your troth too much
captain, I must tell you the whole truth.

MURPHY: The truth? What is that this time of day?

LIL: This infant I had in Carlisle just before I sailed.

MURPHY: I wouldn't blame a woman of your experience
and passion for human exploration for having a child in
a casual way, God help me.

LIL: Captain, it was deformed.

MURPHY: Dear Lord, I've seen such things in the sea on
many a morning. That doesn't worry me at all. Come on.
Give us a kiss and lend us a shilling.

LIL: I always have deformed children. The lucky ones die.
Do you still want to marry me?

MURPHY: I tell you, everything is different in Ireland.
If we are fortunate enough to have progeny between us
I have no doubt they will be as straight and sharp as a
chisel. (*Fades.*)

(*Fade sea sounds and ship at sea atmosphere. Fade in greenwood
atmosphere. Hubbub.*)

PRIOR ALEC: I promised you all a saviour. I promised
you all a sign. I have ridden night and day from Carlisle
to bring it to you.

(*Roar of amazement and horror.*)

Our child, our future! Sprung from a mason's loins!

TURSTIN: (*In his head.*) My child is hammer-headed!

PRIOR ALEC: Praise its deformity! Praise its strangeness!

TURSTIN: (*In his head.*) My poor child. Now it's there I love it. It has knocked down the church in my head!

(*Cry of the hammer-headed CHILD.*)

Give it to me! I am its father.

PRIOR ALEC: Its father? Yes, an unnatural one. You ran away from it. Because you doubted that it could be perfect, you turned your back on your own pride and joy.

TURSTIN: Give it to me. I will care for it. I will bring it up decently. It is of my blood. I don't mind its ugliness. I want it! Give it to me!

(*Scuffle. A blow.*)

PRIOR ALEC: Down! It is ours! It is the sign we have been waiting for. A saviour born of true pride! Kneel, masters, and praise it. I give you the Hammer, born in a pigsty, and it will be wise men who worship it! The child is a sign to rule the world.

(*Cry of the hammer-headed CHILD. Crowd response in awe and prayer.*)

ST THOMAS: (*Voice over.*) The Albigensian heretics say that my Lord Jesus did not die on the Cross. To them He is little more than a trapped tree spirit from a pagan age. I saw Him die. I heard Him, smelt him. They say that the god of the Old Testament is nothing but an evil demiurge. There is no centre to their own mess of ideas except for a peculiar addiction to the notion that light is the essence of God. Matter is evil, to them except when it is tooled by a craftsman's hand to represent the drifting daylight. To them, stone that is shaped to look like light is an argument for heresy. Cathedrals!

PRIOR ALEC: Chartres! Rheims! Amiens! Laon!

(*Hammering of the hammer-head on wood, punctuating the list. Cries of the hammer-headed CHILD.*)

Bourges! Paris! Rouen! Chalon!

(*Hammering of the hammer-head on wood, punctuating the list. Cries of the hammer-headed CHILD.*)

The plans are drawn for these places. Some have already been rebuilt in the style of light, others will be when fires have destroyed them as they presently stand. Our fires of love.

(*Sound of burning.*)

ROBIN HOOD: Our fires of love began a hundred years ago. Since then we have worked hard to clear Europe from its old contamination. We have burnt it out and made the earth ready for our new temples of light. In the last hundred years, while being cursed and persecuted we have burned down with our fires of love eleven cathedrals, eleven sepulchres of darkness, matter and evil. Peterborough!

ALBIGENSIANS: Burn! Evil! Burn! Make light from darkness.

ROBIN HOOD: Exeter!

ALBIGENSIANS: Burn! Evil! Burn! Make light from darkness.

ROBIN HOOD: Canterbury!

ALBIGENSIANS: Burn! Evil! Burn! Make light from darkness.

ROBIN HOOD: Rochester ... Strasbourg ... Chichester ... Gloucester ... Chartres ... Rouen ... Southwark ... Reims ...

ALBIGENSIANS: Burn! Evil! Burn! Make light of darkness.

ROBIN HOOD: And to confirm the virtue of our campaign against the forces of darkness, God sent his earthquake against Lincoln. A mighty victory for the Lord of light! And we have our plans. Amiens will burn in two years time, Coutances will burn in two years time, Beauvais will burn in three years time, and from their ashes greatness will grow.

ALBIGENSIANS: Hosanna! Hosanna to the holy fires of love!

(*Burning of a great building. Music. Fade in special atmosphere, fire continues.*)

ST THOMAS: The heretics dance round their bonfires in the greenwood glade, one for each of the great churches

they have razed to the ground. In their cries of joy
I also hear the screams of craftsmen toppling from
towers and spires on icy mornings like fledglings caught
wrong-footed in a late frost. I hear the wail of the last
hundred years of frenzied building in Europe. Amongst
this hideous medley of pain I hear the last cry of one
carpenter in particular. It is the church that has crippled
Christ. If he came again it would have to be on crutches.
These gambolling fools cannot see Him but He is there
in that huge, twisted church of tree-trunks, the natural
model for all their silly houses of poisoned prayers. I see
Him in the leaves, hanging like a drop of morning dew.

(*Fade special atmosphere. Fade in greenwood. Burning.*)

HAMMERHEAD: (*Sings.*)
The oak, the ash, the elm, the beech,
bears the suffering, weeping leech,
Every tree, rose, thorn and willow,
carries the crying I-am-god fellow,
Even the nut-tree, hazel and wall
boasts of the blood of one who loved all.

PRIOR ALEC: The mason's child sings! It is a further sign
of grace!

ROBIN HOOD: But what is it saying, Alec? What is it
saying?

HAMMERHEAD: (*Sings.*)
Here must I live in the greenwood tree,
far from my home in the cold country,
when comes the carpenter to set me free
taking my place on the greenwood tree?

ROBIN HOOD: Quick, Alec, speak! Cloud the monster's
song!

PRIOR ALEC: And we will expand into Germany at
Cologne, Freiburg, Regensberg and Ulm!

ALBIGENSIANS: Hosanna! To the light! Luminous!

PRIOR ALEC: Into Austria at Vienna. Into Spain at
Burgos, Toledo, Leon, Pamplona, Seville.

ALBIGENSIANS: Hosanna! To the light! Luminous!

PRIOR ALEC: Into Italy at Orvieto, Siena, Florence and Milan!

ALBIGENSIANS: Hosanna! To the light! Luminous!

PRIOR ALEC: Praise the hammer that will beat the light of God from the anvil of darkness. Praise the hammer that will cut the stone of light from the rock of evil.

(*Cry of the CHILD. Fade in special atmosphere. Uproar of delight.*)

(*Music of the spheres.*)

ST THOMAS: We should never have persecuted them. I, Thomas Didymus, disciple, have no doubt about that. These people knew how to fight back. From the time that the Vatican first condemned them as heretics in eleven hundred and nineteen at the Council of Toulouse they have gnawed their way into the guts of every Christian nation, pursuing this policy of arson and demolition to build their new temples. They are so much a part of each government in Christendom that no one can recognise them for what they are. And it is the masons who have served them. I know the masons died in droves, human snow from stone skies, strangled on crane-tackle, struck down by timber in the clutch of gravity's evil, sucking force, choked by dust – and I know that they died anonymous, unsung and often unpaid – but they did it! They built those proofs of heresy that were at one and the same time the Church's hunting dogs of stone, crouched all over Christendom, hounds waiting for the hare of heresy. But the heresy was inside them! And is it any wonder Man became confused? Light is not God. God is God, the small, pitiable fellow hanging on the wooden cross. I do not forgive the masons for their part in this. The beauty they created was that of power, not poor Christ's passion.

(*Fade out special atmosphere. Fade in greenwood. Birds singing in the greenwood.*)

TURSTIN: Where's my child?

PRIOR ALEC: Sleeping.

TURSTIN: What will become of it?

PRIOR ALEC: It will live here in Sherwood.

TURSTIN: Did you hear what it was singing?

PRIOR ALEC: Even that child is innocent.

TURSTIN: That was a free song, nothing to do with Felix the fallen priest, or your corruption. (*Pause.*) Perhaps you'll kill it?

PRIOR ALEC: No. It is one of us. We will teach it new songs, don't worry. And you will help me build my new church at Carlisle, won't you?

TURSTIN: Why should I?

ROBIN HOOD: Surely you're not afraid of hard work? We have been condemned as heretics for a thousand years but no one has ever called us lazy.

TURSTIN: Let me go. I will take my child and find a quiet place to live with it. My wife is a good woman. She will help me. I believe that she might even come to love it as I do.

PRIOR ALEC: Turstin, if you do not join us we will have to grant your extraordinary offspring the privilege of the *endura.*

TURSTIN: You must not hurt my child. It is innocent and a natural Christian.

PRIOR ALEC: Pure souls amongst our most perfect followers are, on rare occasions, permitted to starve themselves to death. That is the *endura.*

ROBIN HOOD: A great honour.

TURSTIN: My child, deformed though it is, is not an Albigensian. Without teaching it sings Christian songs!

ROBIN HOOD: Oh, that's easily changed, Perhaps you want it dead? It's an embarrassment to you? Can we say about you that this mason is made of stone?

TURSTIN: I will join you. You must not hurt my child.

PRIOR ALEC: Fatherly feelings won out. Quite right too. Robin, do you think that in Turstin's case we might waive the *appareillamentum*?

ROBIN HOOD: Unusual to mollycoddle a novice.

PRIOR ALEC: But his position has been made clear already by the birth of the hammer-head. No further information is needed. We know the man backwards. You see, Turstin, the *appareillamentum* is the public confession of sins. Yours have been made flesh in your child. We can see them.

TURSTIN: I said I will join you!

FELIX: (*Fade in.*) Have you finished the preparations.

PRIOR ALEC: Yes. We have tied up all the loose ends. We can proceed. Of course, you two know each other, don't you Felix?

FELIX: We do indeed. This novice commissioned a song from me to be sung by a boy from Lightwater near Hook, near Bagshot to King John for the purpose of persuading His Majesty to pay a debt. You remember?

TURSTIN: I do. It was the worst thing I ever did to myself.

FELIX: It was a good song. It got you here, eventually.

PRIOR ALEC: Now you know just how much we want you to be part of us. We have used every influence we can. What else do you need to know?

TURSTIN: I have one question left: what do you call yourselves? I hear nothing of Albigensians.

ROBIN HOOD: It was thought prudent to drop that name when the persecutions started. Over the centuries we have been called many things: Bogomiles, Arians, Paulicians, Manichaeans, Zarathustrians. Some even call us fireworshippers. None of these names matter, even to be called men of Albi. Truth is truth.

PRIOR ALEC: Mason, it is a matter of policy that we do not have a name for a while. Maybe we will find a new one.

(*Crowd in the greenwood. Many birds singing the evening chorus. Music.*)

FELIX: (*Fade in.*) There is only one question I have to ask of you, Turstin Stacey. All who take our faith must promise that when they see death approaching they will receive the *consolamentum*, the spiritual baptism. Then

you will take your new name to be known by
in the kingdom of light. Will you receive the
consolamentum?

TURSTIN: Is that all you ask of me?

FELIX: For the rest, you may do as you like.
The world is a wicked place and its corrupting
pressures impossible to resist. We share this agony.
So you must help your brothers above all others.
Do you promise these things.

TURSTIN: I do. (*In his head.*) This being one of the world's
evil pressures that I find impossible to resist.

(*Fade greenwood atmosphere. Music of the spheres. Fade in special
atmosphere.*)

ST THOMAS: There is something I should confess.
I, Thomas Didymus, disciple, doubter, lover of Our
Lord, cannot help this poor man with useful arguments.
No one here in Heaven will get down to admitting
evil is at lusty work in the creation as a *servant*. Who
employed him? Who pays his wages? The answer
makes me tremble. In the absence of our courage these
heresies will flower, seed and flower again. Turstin
spends that night wrapped in a cloak at the foot of
a hollow tree where his hammer-headed child is kept
like a human woodpecker.

(*Fade out special atmosphere. Fade in greenwood atmosphere and
nightingale.*)

TURSTIN: Child!

HAMMERHEAD: Father!

TURSTIN: Can you hear me clearly?

HAMMERHEAD: I will ask the nightingale to stop its
song. Nightingale! Shut up!

(*Nightingale stops singing. Pause.*)

TURSTIN: Child, what am I to do?

HAMMERHEAD: Go back to Carlisle.

TURSTIN: And leave you here? These are evil men. They
live a life of lies.

HAMMERHEAD: Go back to Carlisle and build the new cathedral.

TURSTIN: For heretics? For light-worshippers?

HAMMERHEAD: Build it as he wants it built. When it is finished in its inhuman beauty, in its reaching upwards, Prior Alec will die. A new bishop will come. With him you must get into that church and carve the faces of men on every pillar, every roof-boss, every space you can find. Show him smiling and crying. Show him in January and June. Show him drunk and sober. Fill the church with leaves and birds. That way the mason in you will be redeemed.

TURSTIN: I will do it. If I find a place, may I carve a resemblance of you, my child?

HAMMERHEAD: If it pleases you. Nightingale! You may sing again if you wish.

(*Pause. Nightingale starts to sing. Fade greenwood atmosphere. Fade in special atmosphere.*)

ST THOMAS: The nameless company of heretics goes from the greenwood back to its hidey-holes all over England – offices and chancelleries, courts and abbeys, monasteries and palace rooms. To me a web of cynical and greedy exploitation of the Christian mass of souls. To them, just ritualistic realists spinning out their time in sweet, clandestine power. The next day Prior Alec and Turstin started their journey back to Carlisle to begin the demolition of the old grey church, leaving the mason's child behind in the care of Robin, Felix and the merry men of Sherwood. (*Fades.*)

(*Fade in outside Carlisle cathedral atmosphere. Huge clap of a trebuchet, flying of a great boulder through the air, crash of boulder on thick church walls. They boom with the blow. Cheers and applause from a crowd.*)

PRIOR ALEC: What do you think of that? A good shot, smack on the nose! Reload the trebuchet, lads.

(*Sounds of loading heavy stone into the bucket and returning trebuchet to primed position.*)

PRIOR ALEC: Hardly made a dent in it. This is going to be a long business. They built to last, the Normans. Savages! Cheer up, Turstin. Go on, you fire the second missile. It will do your heart good.

TURSTIN: I thought you favoured the fires of love? Why not burn the place down?

PRIOR ALEC: Tried it. We had the same trouble as they did at Laon in eleven fifty. Wouldn't burn. We have to demolish.

(*Clap of the trebuchet as the bucket is tripped. Shouts, whistles and laughter from the crowd. The stone strikes. Boom.*)

PRIOR ALEC: See how they're enjoying themselves? Don't keep that long face. This is a festival. Join in, smile. Do you know what I've done? Each of the burghers of Carlisle has coughed up five shillings for the privilege of firing one projectile. I hope raising the funds for erecting the new church will be as easy as getting the money to knock down the old.

TURSTIN: I thought you had money? King John said that you had found the cash already.

(*Reloading the trebuchet.*)

PRIOR ALEC: Did he? Oh. Don't you worry about the finances.

TURSTIN: You're not expecting me to do this without guaranteed payment, are you?

PRIOR ALEC: Your first major ecclesiastical commission? I'm the one taking all the risks. Albert Magnus! Are you first to fire the machine for God, grace and a handsomer Carlisle?

ALBERT: I am. That's what this old town needs. A torch to light the way. We've been stuck on our own too long up here, doing as we like. We must integrate. Your new church, Prior, will be a sign of our inclusion in the English state, and Christendom at large. Halleluiah! In the name of God and his holy Mother. Fire!

(*Clap as trebuchet is fired. Applause and cheering. Boom as it hits the wall. Crash of falling masonry. Cheers.*)

I did it! I did it! I made the first hole! Get stuck in, lads. Let's pull the old bitch down! (*Fade.*)

(*Fade out outside Carlisle cathedral atmosphere. Fade in TURSTIN's quarters.*)

ALICE: (*Fade in.*) Husband, is that you? Turstin?

TURSTIN: Who is there?

ALICE: It's me, Alice.

TURSTIN: Alice! What are you doing here?

ALICE: You're angry that I've come?

TURSTIN: No. It's good to see your face again. What's this?

ALICE: It's nine months since you left to find King John. Soon we will have a child.

TURSTIN: A child! Alice, what does it feel like?

ALICE: I don't know. I've never had a child before.

TURSTIN: Can you feel its head?

ALICE: Yes, I think I can.

TURSTIN: Is it round?

ALICE: Yes, it's round. (*Pause.*) You're shaking. Are you sick?

TURSTIN: Oh, Alice, Alice. Our world still exists. It's wonderful to have you standing there, so real. Welcome. (*Goes to her. Kiss.*) Yes, it is Alice, my wife. But how did you get here?

ALICE: Prior Alec sent down for me. I had an escort all the way up from Nottingham and a fine horse to carry me. We travelled slowly, resting a lot for the child. I have never travelled such a distance before.

TURSTIN: Sit down. I still can't believe it's you. Did you meet Prior Alec?

ALICE: Yes. He met me at the gates of the town. He seems a good man. Certainly he thinks the world of you. And such a great work he has given you to do. A cathedral! I'm so proud.

TURSTIN: Did he ask anything of you?

ALICE: Yes.

TURSTIN: What was that?

ALICE: That I should make you happy in this, our new life. (*Pause.*) Turstin, our house in Nottingham was lost. It was burnt down.

TURSTIN: When did this happen?

ALICE: In the first week of May. Common soldiers did it, men who had not been paid their wage.

TURSTIN: What kind of soldiers?

ALICE: They said they had been fighting against King John until he died. They said they had no master but lived by robbery.

TURSTIN: And what colours did these men wear?

ALICE: The green of a greenwood! So, I went to live with my mother to await your return. Prior Alec – bless his great charity – sent his agents to find me.

TURSTIN: Did we lose everything?

ALICE: Yes. The morning after the fire your seniors from the lodge brought me money, food and clothes. But the greatest favour that they did was to guide the agents of this holy prior – God bless his thoughtfulness – to find me in the ashes.

TURSTIN: Just so, just so.

ALICE: They said, for the child's sake, we must build a new life here in Carlisle and give ourselves over to God's great work. I think those men saved me from madness. I was in despair.

TURSTIN: For the child's sake? Are we lost, Alice?

ALICE: Things are just beginning for us. My child will have a famous father, a man whose work will be marvelled at. And do you want me to use your old or your new name?

TURSTIN: What is my new name?

ALICE: Prior Alec says that you have a secret name. It will only be used at the hour of your death but, he says, I may know it. He says you are a changed man.

TURSTIN: What is my new name!?

ALICE: Flos.

TURSTIN: Flos. The name of a dog.

ALICE: No. Prior Alec says it is from the Latin – *flos
operatum* – the flower of craftsmen. That you will be.
(*In special memory atmosphere. Music.*)

HAMMERHEAD: Flourish fair flower, my father.

TURSTIN: I hear you, child.

HAMMERHEAD: Flourish fair flower, my father,
friend and fancy of all fit minds,

TURSTIN: Prior Alec is already looking very old.

HAMMERHEAD: Carve me men, animals and monsters,
carve me grotesques and gargoyles with grace,
carve me fox and geese, and girls and boys,
carve me April in pruning-time, my flower.

TURSTIN: On the day that Prior Alec dies I will be
through the door with my bag of tools. I will work day
and night to redeem my work.

HAMMERHEAD: Flourish fair flower, my father,
build beauty out of evil into good.
build beauty out of evil into good.
build beauty out of evil into good. (*Fades.*)
(*Fade special memory atmosphere. Fade in Carlisle outside
atmosphere. Huge rumble of falling masonry.*)

PRIOR ALEC: She's down lads! She's down! Lord, how that
changes thy skyline! Out of this rubble will rise a sacred
bird in stone. It will have a secret song, and sing for
ever.
(*Fade Carlisle atmosphere. Fade in greenwood atmosphere, and
birdsong.*)

ST THOMAS: (*Sings.*) Deep in the greenwood
in a rotten hollow tree
lives the hammerheaded child
on cold, masonic charity,
lives the hammerheaded child
in curious, pure deformity,
lives the hammerheaded child,
in hunger, cold and poverty,

lives the hammerheaded child
in honest Christianity.

HAMMERHEAD: (*Sings.*)

Here must I live in the greenwood tree,
far from my home in the cold country,
when comes the carpenter to set me free
taking my place on the greenwood tree?

The End.

KITTY WILKINSON

Society of Authors Silver Sony Award 1993

For Martin Jenkins

Kitty Wilkinson was first broadcast on BBC Radio 4 on the 30th of May 1992. The cast was as follows:

KITTY, Maureen O'Brien

MAM, Kate Binchy

GUEST/FATHER/TOM WILKINSON, Keith Drinkel

DR FARADAY, John Rowe

HELEN, Helena Breck

JOHN DE MONTE, Peter Gunn

IRISH GIRL, Siubhan Reid

ANNE/HANNAH/BOY, Melanie Hudson

JESSY/WOMAN, Joanna Wake

DEIRDRE/MARY, Veronica Quilligan

CHOLERA (Dr O'Lera), Robert Glenister

DIRECTION, Martin Jenkins

Fade in special atmosphere. Sounds of rhythmic washing in tubs. Music.

FEMALE SINGER: Monday's always washing day,
 No matter what the weather say,
 Heat the copper, cut the soap,
 Watch the sky for signs of hope,
 Let there be a drying wind,
 Mankind hath sinned.

 Monday's always washing day,
 Last week's gone with all our pay,
 Starch this collar, bleach his shirt,
 Your enemy is only dirt,
 Let there be a drying wind,
 Mankind hath sinned.

 (*Music continues in distant background. Chime of glass.*)

Scene 1

DR FARADAY: To Hippocrates!

GUEST: If he were here, Faraday, what would he make of us? Would Hippocrates admire such a hypocrite as myself?

DR FARADAY: Puns, is it? I love a good pun. I'll think of one.

GUEST: No, it's self-mortification and disgust. Guilt, you see, Mrs Faraday. It works from within like the worm. The cholera marches on. After two and a half thousand years of human medicine we can't do a damn thing to stop it. That's shameful.

DR FARADAY: You're in a bad way, old boy.

GUEST: Mrs Faraday, forgive me. I'm adrift. That much I can diagnose. I can even cure it, if I had the will to. I need ... equa ... equanimity ... But it's right that I should be haunted by this killer cholera ... I give you a toast, madam ... to your beauty and the wind which blows upon us all.
 (*Chime of glass.*)

HELEN: The wind which blows upon us all. Is that an old saying?

GUEST: More ancient wisdom? What do you reckon, Faraday?

DR FARADAY: That I should call you a cab.

GUEST: Yes ... Sorry I haven't been at my best ... Haven't got your strength of mind, old chap ... your reason for living, you know ... very lucky man.

(*Chime of glass.*)

GUEST: But, I give you ... the wind, the anti-Hippocratic wind!

(*Fade FARADAY. Dining room atmosphere music continues.*)

SINGER: Monday's always washing day
Now every day is Monday,
Hands red-raw, an aching back,
Hang the corpse clothes on the rack,
Let there be a drying wind,
Mankind hath sinned.

Scene 2

(*Wilkinson cellar atmosphere and sounds of mangling.*)

MAM: What are you writing, our Kitty?

KITTY: Sums.

MAM: I'd rather put my head through this mangle than do sums.

KITTY: Quiet, Mam. They've all gone off to sleep.

MAM: I'm not doing any more mangling!

(*Mangling sounds stop.*)

KITTY: Have a rest, then. Three shillings and four pence ...

MAM: (*Interrupting.*) You and your sums!

KITTY: Mam, it was you who taught me to fear debt. I must keep up to date with my accounts.

MAM: That was long ago. Get into debt as much as you like.

KITTY: Now you're just talking for talking's sake.

MAM: How will you ever prosper with everyone scrounging off you? You're beaten before you start. You're a fool to yourself, Kitty.

KITTY: Shall we do the mangling together? Two hands on the handle, two hands to the wheel?

MAM: I'd like that.

(*Mangling sounds resume.*)

KITTY: Come on, now. We'll sing very quietly in our minds so as not to wake the others.

MAM: Oh, yes!

KITTY: Just in our minds, now. No real singing.

MAM: Like the old days. Sssh. Not too loud now. Very quietly. Are you singing already?

KITTY: I am.

MAM: Which one are you singing?

KITTY: You have to guess.

MAM: The one about the lady who ran off with the tinker?

KITTY: No.

MAM: Good, because that's the one I'm singing. But, whatever it is that's going through your head, Kitty, let it not be lamentation.

KITTY: It's certainly not that.

MAM: You have this fine little cellar with water running down the walls. So, lamentation for you would be entirely out of place.

KITTY: It's wrong to mock the hardness of another's life, Mam.

MAM: It's my life as well. When you let me come out of the workhouse for a while I live it alongside you like a Trojan. (*Pause.*) Why did you bring me out this time? So I could catch cholera as well as being worked to death?

KITTY: You haven't yet guessed what song I'm singing in my mind.

MAM: What kind of a daughter is that?

KITTY: Shall I sing you a bit of it?

MAM: You could never keep your eyes off the men, could you? And you're no good for them. Poor old John de Monte drowned himself rather than come home from sea. Remember him? Your husband before Tom Nobody? And you've driven John's son to drink with your adulterous ways. What a slut you are!

KITTY: (*Sings a phrase.*) It's "The Unquiet Grave."

MAM: I said no lamentation! Let's mangle harder! Oh, God, God, why do I say these things? I can't be a good person with a tongue like mine. Forgive me, darlin'.

KITTY: I told you a little fib, Mam. It wasn't that song I was singing. For mangling there's no better tune than (*Sings.*) 'Onward Christian soldiers'.

MAM: Oh, that's a real workhouse song. Don't put me back in that place, darlin'. Let me have a rest. My arm hurts.

KITTY: We consume so much butter! Three shillings and fourpence's worth in a week! Five pounds in weight.

MAM: When I've got my strength back I'll get on with the mangling. Don't be harsh with me.

KITTY: I suppose that's not all that much for fifteen of us. What is it? Five pounds is ... eighty ounces, divided by fifteen is ... five and a bit ounces each. That's not much, is it?

MAM: Tell you what. I'll use my ration of butter to grease the mangle and stop it squealing. It gets me down.

(*Mangling sounds resume. MAM hums 'Onward Christian Soldiers'.*)

TOM: What's the trouble with her now? Will she never give us any peace?

KITTY: Go back to sleep, husband. You have a full day's work tomorrow.

TOM: Will you stop slandering my wife? You say the most terrible things about the poor woman, none of which she deserves.

MAM: I'm only talking.

TOM: If you must talk about her, then tell the truth, for God's sake!

(*Cross cellar atmosphere into sea sounds and a sailing ship leaving harbour – flashback on echo.*)

Scene 3

MAM: Kitty say a prayer for Ireland. Who knows when we'll be seeing her again.

KITTY: (*As a girl.*) God bless Ireland, and feed the people.

MAM: When things are better we'll come back and look after your Dad's grave, God rest him. Things will be better then.

KITTY: Will anyone take care of an English soldier's grave, Mam? Won't it get grown over?

MAM: Oh, someone will pass a scythe over it now and again. Here, Kitty, hold the baby for me, there's a good girl. My arm is dropping off.

(*Sound of BABY being handed to KITTY. It cries a little.*)

KITTY: Shush, now. You're all right. Isn't this a fine ship? (*Pause.*) What'll it be like in Liverpool, Ma?

MAM: Not bad, I hope. We might not be so skint.

KITTY: Will we get rich, then?

MAM: We'll have to wait and see.

KITTY: Do they speak our language there?

MAM: Near enough.

KITTY: That will help us some.

(*BABY cries a little.*)

KITTY: Shush, now.

MAM: You're good with that child.

KITTY: He knows me well enough.

MAM: I don't like the look of the weather.

KITTY: It's only rain.

(*Fades. Cross sea atmosphere and sounds, into Wilkinson cellar atmosphere with sounds of mangling and mangle squealing.*)

MAM: Where's my baby? Oh, Jesus, he's been swept overboard!

KITTY: Shush, Mam. Don't punish yourself.

MAM: It was you who let go of him! Why did you do that, you wicked girl?

KITTY: Mam, that's all over. Don't bring it back.

MAM: The poor little mite, drowned! Oh, God in heaven!

Scene 4

(*Pause.*)

MAM: But I held on to you, Kitty, didn't I? I didn't let you go.

KITTY: You did, Mam, and you didn't.

MAM: I'm a good woman, aren't I?

KITTY: Of course you are. Watch your bib in the mangle.

MAM: And I give you my help unstinting, don't I?

KITTY: All the time, which is most of the time.

MAM: So much mangling. My arm's got so strong.

KITTY: You can mangle better than most men, Mam.

MAM: And they'd let me, the loafers. What a mountain of mangling, eh? It's going to take us all night, darlin'.

KITTY: We'll be done soon.

MAM: There are women who can mangle in their sleep.

(*A knock. The mangling continues. Footsteps to the door. Door opens.*)

DEIRDRE: Would you be Kitty Wilkinson?

MAM: I'd be her mother and a good woman. What do you want?

DEIRDRE: Is she here?

MAM: She's working.

DEIRDRE: Could she come? My name is Mrs Deirdre Flannery and we have the cholera.

MAM: Don't think you're the only one.

DEIRDRE: Are you Kitty Wilkinson?

KITTY: (*Coming to the door.*) I am.

MAM: Oh, the filthy state they walk around in.

DEIRDRE: Thank God I've found you. We have the cholera.

KITTY: Come in.

(*Door closes. Footsteps. Mangle starts up again.*)

KITTY: You'll pardon us if we keep working. You're ill, yourself?

DEIRDRE: Yes. My old man got it first and he's passed it on to me. We've tried to keep ourselves apart from the childer but they're everywhere in our small place. They're sure to catch it soon. Help us, if you will.

KITTY: How many have you?

DEIRDRE: Fourteen.

MAM: A beast of the field!

KITTY: Where are you living?

DEIRDRE: A cellar in Donaby Street.

KITTY: What number?

DEIRDRE: Thirty-seven. Will you come?

KITTY: You walked here from Donaby Street?

DEIRDRE: I did. Will you come?

KITTY: What stage is your husband at? Is he awake, purging and vomiting, in collapse?

DEIRDRE: That's him, the latter.

KITTY: When you touch him is he cold and clammy?
(*Silence.*)

KITTY: Sunken eyes, cheeks hollow, husky in the voice, blue about the mouth?
(*Silence.*)

MAM: A good half die, darlin'. The men go more than the girls. That's because they're not so clean.

KITTY: Why do you think you have the disease?

DEIRDRE: It's the same start as he had. Suddenly I began to purge and vomit everything I had out of me. It just came until I thought I must be empty, surely! But more came, and it was white.

KITTY: You should have sent someone, not come yourself.

DEIRDRE: (*Retches.*) I'm sorry ...

KITTY: Sit for a while.

MAM: All over my clean floor. Now I'll have to scrub it again.

DEIRDRE: I'll do it.

MAM: They could help themselves if they tried.

DEIRDRE: How? What can we do?

MAM: Keep clean!

DEIRDRE: Clean! God help me, I'm washing from morning till night. I keep my family clean, I do. It's a point of pride with me.

KITTY: Don't talk. It'll tire you.

DEIRDRE: She has to be told! We're decent people!

MAM: Yah! I know your sort, sitting around drinking stout.

DEIRDRE: I do not! Stout has never passed my lips.

KITTY: Take no heed. It's my mother's way of talking.

DEIRDRE: If I could do without your help, I would.

MAM: Then get on with it. (*Pause.*) You're whiter than a sheet. Was there ever a time you can remember not being with child? You have one. Within a month you let your husband back into you after you've both been drinking stout and it all starts again. Then you get the cholera and come running. What good is that?

DEIRDRE: (*Retches.*) Oh, God, let me die.

KITTY: Leave her be, Mam.

MAM: Well, they should be told. She should be told.

DEIRDRE: I'm going.

KITTY: Have you any savings?

DEIRDRE: You charge? Oh ... I heard ... How much is it you want?

KITTY: Nothing. If your husband is sick he'll have no wages to bring home. Your children will need feeding.

DEIRDRE: We've borrowed all we can. There's nothing left.

KITTY: We'll find a way.

MAM: Beg, beg, beg.

DEIRDRE: Shut your mouth!

MAM: You'll let her talk to your mother ...

KITTY: Mam – please be quiet. My mother will go home with you and get things going. I'll come along as soon as I can.

DEIRDRE: God bless you. Pardon me for saying this, but they say the old lady's not all there. I only mention it because I haven't got much strength to deal with things as they arise.

MAM: I'm all here, darlin'. I'm her good luck. Without me she couldn't manage, could you?

KITTY: Mam's competent. Let her help you.

MAM: I'm strong too, so don't start a fight.

DEIRDRE: But you'll come, yourself? If my old man knows you're coming it will be easier for him. He worries about the childer. Just your name will comfort him.

MAM: And you're having another baby.

DEIRDRE: And what's that to you?

MAM: Next time I come to earth I'll die curious. All the children in these streets are engendered in drink and wildness. Not one of them is created in peace and decency. Listen to them. No wonder their wives lie quaking in their beds.

(*Edge in sound of drunks in the street.*)

Scene 5

(*Faraday house bedroom. Distant clock striking eleven.*)

DR FARADAY: Sorry that so much shop was talked at table. That fellow would go on and on. Shan't ask him again.

HELEN: (*In bed.*) I've never encountered such melancholy. He was in pain.

DR FARADAY: Posing!

HELEN: He said he was haunted.

DR FARADAY: Yes, yes. We're all haunted. All doctors are haunted, darling. What are we dealing with? The unknown. God, we're stumbling around in the dark most of the time but one doesn't have to beef about it.

HELEN: Don't you ever feel helpless?

DR FARADAY: (*Gets into bed.*) I value my sanity.

HELEN: D'you think that poor man is going mad?

DR FARADAY: (*Trying to kiss her.*) I think he was intent upon making an impression.

HELEN: No.

DR FARADAY: Upon you.

HELEN: Oh, give him some credit.

DR FARADAY: He never took his eyes off you. And I know why.

HELEN: Not now, please. (*Pause.*) Think of him going home through the streets, haunted ... by a disease.

DR FARADAY: It's made you sad?

HELEN: Yes, I suppose it has.

(*Cut into mangle/water sounds. Then cross into Flannery cellar atmosphere.*)

Scene 6

(*The sound of many children sleeping.*)

KITTY: You've done nothing, then? You've just been sitting here in the dark?

(*Cellar door shuts.*)

MAM: They've no candles and I forgot to bring any.

(*DEIRDRE cries out.*)

KITTY: The cramps are racking her.

MAM: Every one of her children has got red hair, she tells me.

KITTY: Are the girls pretty?

MAM: How would I know? They're all in the dark with their red hair. Quite a stink in here, eh?

KITTY: They can't have the window open with that wind blowing.

MAM: Worse smell than pigs. Turns my stomach, it does.

KITTY: If they had more space they'd smell less.

MAM: No, they wouldn't. Whatever space they had they'd smell.

KITTY: Now you're being hard again.

DEIRDRE: (*Groans.*) It's coming ... oh, not into this ...

KITTY: Mrs Flannery, it's the cramps.

DEIRDRE: No, it's the child ... I can feel it ...

KITTY: It's the cramps. Be brave, now.

DEIRDRE: (*Angrily.*) D'you think I've not had a baby before?

KITTY: Quiet, now. Don't wake the others. Pray to God in your mind.

DEIRDRE: (*Crying out.*) Oh, what'll I call this child?

(*Mocking laugh caught in sound of wind as it blows harder. Then into music.*)

Scene 7

CHOLERA: Doctor O'Lera is my name, physician to the unpurged and over-hydrated, those who have lost the power to expel waste, those who are slow to regurgitate, all these necessary emissions and voidings which clean out the system. I work hand in hand with Nature, which abhors the prolific, the myriad nests of the copulating poor, the places too rich with life. It is my occupation to keep mankind in its fundamental and minimal state, that sought by the saints in the desert, the anchorites, fakirs and holy men: dry, drained, physically apathetic but spiritually alight, ever-ready to be slotted into the eternal earth.

(*DEIRDRE cries out – on echo.*)

CHOLERA: Would she name her child after me, this Mrs Flannery who twists and groans on the rack of the cramps which I have induced? The blood pressure fails. The pulse cannot be felt at the wrist. The urine is suppressed. Circulatory failure sets in, vital power diminishes, and I, C.H. O'Lera, M.D., physician to the poor of all nations –

DEIRDRE with a labour pang – on echo.

CHOLERA: – midwife another death from the womb of the world.

(*Cross music into:*)

Scene 8

(*A few chirrups in the distance.*)

MAM: Morning's come.

KITTY: Already? You've good ears.

(*Morning chorus starts up after muted beginning.*)

MAM: Thank God for the birds. When I was sitting here in the dark I could only hear the sea beating against the walls. I don't like that!

KITTY: Where is the mother?

MAM: By the stairs. Do you never listen to a word I'm saying, you evil creature? I can hear it! Oh, merciful God, here comes that wave with you riding it!

KITTY: Be quiet, Mam. (*Moving across the cellar.*) Mrs Flannery.

DEIRDRE: (*Waking.*) Uh?

KITTY: Is there somewhere the children can play?

DEIRDRE: Eh? Oh ... you've come ...

KITTY: Somewhere they can go. We have to start work.

DEIRDRE: Tell Anne – she's my eldest. Please keep them all together. Get my husband to tell them not to wander.

KITTY: He's gone to a better place, Mrs Flannery.

DEIRDRE: Has he? Oh ... Tell Anne to take the childer to Mrs Rowledge at number forty-three. She'll help out.

(*Children starting to wake up. Coughing, sniffing, whimpering.*)

KITTY: Are you Anne?

ANNE: I am.

KITTY: My name is Kitty Wilkinson.

ANNE: You've come, then? Ma said you would.

KITTY: You're a big girl and I can trust you to be good and sensible. Your Mam is very ill with the cholera and your father died during the night. It's a terrible morning for you, child, but we have to clean your home out from top to bottom and wash all your things. Take your brothers and sisters to Mrs Rowledge at number forty-three and ask her to help out.

ANNE: Do I do that in your name?

KITTY: If it will help.

ANNE: It will. Why are you so good to people you don't know?

KITTY: Nobody was any the poorer for what they gave to a neighbour in distress.

ANNE: Will my Mam die?

KITTY: No one knows. You must all pray to God for her life.

ANNE: Should I say goodbye?

KITTY: I'll send for you. Take this sixpence and buy bread and milk. Before you go I'll need all your linen and woollens, all your clothes, every scrap. I've brought a bundle of clean things for all of you to wear. But now I want every one of your brothers and sisters to stand naked so that I know that not one item of infected material is escaping me.

ANNE: Is that how my Mam and Dad got the cholera?

KITTY: That's where it hides, I believe.

ANNE: (*Screams and rips at her clothes, tearing and rending.*) Come out! Come out of my clothes!

KITTY: (*A slap.*) Stop that! Those clothes cost money. Now, be good like I asked.

ANNE: Yes, Kitty Wilkinson. (*Pause.*) Will you be washing my Mam's clothes just in case she lives?

KITTY: I'll look after your mother. Now don't let the children stand around in the cold too long. Get them going. Hurry up.

ANNE: Come on. You heard what Kitty Wilkinson said. Get undressed and put these other clothes on! Quick!

(*Children crying, grousing.*)

KITTY: What religion do you have, Mrs Flannery?

DEIRDRE: Eh?

KITTY: What religion?

DEIRDRE: Oh ... Protestant ...

KITTY: With a name like Flannery? Well, well. So, it's a Protestant burial you want for both of you?

DEIRDRE: Whatever you can fix, for no payment ... the children are all naked ... my children ... how thin and pale they are.

KITTY: They're beautiful. Such wonderful red hair.

MAM: God love them, they're shivering.

DEIRDRE: Who owns those clothes they're putting on?

KITTY: No one. Close your eyes now.

DEIRDRE: No, I want to watch ... there's such a host of them ... my sweet childer. They shine, don't they? And all from me? That's hard to believe ... (*Retches.*) Oh, come, come ...

(*Cross into music plus mangle/water/sea sounds, then:*)

Scene 9

CHOLERA: My passion is travelling the earth. Fifteen years ago I set out from India, went by land to China, by good ships to Ceylon, Mauritius and East Africa, then on, on to the Philippines and Japan, then home to India for a visit, crossing on foot to Persia and Arabia and thence to Russia via Astrakhan where I rested a while, then moved on to Mongolia and Manchuria, retracing my steps to Moscow and thence on to Saint Petersburg which gave me access to Germany, from there it was a short sea-voyage to Edinburgh, leaving me a leisurely stroll down to Liverpool.

(*Cross from music into:*)

Scene 10

(*Wilkinson cellar. A hubbub at door.*)

TOM: I've told you, I don't know when she'll be back ...

WOMAN: Tell her we're desperate, Mr Wilkinson.

TOM: I will, I will. But you must be patient. She can't be in two places at once.

JOHN: (*Pushing through the crowd.*) Let me through!

MAM: Wait your turn!

JOHN: I lived here! God, you've got my poor mother under siege. Where is she, Mr Wilkinson?

TOM: I can't say in front of this lot or they'd be round there straight away. Come in, come in.

(*Door being shut against crowd.*)

TOM: It's like this day in, day out.

JOHN: You shouldn't have to put up with it.

TOM: Have you come to help? Your mother needs you, badly.

JOHN: No, I've done all I'm ever doing. She'll bury you along with the rest, but not me. I called in to see how she was but I can guess from the mob outside. You can't live like this for ever. It'll kill you both.

TOM: It's her way, John. I can't change it.

JOHN: It's idolatry. She can't cure cholera with a scrubbing-brush. These people grab at anything. Where's the sense? Take her away.

TOM: She wouldn't go. All right! All right! Go easy there!
  (*Edge out. Edge in Flannery cellar atmosphere.*)

Scene 11

DEIRDRE: ... don't lay me alongside him ... don't let them
  lie us side by side ...

KITTY: Now, now, be forgiving, Mrs Flannery.

DEIRDRE: I want my own grave. Promise. Peace and quiet.

MAM: Let go, darlin'. I need my hand for the scrubbing.

DEIRDRE: Oh, the baby will be with me. Even in the earth
  I won't have room to myself. Please ... please ... don't let
  my childer watch me die. They must go out and play ...

MAM: They're out now, darlin'.

PETER: (*Coming in through an open door.*) Kitty Wilkinson,
  you're needed at home.

KITTY: Ask Mr Wilkinson to deal with it until I get back.

PETER: He's not there. You have twelve people waiting for
  you. They're sitting out in the street.

KITTY: Are they all to do with the cholera?

PETER: Not all. One is a man says you owe him money
  for shoes.

KITTY: Peter, you're a good boy. Take over this scrubbing
  for a while.

PETER: I'm on my way to my lessons.

KITTY: We'll tell the teacher that someone was sick.
  (*KITTY exits.*)

MAM: And scrub properly! Hard! Or there's no point in
  doing it.

PETER: I've done scrubbing before.

MAM: They're in these you know, the cholera things. They're
  brown. If you see brown then batter it with the brush.
  (*Sounds of bricks being moved, clanking sounds of dolly tubs.*)

PETER: I'm better on the washboard, Mam.

MAM: We haven't got a washboard. Put your back into it now.
  (*Cross into O'Lera music.*)

Scene 12

CHOLERA: The boy and the mad old woman bend to
their task while the mother lies dying beside them,
dying double with her child locked in her fevered
womb. The father's fouled clothes are under the brush
of the innocent and the insane, the dashing paintings
of my dysentery fading in the suds of the chloride of
lime soap, the only defence against O'Lera, the driving
dehydrator, the expeller of life's precious fluids, the
burner, the smeared traveller with the dust of a hundred
suffering nations on my feet. Chloride of lime is sad.
It does so little. It takes so much elbow-grease, as the
washer-women say. Mrs Flannery is fading, burned
brown.

(*Cross on music back to Flannery cellar.*)

Scene 13

PETER: I think that woman is dead.

MAM: She is, God save her. There's a soap-bubble, Peter.
Pop! (*Continues humming.*) Pop! Pop! Pop!

(*Cross on Mam 'Pop! Pop!' into:*)

Scene 14

(*Wilkinson cellar.*)

KITTY: If there's nothing more to be done than we're doing
already, then that's it, Doctor.

CHOLERA: Chloride of lime is your only answer, Kitty
Wilkinson, and even that's not very effective

KITTY: And the badness of the water and the sanitation in
these old quarters have nothing to do with it?

CHOLERA: Who knows?

KITTY: People up in the finer parts of the city don't seem
to get afflicted.

CHOLERA: Now, now. No more of that. Just you keep your
mind on scrubbing. Don't be resentful.

KITTY: I'm not resentful. What I'm thinking is 'why?'

CHOLERA: Is it such a bad thing that, now and again, these slums should suffer a reduction in population? What good do these people do? They produce nothing, they create nothing except more of themselves. The poor have to be culled, Kitty. Ah, now I've shocked you. I'm only playing Devil's advocate, you know.

KITTY: These people are the salt of the earth.

CHOLERA: Salt that will kill it. I say, let cholera run free. Let it thin out the numbers. Not everyone dies. Those with good constitutions can survive so that will improve the breeding stock. And it is the males who are worst affected. They form the most dispensable part of the surplus. Take away the idle males and you will lessen violence, perhaps even lessen war. It would be more of a woman's world.

KITTY: Is there no useful advice you can give us?

CHOLERA: It's a matter of simple sums. It will not be more than a few hundred years before the world is suffocated by the unproductive poor. Read your population scientists. It's a grim prospect. Long term.

KITTY: I have no time for that.

CHOLERA: I foresee a day when diseases which have been conquered by medical science will be deliberately re-introduced in order to reduce the population.

KITTY: God help us, Doctor. What a terrible thought to have when innocent people are dying in their hundreds all around us. Your banter is too cruel.

CHOLERA: We must look truth in the eye, Kitty, always. You cannot fight mathematics. Now, I have many calls to make in the area and I must be about my business. But I'll be back to see how you're getting on.

KITTY: Thank you for taking the trouble to talk to me, Doctor. It is much appreciated. I wish more members of the profession would show the same concern.

CHOLERA: Oh, you know those chaps. They don't have the love for the poor that I have. They won't take the risk of coming down here. (*Pause.*) Don't you find it odd that you've never caught cholera? It's nothing short of a miracle. Don't you ever wonder about that?

KITTY: No.

CHOLERA: Hm. I thought it must be an obvious thought for you to have. But then, you're not an obvious woman, are you, Kitty Wilkinson?

KITTY: I wouldn't be knowing.

CHOLERA: No, you're a supple, strong warrior of a woman. You shimmer amongst the suds and steam like Diana bathing under the moon ... ah, yes, I have an idea of you, Kitty Wilkinson.

KITTY: Well, Doctor, it's a lot more elaborate than the idea which I have of myself.

CHOLERA: Quite proper of you to tick me off. How dare I compare you to some cruel old pagan goddess? You're all heart. In many ways I'd say that you are a very modern woman, Kitty Wilkinson.

KITTY: No, no, I'm very old-fashioned. There's nothing modern about me. I'm ignorant and uneducated that's the sad thing.

(*Cross on mangle/water, into O'Lera music for:*)

Scene 15

CHOLERA: The poor, deluded wretch is scratching at the surface, I'm afraid. Her instinct to scrub and clean is telling her that this is some use. If she gets rid of all visible dirt then the battle is won. She is, essentially, one of those women who believe that water is the answer to everything. When I look over the flooded fields beside wide rivers, fields where the populations of great cities creep out to defecate, and I watch what they think they have got rid of from their bowels going back into their cups and kettles, I have to agree with Kitty Wilkinson. Water is the answer to everything. It is the first element. It is the means of the cycle. It enables death to sail upon the surface of life.

(*Fade. Bring up water noises. Then cross into busy waterfront pub.*)

Scene 16

(*Fade in pub atmosphere.*)

KITTY: (*Fade in.*) John, at last I've found you. Your step-father said you were trying to find me. I've been looking everywhere.

JOHN: Mam, you mustn't follow me into an alehouse, for God's sake!

KITTY: You called round to see me but you didn't wait.

JOHN: I would have been kicking my heels for a week.

KITTY: Today has been such an ungrateful time. I've felt a fool standing at the tub washing as if I, a stupid woman, could fight cholera all on my own. (*Pause.*) Why did you come?

JOHN: Still up to your old tricks, eh, Mam? I came to see how you were bearing up. But I didn't come to re-enlist.

KITTY: That's cruel. Couldn't you do a bit of teaching for me? We're crying out for help from people with some education.

JOHN: No.

KITTY: John, pass on what learning we got you. It would only mean a few hours a day. Think of the children ...

JOHN: (*Passionately.*) No, curse you! You've driven me away from all that, ground all the good out of me. It's me from now on.

KITTY: John, no one is more precious ... (*Pause.*) Did I ask too much of you? Too much fetching and carrying? (*Pause.*) No, everyone must give all they can. I don't understand what's happened to you.

JOHN: So you say. What choice was I given? What choice is that poor, biddable dog of a husband of yours given? Do this, do that!

KITTY: You know, Tom, fine man that he is, would be distressed to hear you talk about him that way.

JOHN: And I'm distressed that I can. Barman, give us another here, and make it a large one! Will you take something since you're here, Mother?

KITTY: Just have a sip of yours.

JOHN: You will not. I've taken all the risks I'm taking for you. Haven't you learnt anything? You know how cholera works.

KITTY: I do. I can't point to it, but I know it's there. But a clean person won't give it to you.

JOHN: D'you dream about dirt?

KITTY: It's not just dirt, John. It's a live thing.

JOHN: If you say so. I've stopped thinking about it.

KITTY: Once the pestilence is active in the blood then all my tubs and coppers and plungers and brushes are of no use. I cannot go inside the body like a surgeon, though, God knows, I would love to. What I would give not to be ignorant; to have a great laboratory myself and find this live thing.

JOHN: It's vile, disgusting – a killer and yet you speak of it with great respect.

KITTY: We're losing the fight, son. My strength keeps failing.

JOHN: You'll win in time. Nothing can stop you once you start.

KITTY: Come home. I need your help to fight it.

JOHN: I'm expecting a ship any day.

KITTY: While you're sitting here drinking, people are dying.

JOHN: One or two I've had, that's all. (*Pause.*) I can't, Mam, I can't. I say to you as a man, I can't. A ship will come up shortly.

KITTY: Your father would be ashamed of you, John de Monte. He's watching everything you do. We need your arm.

JOHN: Mam, I've left all that behind. I turn the windlass not the mangle. I've done my bit for you, be honest.

KITTY: Your Gran should be in a proper place where they can look after her, but I keep the poor lamebrain up all night working. That's not right. Come and help.

JOHN: No! I've a ship. It's in the Pool right now, waiting. My things are packed. This was my last drink before I join her. We'll be out on the morning tide.

MARY: (*On approach.*) I'm the ship he's talking about, Missus, and he's paid his fare in advance. What's it to be, John? Do you want me to blow with the wind or do we go against the current tonight?

JOHN: Mam, this is a whore I must spend time with before I set sail, so I don't go mad on board, you understand.

KITTY: You're a disgrace, John.

JOHN: And what are you, Mam? Fifty? With the face of a hundred-year old whore.

KITTY: After that insult, I'll be going.

JOHN: I'm your loving son. Don't hope I get washed overboard.

KITTY: You've got no ship, John. Not any more.

JOHN: I have. Any vessel that leaves Liverpool is mine. Curse this city of shit! You'll scrub at it for the rest of your life and not get past the first layer. I'm heading for San Francisco. I may write once in a while. Give me your blessing. (*Pause.*) Mam?

KITTY: God forgive me, I can't.

(*Dip pub sounds into O'Lera music and sea/wind.*)

Scene 17

CHOLERA: John de Monte – his father was washed overboard on a voyage home from Canada. His baby brother was washed overboard on a voyage from Derry. All this washing by the sea and the mother. What is being cleansed? Beneath the filth is … what? And who can help Kitty to find it?

(*Cross into coach and four. Then cross into drawing room atmosphere with french style clock.*)

Scene 18

HELEN: Mrs Wilkinson, it's so good of you to come. Did my driver take proper care of you?

KITTY: He did, but your carriage caused a lot of excitement when it came to our door, which is why I'm late.

HELEN: No matter, you're here. Now that we're face to face, what do you think about my offer of help?

KITTY: Money would do most good. These people have no strength because they have not enough good food. If they ate better then they could fight the cholera with what God gave them.

HELEN: The ladies who wish to join me in this have all said that giving money is all very well but they want also to participate somehow, to actually do something.

KITTY: To participate? They wouldn't like the work, Mrs Faraday.

HELEN: Teach us.

KITTY: It's washing, scrubbing. None of you will know how.

HELEN: Surely it's not that difficult? Any woman can be taught how to launder.

KITTY: Are you strong enough?

HELEN: We eat well.

KITTY: I am sorely in need of hands, I admit. The places you will have to work in are dark and damp. You will have suffering thrust at you. Then, there's the cholera.

HELEN: You haven't caught it.

KITTY: I'm meant to do this work of mine. Other people die of it in their thousands. Think about it, Mrs Faraday.

HELEN: How is it spread?

KITTY: On everything, in everywhere. The doctors have told me that all that can be done is washing it out with chloride of lime.

HELEN: Is that what you'd want me to do?

KITTY: It's either that or looking after orphan children – scores of them. This is a big house you've got.

HELEN: (*Urgent.*) My husband must not know about what I'm doing.

KITTY: I won't tell him, but nor can I lie for you.

HELEN: Leave that to me, please.

KITTY: If you should fall ill, would I be blamed? I can't afford to waste my time arguing over that kind of thing.

HELEN: I shall cross that bridge when we come to it.

KITTY: Do you have any children, Mrs Faraday? You have so much room here for them to run about in. We could start up a school.

HELEN: It wouldn't be practical, I'm afraid.

KITTY: Then you must help with the washing.

(*Cut into sounds of mangle. Then edge down for:*)

Scene 19

(*Wilkinson cellar. Sounds of washing, scrubbing.*)

CHOLERA: Mrs Faraday! What on earth are you doing in a place like this? Your lovely hands! And all those silks, your wonderful dress, everything will have to be disinfected. Indeed, they must be boiled. I hate to tell you, Mrs Faraday, but they will certainly lose their shape and shine.

HELEN: Why, Doctor O'Lera, in your own strange way I do believe you're flirting with me.

KITTY: I did advise you to come in some old cotton clothes which could be easily washed.

HELEN: But I have no old clothes.

CHOLERA: Ah, how he spoils you, that husband of yours. He idolises you. Who can blame him?

HELEN: Can you find me some old clothes to work in, Mrs Wilkinson? If I buy some it will arouse his suspicion. He must never know I am here. He would go mad.

KITTY: There are plenty of old clothes in these parts. Go to any street market and buy some. You can keep them here and change.

HELEN: I'll do that immediately.

(*Exit. Fade.*)

CHOLERA: Lovely. Oh, how I'd be good to her!

KITTY: She works hard.

CHOLERA: If her husband found out he'd be terribly upset. The thought that she was down here, putting herself at risk ... oh! He'd be outraged to discover how you'd tempted her. If she died ...

KITTY: I had to have the help. I've got a few rich ladies working in different places now. They roll their sleeves up and, d'you know, in a couple of days it all comes to them naturally. From what I can tell, it makes them happy.

CHOLERA: Well, it won't make her husband happy, I assure you.

(*Cut into mangle/water noise then dip into:*)

Scene 20

KITTY: Old clothes don't suit you, Helen.

HELEN: If they were all I had, might that not change your opinion?

KITTY: What would Doctor Faraday think if he could see you now? (*Pause.*) 'Is that my wife?' he'd say. 'I don't recognise her.'

HELEN: You're teasing me.

KITTY: Why didn't you tell me your husband is a doctor? (*Pause.*) I could ask him to help.

HELEN: Please don't.

KITTY: Is he not a medical man?

HELEN: What could he do? Wash clothes? The doctors are in the dark about cholera. They don't know what to do.

KITTY: But the suffering from the symptoms could be eased. People like to have a doctor near, even when they know that he cannot cure the disease. It's a comfort to them.

HELEN: My husband isn't very good at that. He's more of a business man. Good works annoy him, I'm afraid. He would find what we're doing ... pointless. Needless to say, I'm very ashamed. (*Rubs harder at the washboard.*) Very ... very ashamed!

KITTY: Couldn't you talk to him? Persuade him ...

HELEN: Ornaments don't have ideas.

KITTY: Then let me speak to him.

HELEN: What would you say? He'd want reasons, Kitty. Why do you do this work? It's useless, he'd say. Or you're only doing it to save your soul. He doesn't believe in natural goodness at any price.

KITTY: Hasn't he seen enough natural evil? Send him down here. I'd show him plenty! (*Rubs harder at the washboard.*)

HELEN: Now you're angry.

KITTY: Yes, I am! Isn't he supposed to be intelligent, this husband of yours? A man of medicine?

HELEN: How would you answer him?

KITTY: Answer him? I owe him no answers.

HELEN: But why do you live like you do? Fifteen people in your tiny house. Anyone who needs your help can just walk in. You wash their clothes; you give them food; you set up schools for their children; you arrange homes for orphans; you visit the workhouse to care for your sick old mother; you never rest. I don't know why you' re not dead from exhaustion.

(*Washboard sounds stop.*)

KITTY: I have help. My husband Tom does what he can ... You help ...

HELEN: (*Pressing the point hard.*) But why do you do it?

KITTY: I haven't thought. (*Resumes rubbing at washboard, humming 'Onward Christian Soldiers'.*) Come on, Helen! Back to work! That's what we're here for. Rub all that dirt away! There's no time for stopping and thinking.

(*Peak washing sounds. Edge in O'Lera music.*)

Scene 21

CHOLERA: I rage. In the delta of the Ganges and in lower Bengal I claim two hundred thousands lives a year, but after my travels my potency is weaker, so Liverpool is fortunate. In this Year of their Lord, eighteen hundred and thirty-two, in the spring of April, a welcome month, I visited a man in Tolson Street first.

Although I felt tired from my voyages and wanderings about the earth, I killed him quickly. After he was dead the doctor would not allow the corpse to be washed. When the neighbours heard this, a riot began, the people insisting that the dead man should not be buried unwashed as it flew in the face of custom. Kitty Wilkinson, who lived not far away in Denison Street, had been called by the dead man's wife, hoping for help. At first the people would not let her speak, so she stood and waited for the tumult to die down. When there was sufficient quiet, she spoke to them in that way of hers:

KITTY: (*In echo.*) We should be very sorry to do anything wrong, but this man was no more to us than he is to you. We have done all we can for him, and if any of you is ready to wash the body then we will find you everything necessary.

CHOLERA: There were no volunteers, needless to say, and the mob dispersed. The man was buried unwashed. But what I liked about Kitty Wilkinson from this first time of meeting was her use of the royal we. She knows that she is a queen. An empress of do-gooders. And it all comes … naturally.

(*Fade cross from O'Lera, move into carriage rattling over cobbles.*)

Scene 22

HELEN: (*In her head.*) Why? Why does she do it? She seemed not to know. Do I believe her? She really doesn't know? Why didn't she come out with it and say that people are worth the trouble?

(*Cross back to O'Lera music.*)

Scene 23

CHOLERA: (*Fade in.*) But are they? When there're so many of them? It is natural that culling of the superfluous and inadequate should regularly take place otherwise they

will outbreed those more blessed with brains and energy.
And then what? Mankind will return to his primitive
beginnings, becoming little more than a disease himself.
So what is Kitty Wilkinson saving but that which Nature
has deemed to be worthless? She paddles in their filth,
embraces their infestations. Does she believe that she is
immune? Untouchable? Suddenly I saw this pride of hers
as a challenge! And I accepted it as one. This was only a
woman, after all. A receiving vessel. Why should she be
impenetrable?

(*Cross O'Lera music into Wilkinson cellar.*)

Scene 24

(*A knock.*)

CHOLERA: (*Calling.*) Ah, Kitty, Kitty! Open up to an old
friend and colleague.

(*Door opening.*)

KITTY: Doctor O'Lera. You come visiting late.

CHOLERA: I've been on my rounds. May I enter?

KITTY: I'm very busy.

CHOLERA: So am I. But I was passing and I thought, I'll
drop in on the off-chance that I'll catch that brave little
woman with her feet up, but here you are, still hard at it.
You're a marvel. Everybody says so.

KITTY: Well, don't stand on the doorstep, Doctor. You'd
better come in.

(*Door closing.*)

CHOLERA: Here, let me mop your brow. You mustn't
overdo it, Kitty.

KITTY: We're not winning. (*Resumes scrubbing.*)

CHOLERA: Come and lie down for a little while.

KITTY: No, no. I must keep going.

CHOLERA: Let me give you something to make you rest.

KITTY: Why don't you lend a hand?

CHOLERA: Me? I'm better out of the way. Perhaps I'll go.
There's plenty for me to do elsewhere.

KITTY: (*Pausing in her work.*) You've only come to
    torment me, I think, but that gives me a laugh.
    There're so many long faces around me, Doctor. Will
    we have a cup of tea together?

CHOLERA: One cup? Should we share it?

KITTY: I can find another.

CHOLERA: No, I'd be proud to drink from the same vessel
    as you.

KITTY: The tea's mashed. My hands are aching, Doctor.
    Will you do the honours?

CHOLERA: With reverence.

    (*Tea being poured.*)

CHOLERA: Sugar? Sweets to the sweet?

KITTY: Two spoons.

    (*Sugar being put in cup and stirred.*)

CHOLERA: Kitty, my dear colleague, my respect for you
    borders on adulation.

KITTY: Doctor, you've kissed the Blarney Stone at some
    time or other.

CHOLERA: May I drink first?

KITTY: Go ahead.

CHOLERA: Take this as a kind of kiss. (*Drinks.*) Now, you.

    (*Cut into O'Lera music.*)

Scene 25

CHOLERA: She drank. With her iron-grey hair plastered to
    her forehead, sweat running into the corners of her eyes and
    off the end of her long nose, she put her lips exactly where
    mine had been and I shuddered with delight as I entered
    her. No lover has had more affairs than C.H. O'Lera.
    Casanova and Lothario must hide their heads when my
    name is mentioned. But my pleasure was soon in the grip
    of a strong force that bent me down, that almost broke my
    back, then cast me out of her into desolation and failure.
    I knew that soon it would be time to go.

    (*Cross music into:*)

Scene 26

(*Fade in Faraday bathroom. Sounds of basin being filled and face-washing.*)

HELEN: (*Off.*) Darling.

DR FARADAY: (*Who is washing his face.*) Yes?

HELEN: What do you really know about cholera?

DR FARADAY: Not much. There isn't much to know.

HELEN: Do you know if anyone is trying to discover what causes it?

DR FARADAY: (*Drying his face with a towel.*) Oh, I expect they are, somewhere.

HELEN: Does dirt have anything to do with it?

DR FARADAY: Dirty people get it more often than clean ones do, but then, there're more dirty people than clean, aren't there, darling? Pass me my hair brushes, will you?

HELEN: Have you ever known anyone who's had it?

DR FARADAY: Yes, actually, I have. (*Brushing his hair.*) A couple of men who studied with me. They went out to India with the Army.

HELEN: Did they die?

DR FARADAY: Yes, they did, both of them. (*Pause.*) Quite good friends of mine as it happened. Are you ready to go down to dinner?

HELEN: Have you ever been professionally involved with a case of cholera?

DR FARADAY: I saw one case very early on in this epidemic. I was on my way across town and a crowd actually stopped my carriage and forced me to look at a chap in Tolson Street. He was already dead and I told them so. But they wanted me to examine him, to touch him, as if they wanted me to catch it. I refused, of course. To have taken the risk would have made no sense. I must say that I think there were elements in the crowd that were using the situation to make a point ... Where are you going?

HELEN: Down to dinner. You're cleaned up and ready,
aren't you?

(*Cut into O'Lera music.*)

Scene 27

CHOLERA: I prepared to leave Liverpool. There was
something about the place which was uncongenial to
me now; the constant wind and dampness, that grey sea,
those endless docks bulging with plenty, the great ships
thronging the river, waiting to unload the riches of an
empire under the noses of the suffering poor. There was
too much energy, too much challenge, too many
contradictions to sustain my simple task of reaping the
unfortunate. There was not the lassitude which I love;
the heat, the idleness of all. But before I set out on my
travels again I wanted to pay Kitty Wilkinson back a
little. Pay her back for lessening my influence.

(*Cross O'Lera music into:*)

Scene 28

(*Club atmosphere.*)

CHOLERA: Doctor Faraday?

DR FARADAY: Sir?

CHOLERA: C.H. O'Lera at your service, physician,
though not an eminent man like yourself. I have heard
of your reputation in the field of rheumatology, also
I have had the pleasure of meeting your beautiful
wife.

DR FARADAY: Are you a member of this club, sir?

CHOLERA: Oh, I'm a guest, always a guest.

DR FARADAY: And where did you meet my wife, may
I ask?

CHOLERA: At a charity function, I think it was.

DR FARADAY: Charity? Well, that could be any number of
places. Now, if you'll excuse me ...

CHOLERA: And have you heard about this extraordinary woman, Mrs Catherine Wilkinson? A low-born Irish person, a washerwoman, who has become the saviour of the slum-dwellers.

DR FARADAY: Really?

CHOLERA: Oh, yes. A nobody. The woman's energy is astonishing, sir. She is only just this side of fifty, the mother of several children, house-wife to a dozen or more persons, yet she gives all her time and money to the sick and dying, to orphans, the poor and afflicted, and labours night and day washing the garments of cholera victims and those nearest to them in order to reduce the spread of the disease. Don't you find this remarkable, sir?

DR FARADAY: No doubt she will get her reward in a better place. Now, if you will forgive me ...

CHOLERA: Purely by accident I observed your lovely wife and this Mrs Wilkinson standing side by side in the street taking the air. Your wife was wearing ill-fitting, old clothes – second-hand, I'd say – and smelling strongly of soap.

DR FARADAY: What? Where did you see this?

CHOLERA: Denison Street, sir. A very low part of town. And, I should add, they were arm in arm with each other. The conjunction of these two, the light and beauty of your wife, the darkness and severity of this Wilkinson woman, was extraordinary to behold.

DR FARADAY: You amaze me! No, you must have been mistaken.

CHOLERA: Your wife, Doctor Faraday, has a delightful birthmark at the top of her left breast, which was open to the air, she had been so hot at work.

DR FARADAY: God, damn it! What's going on? What work is this? Tell me everything you know.

CHOLERA: With pleasure. What a Venus she looked there in the street, gaped at by the idle scum who crowded

round her, admiring ... Why, sir, you're trembling!
Compose yourself. It was all in a good cause, trying to
beat the cholera.

(*Out.*)

Scene 29

(*Another slum cellar. Cries of keening and children.*)

KITTY: Help me turn him over so we can get at his back
button.

(*Sounds of effort as they turn over a corpse and undress it.*)

HELEN: If only they weren't so cold. (*Pause.*) Do you ever
think of anything that you want for yourself?

KITTY: I dream.

HELEN: What would you like most in the world?

KITTY: Let me think.

HELEN: I've wanted for nothing, I'm afraid. Never.

KITTY: Except to come here. To work with the afflicted.

HELEN: Yes. (*Pause.*) I would do anything for you.

KITTY: Not for me.

HELEN: Yes, for you. Your goodness overshadows
everything I have. Fortune gave me those things and can
take them away again. But that cannot happen to your
goodness. That is the only eternal thing I know.

KITTY: I am filled with dread when you talk that way.

HELEN: Don't be. (*Pause.*) Now, tell me what your heart's
desire is. You guessed mine.

KITTY: Oh, I don't know.

HELEN: (*Urgently.*) Do tell me.

KITTY: You have to guess. Take the bottoms of his breeches
and pull.

HELEN: Money?

(*Sound of breeches being dragged off.*)

KITTY: I'm not sure that I'd be good at being rich.

HELEN: You'd give it all away.

KITTY: No, no, you're supposed to be guessing at what I want for myself. Should I do the rest of him?

HELEN: No, no. I'm all right. I'll keep going.

KITTY: Are you steady? You don't feel faint?

HELEN: Let me keep guessing. Oh, God, this poor fellow can't have changed his underclothes for months.

KITTY: No, you're misjudging him. After death there is no control over the bowels.

HELEN: I know, I know. I must get used to these things. Learn!

KITTY: It's something very straightforward, my heart's desire.

HELEN: Why are we undressing him? Shouldn't he be buried as he is?

KITTY: The family need his clothes. Once we've washed them: they'll be as good as new.

HELEN: Oh! (*She is near to fainting.*)

KITTY: Come on, now. You insisted. See it through if you can.

HELEN: So, heart's desire? A little cottage somewhere, with a garden full of flowers?

KITTY: I like the country well enough, but the city has hold of me now. I'll give you a clue. It's something to do with being a lady.

HELEN: Fine clothes?

KITTY: Not with all the washing I've done.

HELEN: Servants?

KITTY: Well, you're my servant, aren't you? (*Pause.*) Well, aren't you?

HELEN: Why do men have tattoos? They're so hideous.

KITTY: Don't be ashamed.

HELEN: I'm not at all ashamed! But you see I can't forget who I am, where I come from. I find myself hating all this filth and poverty, looking down upon people, and I cannot even dress my hair without my hands shaking with indignation. Why does it have to be this way? Surely, in this fertile world there's enough for everyone? We never want for anything.

KITTY: Some would say that your arithmetic is innocent.

HELEN: I don't feel an innocent any more, not with this naked sailor with a fierce god tattooed over his heart staring up at me. I feel that I should know everything, but I don't. I depend upon you to explain it.

KITTY: I can't explain anything.

HELEN: No one believes that. Everyone who knows about you admires your faith.

KITTY: My faith? In what?

HELEN: Isn't it faith?

KITTY: My faith is no better or worse than any other owner of a prayer-book. But I can scrape up the pluck to lift the tender parts of this dead lad and wash him. You do the same.

HELEN: Oh, no! I couldn't, really.

(*Washing sounds.*)

KITTY: It's nothing. A simple step. Here, take the soap.

HELEN: I can't.

KITTY: Would it help to know his name?

HELEN: No, that would make it worse.

KITTY: A wanderer then. His mother tells me that he hadn't come home for three years. Voyages to India, the Far East, and in all that time he was never sick. The moment he's back he gets cholera. So, she says, don't talk to me about the filth of Calcutta.

HELEN: What terrible luck.

KITTY: Luck? He was a fool. He should have stayed away. He should have let his family forget him. Like you should stay away and let us forget you.

HELEN: You're deliberately trying to horrify me.

KITTY: Only to make you into a better servant. (*Pause.*) Are you going to do it?

HELEN: My husband would die if he knew.

KITTY: Tell him that I'd do it for him should the need arise. At last you're smiling. Don't you think a sailor would rather have it that way? He could have been my son. He could have been your son. When we bathed him, what mysteries would there have been?

HELEN: As you know, I would have had someone to do that for me. (*Pause.*) Here goes.

(*Washing sounds.*)

KITTY: Think of all the children he would have made from something that seems so harmless now. Where would they have lived? Who would have fed them? (*Pause.*) Well, since we're sisters now, perhaps you can guess what I want most in the world?

HELEN: (*Whispering.*) No, I still can't.

KITTY: A silver tea service.

HELEN: (*Laughing softly.*) I would never have guessed that.

KITTY: One I can polish till I can see my face in it.

(*Out washing/sea noises into:*)

Scene 30

(*Fade in exterior street atmosphere. Knock at the door. It is opened.*)

KITTY: Yes?

GUEST: Am I addressing Mrs Catherine Wilkinson?

KITTY: You are.

GUEST: My name is Guest. May I come in for a moment?

KITTY: What is your business with me?

GUEST: It concerns Doctor Faraday.

KITTY: Oh.

GUEST: I am a friend of his, a fellow doctor. The poor fellow is deeply perplexed by his wife's behaviour; so much so that he has asked me to act for him.

KITTY: Act?

GUEST: To represent his feelings, you understand.

KITTY: He couldn't do that for himself?

GUEST: No. This issue has greatly disturbed him.

KITTY: Yet his carriage is in the street.

GUEST: He wanted to cast an eye, as it were ... Please try to understand, Mrs Wilkinson. He has had the most fearful shock.

KITTY: Well, he's come to the right district for shocks.

(*Footsteps.*)

GUEST: Where are you going?

KITTY: If he hasn't got the courage to come to me, I will go to him!

(*Fade street exterior atmosphere. Fade in carriage interior atmosphere and door being opened.*)

GUEST: Henry, may I introduce Mrs Catherine Wilkinson to you? (*Whisper.*) Be pleasant to her, please!

DR FARADAY: Oh … er … yes, how do you do? …

GUEST: We can talk here in the carriage, I think. Will you step inside, Mrs Wilkinson?

KITTY: Thank you.

(*GUEST and KITTY getting into carriage and door closing.*)

GUEST: This is the way Mrs Wilkinson preferred. Would you like me to leave you alone to talk?

DR FARADAY: Oh, no! Do stay.

KITTY: Don't be afraid, Doctor.

DR FARADAY: I am not afraid.

KITTY: Then why send someone else on such a delicate mission?

DR FARADAY: Because I do not have the amount of self-control that I would like in any matter concerning the safety of my wife. Does that seem odd to you?

KITTY: Perhaps not.

DR FARADAY: Also, it has to be said, my friend here is known to be more au fait with this end of town.

KITTY: So, you needed a guide? That speaks for itself. But let's get to the point.

GUEST: Now would you like me to go? I can walk back.

KITTY: If we have your sympathy, Doctor Guest, I'd like you to stay. It might be that I can persuade you to help us beat the cholera.

GUEST: (*Laughing softly.*) They do say that you never stop working.

DR FARADAY: (*Abruptly.*) How did you manage to cajole my wife into coming down to this dreadful place? She doesn't belong here!

GUEST: Henry, calm down ...

DR FARADAY: She would never have come of her own volition. You appealed to her for help, didn't you? You bullied her.

KITTY: I did not. The woman has her own conscience.

DR FARADAY: I'm going to lose her by one means or another, all of which are governed by you! If that happens, beware of me, Mrs Wilkinson. One cannot ruin other people's marriages with impunity.

KITTY: Take her away, if you can. Keep her at home until the epidemic is over. If you can.

DR FARADAY: You are mocking me. I will not have that.

KITTY: I mock no one. But I am challenging you. Your wife is becoming a useful woman, and knows it. She can never go back to what she was.

DR FARADAY: How dare you! (*Pause.*) Mrs Wilkinson ... I plead with you ... She is my one delight in this life. You know her ... Surely my feelings as a husband need to be taken into account?

KITTY: I have given you all the time I can afford. Good day to you, gentlemen.

(*Door opening in carriage. KITTY stepping out. Door closing.*)

DR FARADAY: Damn that woman! Damn! Damn! Get me away from this hell-hole!

(*Crack of whip. Carriage moving off.*)

GUEST: Henry ...

DR FARADAY: Don't make excuses for that ugly, meddlesome harridan whatever you do.

GUEST: You asked me to help you because you thought I'd make an appropriate go-between. Allow me to modify the disaster we've made of this so far. It's only a thought, a mere thought, but it may help.

DR FARADAY: Whip up those horses! Get me home!

(*Crack of whip. Carriage goes faster.*)

GUEST: May I speak?

DR FARADAY: If you must.

GUEST: I put this to you: should anyone consciously prevent another from doing good?

DR FARADAY: (*In anguish.*) Yagh!

(*Fade on carriage sounds.*)

Scene 31

(*In DR FARADAY's bedroom.*)

DR FARADAY: (*Fade in.*) My darling ... sweetheart ... Ouch! Careful!

HELEN: Did I hurt you?

DR FARADAY: Only a little ... No, don't go away ... Don't mind me saying this, darling, but your hands seem to be rougher than usual.

HELEN: Are they? I'd better get some cream.

DR FARADAY: Not now. But your hands used to be so soft and delicate. And there's a smell that's always in your hair these days ...

HELEN: Perhaps we should just go to sleep?

DR FARADAY: No. I don't want to.

HELEN: Well, if I'm so repulsive ...

DR FARADAY: I didn't say that. (*Pause.*) Don't you think that it's about time that you owned up?

HELEN: What about?

DR FARADAY: Your good works.

(*Pause.*)

HELEN: Well, since you know then I needn't tell you. I have no intention of feeling guilty about it.

DR FARADAY: Darling, you're not the only one who's been noble. I've shared the same bed for days, knowing that you've been close to cholera, keenly aware of the risk ...

HELEN: I needed to do something to help.

DR FARADAY: You don't feel these people might be laughing at you behind your back?

HELEN: Oh yes they are – they mock everyone except jockeys and prize-fighters. (*Pause.*) I had to make up for you somehow.

DR FARADAY: Me?

HELEN: (*Flaring up.*) For doing nothing! For ignoring their suffering.

DR FARADAY: I have my own work. Don't I relieve suffering in my way?

HELEN: Gout and rheumatism! For very high fees! What a way to earn a living. How admirable. What a great deal it will teach you.

(*Pause.*)

DR FARADAY: This Wilkinson woman has made you lose all respect for me, it seems. No wonder you were so secretive about what you were doing.

HELEN: (*Passionately.*) I would do anything for Kitty Wilkinson, anything! She's given my life some meaning at last.

DR FARADAY: And where does that leave me?

(*Silence.*)

DR FARADAY: Very well! I shall sleep in the other room tonight.

(*Sounds of getting out of bed.*)

DR FARADAY: But your Good Samaritan will discover that she cannot wreck my happiness and get away with it. She will be hearing from my solicitor!

HELEN: (*Bursts out laughing.*) Go on, get out, you pompous idiot!

(*Door opens and slams shut. Then cross on HELEN's tears, into:*)

Scene 32

(*Song sung outside Wilkinson cellar.*)

SINGER: She's nothing much to look at, Lord, you'd pass her in the street,

but she's the only one of us,
who's fit to wash Thy feet.

Should the meek inherit, Lord,
and the poor be blessed above,
this brave, good washerwoman,
deserves Thy perfect love.

HELEN: Don't they ever tire? They've played all morning
for you.

KITTY: It's their way. If they had money they'd still offer
me the music first but give me the money if I had the
bad manners to ask for it.

HELEN: Does it make you feel proud? They're so grateful.
Making up songs just for you.

KITTY: Well, they all had the cholera, every one of them.

HELEN: So, without you ... silence.

KITTY: I doubt that. Somewhere they'd make a noise.

HELEN: I'm going to leave my husband and come to live
down here with you.

KITTY: No, you're not! Never mention that again.

HELEN: But this is everything to me now! My life's work!

KITTY: I will not destroy, or be part of destruction. Go
home.

HELEN: But ...

KITTY: Go home. And don't come back until you have
re-taken your marriage vows in your mind.

HELEN: Don't drive me away, I beg you. Whatever happens,
I'll talk him round ... I must come back ... I must.

(*Door opens and music floods in.*)

BOY: Hello to the Golden Angel ...

HELEN: Please, don't call me that! Kitty Wilkinson's your
angel ... (*To herself.*) and my god.

(*HELEN leaves.*)

BOY: Will you come to hear our music, Kitty Wilkinson?

(*Other voices join in, calling: "Will y'come, Kitty Wilkinson?"
The wind rises.*)

CHOLERA: You're celebrating your victory then, Kitty?

KITTY: The cholera seems to be abating, Doctor O'Lera.

CHOLERA: I've come to say goodbye ... au revoir, possibly.

KITTY: Where are you headed?

CHOLERA: I've been thinking about South America. When I return from my travels it would be good to find you still here, washing and scrubbing away.

KITTY: I'll be here, Doctor, God willing.

CHOLERA: Don't get downhearted. It's all a cycle, you know. Your time will come. Don't get too frustrated that people ignore the opinions of a mere washerwoman.

KITTY: I'll make them listen. Perhaps you would lend your support to my campaign for a public wash-house?

CHOLERA: I'm not one for causes, Kitty. Two and a half thousand years ago, the Greek philosopher, Thales, said that water was beautiful and holy, but people still don't listen. Mankind always has wax in its ears and dirt under its nails. Will you come down to the dockside to see me off?

KITTY: Forgive me, but I can't. I've to go to a meeting with the city fathers. Dr Faraday has arranged it out of nowhere.

CHOLERA: I've warned you. Don't expect too much. The city fathers don't live in the slums, and they have short memories.

KITTY: I could tell them about Thales.

CHOLERA: Oh, they'll be men of a classical education, I've no doubt, and they'll know how useless it is. Au revoir.

(*Music has been playing throughout and it now comes to a conclusion. Out of it comes O'Lera's music.*)

Scene 33

CHOLERA: It would be churlish of me to deny Kitty Wilkinson her moment of beauty. In that decaying street under a sunless sky, with the wind blowing her grey hair out of its restraining pins, she had all the loveliness of those gods greater than the Greeks could ever imagine, because they loved. Don't imagine that I do not understand this emotion. A disease embraces its victim with all the fervour of a lover. It racks and bites and plunges with the same terrible passion. But where did her strange, laving love begin? Where did the washerwoman's wealth of feeling pour from? Was it from the sea which had swallowed her infant brother when he slipped like a piece of soap from someone's hand?

(*Fade in Faraday drawing room atmosphere.*)

DR FARADAY: No doubt, Mrs Wilkinson, you will be pleased to learn that the city has ear-marked funds which will supplement those raised by our campaign for the new wash-house. I'm told by a very reliable man on the inside that the project, now it has this necessary blessing, will sail through the rest of the procedure.

HELEN: Isn't that wonderful?

KITTY: Wonderful but late. No matter. Let's hope that the cholera doesn't return before we have the place up.

HELEN: And it needn't be the only one. Other public wash-houses will follow, perhaps.

DR FARADAY: A step at a time. First, we must get the scheme going in Frederick Street and see how we do. (*Pause.*) Mrs Wilkinson, I have been asked to sound you out – unofficially you'll appreciate – about the possibility that you should be the first superintendent of the new wash-house. How would you feel about that?

KITTY: Me? A superintendent? (*Laughs.*) I find that a very strange idea indeed!

DR FARADAY: Oh? Don't dash our hopes so swiftly. Do take time to think about it.

KITTY: I've never been anything but myself. No one's ever called me this or that.

HELEN: Kitty, dear, there must be a superintendent to organise the place properly. Why shouldn't it be you who's worked so hard for it?

KITTY: Why don't you do it?

DR FARADAY: (*Quickly.*) Oh, no! That would be entirely inappropriate.

KITTY: I don't know why, I must say. Your wife is held in great respect. She could easily run a wash-house.

DR FARADAY: The position will need your er ... energy, robustness, in-built authority. She must be able to deal with large numbers of undisciplined people and be able to talk to them.

KITTY: Doctor Faraday, I don't know if you're aware of this, but they call your wife The Golden Angel of the Slums. It is a high compliment and one to be proud of.

HELEN: Oh, don't, don't. I find that very embarrassing.

DR FARADAY: Quite. I should add, Mrs Wilkinson, that there is a salary attached to the post of superintendent. It is not unheard-of wealth, I admit, but it is adequate.

KITTY: I couldn't consider it.

DR FARADAY: How disappointing. I was sure that you'd accept.

KITTY: It never does to take me for granted. But the real reason is that I couldn't humiliate my husband, Tom.

HELEN: But Tom would be delighted!

KITTY: For me to be a superintendent while he has no status at all would be crushing for him.

DR FARADAY: I must confess that I was not aware of the existence of a Mr Wilkinson. By some mishap I had assumed that you were a widow.

HELEN: But you've always been the leader, Kitty. Tom has never resented your place, your reputation ...

KITTY: But it has never been made formal. Men feel these things, don't they, Doctor Faraday?

DR FARADAY: I believe they do. (*Pause.*) Would it satisfy you if I could persuade the powers-that-be to create two equal positions; joint superintendents?

KITTY: It would, provided Tom agrees. Which he will, probably, when I ask him.

DR FARADAY: (*Laughing.*) If you were in diplomacy, Mrs
  Wilkinson, I think the men might have to look to their
  laurels. But if I know the treasury you will have to share
  the one salary.

KITTY: That would be acceptable. Will you convey this to
  ... well, wherever it needs to go.

DR FARADAY: I will, rest assured.

HELEN: Then it's all settled! Oh, Kitty. I'm so pleased.

KITTY: Thank you for your efforts on my behalf, Doctor.

DR FARADAY: That has become my pleasure.

HELEN: I'll come to the door with you.

(*They go through an open door.*)

HELEN: Are you completely happy with those
  arrangements, Kitty?

KITTY: We'll give it a try. The wash-house has yet to be
  built. People have short memories.

HELEN: It will be built. We will see to it, won't we?

KITTY: We must have it working before the cholera comes
  again.

HELEN: Now everyone knows that you'll be part of it, the
  wash-house will be built, never fear. They'll have to.
  Your name will see to that.

(*Fade hall to drawing room atmosphere. Fade in special atmosphere.*)

CHOLERA: I heard about the erection of this public
  wash-house in Frederick Street, Liverpool – the first of
  its kind – while I was very busy killing in Bengal.
  Feeling threatened by the mere idea, I hurried back to
  England. But I had over-taxed my strength and arrived
  tardily, much weakened. By the time Kitty was
  ensconced as the guardian spirit of this municipal holy
  well, the famous Frederick Street wash-house, I was
  driven out of my nature by failure and forced to labour
  and do lay-preaching to earn a few pence. It was in the
  latter role that I helped to bury Tom, Kitty's
  uncomplaining spouse, only two years after his
  elevation to the joint superintendency. He died worn
  out by his wife's indomitable, relentless goodness; glad

to go to Heaven where such superhumanly virtuous endeavour is not extraordinary but an unremarkable part of everyday life. (*Fades.*)

Scene 34

(*Wash-house atmosphere and sounds of WOMEN scrubbing.*)

MARY: Doctor O'Lera's speech at old Tom's funeral was full of double meanings, I thought. Do you reckon he might be a little bit in love with Kitty himself?

JESSY: What d'you know about love, you hard-faced whore?

MARY: You shut your gob or I'll break your nose.

HANNAH: I found much to think about in what Doctor O'Lera put forward. What was that he said? 'Surely the cure should love the disease.' That's tantalising in a general kind of way, isn't it?

JESSY: God, would you believe your ears? She's been fornicating with a professor, that one.

(*Big door opening and clanging shut. Footsteps on tiles.*)

MARY: Kitty's coming on her round of inspection with one of her fine ladies. Ah, it's the divine Helen, Mrs Faraday, no less: the Golden Angel of the Slums, God bless her.

JESSY: She wins her arguments with her arse just like the rest of us, the darlin'. Hey there, Kitty Wilkinson. Cheer up! Why the long face now you're single again and fancy free?

MARY: Crack us a smile, Kitty Wilkinson!

JESSY: If you'd turn Catholic we'd make you the Pope tomorrow! Honest, we would!

(*Laughter. Sloshing of water.*)

MARY: (*Calling.*) How's your John, that Cape Horn sailor son of yours? He's a friend of mine when he has a shilling to spend.

(*Laughter.*)

KITTY: We close in ten minutes, ladies. Leave the wash-house as clean and tidy as you found it, please.

HANNAH: We're not ladies, your worship. Are you feeling
  lonely now your husband has gone, God rest him?

KITTY: Yes. Thank you for your concern. Ten minutes.

HANNAH: Why do you do all those good deeds, your
  ladyship?

MARY: Isn't she a girl for questions?

KITTY: Come on now, I must close up. (*Jangle of keys.*)
  Gather your things together.

HANNAH: I've not been this side of the water all that long
  but even back on the Auld Sod your name rings out.
  But the greatest of the legends concerns a silver tea-pot.
  Will you give me the truth of it?

JESSY: Holy Mother, would you have us here all day and
  night when we only have ten minutes? The silver tea-pot
  story? That's an epic!

MARY: Will I tell it to her for you, Kitty Wilkinson?
  You have enough to do, standing there supervising.

JESSY: I tell it better than you. Imagine yourself out
  at the Carnatic Hall. Orchards, fields, the clean and
  daicent countryside of old England. Not a whore or
  a beggar in sight. Even the land itself has a well-
  laundered look to it. All the cream of Liverpool's rich
  females are there. The perfume in the hall is enough
  to make an entire regiment of dragoons lower their
  breeches in hopeful anticipation. Our Kitty is there,
  her expression thoughtful and serious. It has to be said
  that she'd splashed out on a new dress and bonnet, but
  nothing too fancy. Then the place goes quiet as the wife
  of the Lord Mayor of Liverpool, clad in green
  shantung, (was it not an Irishwoman to be honoured?),
  mounts the platform and throws out a mighty arm.
  'Ladies!' says she ...

WASH-HOUSE WOMEN: Ladies!

  (*Laughter.*)

JESSY: Quiet, now! 'Ladies!' says she, 'we're gathered here
  today to pay tribute to that queen of scrubbers and
  manglers, Liverpool's own, Mrs Catherine Wilkinson!'

(*WASHER-WOMEN shout and cheer.*)

JESSY: Jolly good show!

MARY: Well done, old girl!

JESSY: And with that, she thrusts into Kitty's waiting hands a silver tea-pot.

MARY: Jaysus, this part always turns me over.

HANNAH: Did I hear you say a silver tea-pot?

JESSY: You did.

HANNAH: But I heard that Kitty Wilkinson told the Faraday woman herself that her heart's desire was for a silver tea-service. The lot! The sugar bowl! The little silver spoon! The jug for the milk! The jug for the hot water! The big silver tray! She was going to polish it all so she could see her face in it.

JESSY: Yes – and all the bastards gave her was the tea-pot, and a small one at that.

MARY: Terrible to think that's all you get for saving a great city from the cholera.

KITTY: Well, now you've had your fun, I'll be on my way.

HANNAH: So, in England a saint gets a silver tea-pot and not a shrine. Is that the way of it?

MARY: Sssh. Our Kitty doesn't like to be called that. Surely to God you know that only Roman Catholics can be saints? Protestants have to be welfare workers.

HANNAH: But this place is your shrine, is it not? This great church of a wash-house? And you with your keys like Saint Peter deciding who comes in and who stays out, who gets clean and who stays dirty. I wouldn't use your silver tea-pot to piss in!

JESSY: Shame on you! And saying that in front of the good woman. You're not fit to fasten up her shoes, you dirty slut.

HANNAH: To hell with her, sanctimonious old cow!

JESSY: You roar in here, fired up from the alehouse, your lousy rags tucked under your arm, and take the place over. Who the hell d'you think you are? The Queen of the Gypsies?

(*Screams. Splashing. A cat-fight starts in the wash-house.*)

MARY: In the tub with her!

KITTY: Stop this! (*Blows a whistle.*) Behave yourselves!

JESSY: Get soap in the whore's filthy mouth! Running down our Kitty like that!

(*An alarm bell starts ringing.*)

WOMEN: Fight! Fight!

KITTY: The wash-house is closed! (*Blows the whistle.*) Go home!

JESSY: She should be banned. Coming in here drunk. She's evil, that one.

HANNAH: I hate hypocrites, that's all.

MARY: Ah, shut up, you! Now you've got us all into trouble. We're sorry, Kitty Wilkinson. You carry on with your duties. Don't report us, for God's sake.

KITTY: Go home. Go away. Tomorrow I shall expect the place to be clean and tidy.

JESSY: Come on, girls. Hurry up and let's get out of here. This flare-up has given me a terrible thirst.

(*Door opening and clanging shut the empty wash-house. A tap can be heard running. The tap is turned off. Pause.*)

KITTY: (*Weeps in the echoing wash-house.*) What have I done to deserve their contempt? (*Pause.*) Come on, Kitty ... come on ... sing ... inside ... (*She hums.*) 'Onward Christian Soldiers'

(*Cross into:*)

Scene 35

(*Hissing steam. Boiler house. Sounds of coal being shovelled into furnace.*)

KITTY: Good evening, Doctor O'Lera.

CHOLERA: Madam, please don't use my title, not as I've been struck off the register. A humble stoker in the public wash-house is all I am now, and your servant.

KITTY: I can't get out of the habit of treating you with respect.

CHOLERA: We have a good head of steam this morning.

KITTY: One of the young women in the wash-house just challenged me. I have to admit that I've come away upset.

CHOLERA: How? (*Pause. Shovelling stopped.*) You were challenged for being good?

KITTY: Don't let me interrupt your work.

CHOLERA: They say you're a saint, Kitty. It's a very powerful idea, sainthood, even in an irreligious age. Those women in the wash-house venerate you in their hearts.

KITTY: Yet they mock me ... abuse me.

CHOLERA: What do they swear by in their foul-mouthed way? Their gods. They worship you.

KITTY: That thought makes me shiver. It makes me try to remember all the evil I've done.

CHOLERA: Why is that?

KITTY: To stay in touch. To keep some company.

CHOLERA: Oh, Kitty. How can anyone find redemption if they're struggling to be bad? It makes no sense.

KITTY: A man has started to write a short book about me.

CHOLERA: Ah, a short book. But, then, you've got time to go. The next one will be long.

KITTY: The tone of it is like a sermon. And those wash-house women fought over my name. What's happening to me, Doctor?

CHOLERA: Are you really so naive? You're becoming a legend. They quote your sayings. They tell stories about you: how Kitty was left her first mangle in an old lady's will: how Kitty made porridge for sixty in her kitchen every morning. It won't be long before miracles are attributed to you. People will collect your nail-parings and drink your bath-water. And what will be the effect of all this? The real Kitty Wilkinson will die and a new one will be born. A myth.

KITTY: No! I don't want to be shut out like that! I'm one of them!

CHOLERA: You were never one of them.

KITTY: I am, or I'm nothing.

CHOLERA: Don't be a coward, Kitty. Accept your sainthood. It's what you've earned. Be two people: the myth, and the real woman known to yourself.

KITTY: How can I do that?

CHOLERA: Plenty do.

KITTY: You want all my secrets, Doctor?

CHOLERA: I'm an old admirer, Kitty. One you can trust.

KITTY: Why should I tell you, of all people?

CHOLERA: Goodness does not naturally intrigue the race of men, though they are prepared to respect it against the day when they might need some. But the other powers at work in the world ... ah! They watch, they analyse ...

KITTY: And what do they say about me?

CHOLERA: That you must feel nothing. If you did then the suffering would break you.

KITTY: There's your answer, then. I'm empty. An empty vessel.

CHOLERA: You do good under compulsion.

KITTY: What compels me?

CHOLERA: What you don't do it for is the sake of another. You have no sense of 'other'. There is you, and the corruption of you. You and the pestilence of you. You and the absence of you, which you call God. Every saint has been the same way. Not one has had an atom of compassionate imagination.

(*Out into song.*)

SINGER: When the cholera came, time after time,
Kitty said 'Wash it with chloride of lime.'
Your kecks and your drawers, your fancy man's shirt,
Get rid of the germs, get rid of the dirt.

Yaah, cotton rag dub!
Frederick Street rub!
Cock-red in the face,
wool, linen and lace,
this soap's gone all gritty,
come change it, our Kitty.

The cholera came and the cholera went,
raging at Christmas, beaten by Lent,
rampant for Easter, done by Saint Bride,
washed up and gone on a Mersey high-tide.

Yaah, cotton rag dub!
Frederick Street rub!
Cock-red in the face,
wool, linen and lace,
this soap's gone all gritty,
come change it, our Kitty.

(*Cross into boiler house.*)

Scene 36

KITTY: I'd like to go to Derry again before I die.
Ever been? Would you consider coming with me?

CHOLERA: You'd want me as a companion? Kitty
Wilkinson, come now, you know full well who I am.

KITTY: Of course, but you work for me now. Will you
come?

CHOLERA: The Irish have sheltered themselves from too
many realities. Do you want to flush them out into the
light of day? Surely it's much too late for that?

KITTY: From what my Mam used to say, it's too harsh for
any reality to thrive other than hunger. I have a memory,
a green hill, the walls of a grey town. There's something
there for me. Something in the air.

(*CHOLERA laughs. Cross into sea/sailing ship. Then into Derry street.*)

Scene 37

CHOLERA: These people are very poor. Why haven't
I visited here until now?

KITTY: Can't you tell? They're clean. Thank God that
I came from a clean place. I praise God for it.

CHOLERA: Perhaps you're the person to enlighten me
on a point of Christian theology: why is cleanliness

supposed to be close to godliness? And which doctor of the Church ever said it was?

KITTY: Be careful what you say: in this town it is a matter of which church.

CHOLERA: At last I have a glimmer of understanding. In its small, sea-washed way, Derry is the City of God, which is a place divided unto itself.

KITTY: You're mocking me now.

CHOLERA: Not at all. I always thought of Christianity in the wrong way, something which crawled out of a crucified man: blood and sweat and excrement. It came out of human filth and death which seemed to be its strength. Is that it? You wanted him clean? Down off the Cross and given a good scrubbing?

KITTY: I suppose it's allowed that you should use the Devil's arguments. (*To a passer-by.*) Son!

BOY: Yes, Missus?

KITTY: Where can we find a bite to eat?

BOY: There's nowhere.

KITTY: We're hungry. Don't you have a duty to us?

BOY: Come to our house.

(*Out. Edge in.*)

Scene 38

(*A poor house in Derry. Family at table.*)

FATHER: What there is to share out between twelve of us, you can count for yourselves.

CHOLERA: This is most kind and hospitable, sir.

FATHER: There are seven potatoes, and the water they've been boiled in. Eat and drink your fill. My wife's in milk with the infant and you can have a pull at her if you want to. Beyond that there's nothing, which you're welcome to as well.

CHOLERA: We'd eat elsewhere but we could find nowhere that was open, it being Sunday.

FATHER: Give our guests the big potato to have between them. As you can see, the worst of the bad and blight has been cut out of it. Now we'll have grace if you'll bow your heads.

Silence.

KITTY: Would you like me to say something?

FATHER: That won't be necessary. Here we do it in the mind.

(*Edge in O'Lera's music.*)

Scene 39

CHOLERA: That seemed to satisfy her and she became calmer in herself. To me a bad potato is a bad potato, and nothing divided is nought, but to Kitty Wilkinson it seemed to be everything. Back to Liverpool she went, with joy, and lived to a good old age, helped by the charity which she had extended to so many, which made the acceptance of it fairly painless. In later years her son John returned from the sea, filling her little house with his friends and their trollops. It was rowdy, but life of a kind.

(*Cross O'Lera music into:*)

Scene 40

(*KITTY's parlour. Ticking clock.*)

JOHN: Ah, Holy Mother, it's good to be back. I've done with the sea, I've done with the stars. From now on I'm devoting my life entirely to you.

MARY: If he said that to me I'd be a scared woman.

JOHN: There's no one like my mother. Few men can say that and not have sneaking feelings that they're exaggerating. Sent me to Bluecoat School, she did. Slaved for me. Slaved for everyone. And what thanks did I give her? I ran away.

MARY: The sea was in your blood, John.

JOHN: If I'd only listened to her ... (*Sobs with alcoholic remorse.*)
God, what have I done to you, Mam?

KITTY: Nothing, son. I'm very well.

JOHN: You're a wonderful woman. (*Pause – he fills his glass.*)
Did I tell you that while I was in Peru I met an old
admirer of yours? He was sitting outside a tavern with
a drink, watching the sun go down over the sea. A dark-
skinned fellow, distinguished, sophistication written all
over him, he had, with those red-haired Irish-Indian
looks you see everywhere. As I was passing with my
mates he singled me out and invited me to join him.
'I know your mother,' he said. 'Without even knowing
my name?' I asked him. 'I could feel her influence
coming when your ship was only a dot on the horizon,'
he replied, 'and the surf of the sea reminded me of that
ceaseless washing of hers.'

KITTY: And what was Doctor O'Lera doing in Peru?

JOHN: He said you'd know him immediately. The man was
doing a reconnaissance for some scheme he'd set up on
behalf of the natives.

KITTY: Is it far to Peru?

JOHN: God, yes. The other end of the earth.

KITTY: (*Getting up with an effort.*) I must go.

JOHN: Get back in your chair. I haven't finished my story.

KITTY: I have no time to listen.

JOHN: And where d'you think you're going?

KITTY: To do the washing.

(*The 'Monday's Always Washing Day' song, mixing into the triumphal music of the street band. Mixing into sounds of washing. Sounds of the sea.*)

The End.

UNDER THE TABLE

Society of Authors Silver Sony Award 1996

Under the Table was first broadcast on BBC Radio 4 on the 6th of May 1995. The cast was as follows:

STORYTELLER, David Calder

SETH, Kenneth Cranham

MAY, Maureen O'Brien

RUSTY, Becky Hindley

CHURCHILL, Robert Lang

STALIN, Andrew Sachs

ROOSEVELT/TRUMAN, David Healy

HITLER/
LOUIS ARMSTRONG/CPO, Jonathan Keeble

ROUILLE/WOMAN, Natasha Pyne

JACK, Oliver Senton

BAGS/JOHN, Andrew Branch

MR HUNT, Peter Yapp

TREVOR, David Antrobus

DIRECTION, Eoin O' Callaghan

Scene 1

First world war artillery command post. Officer giving sequence of orders to a field gun team. Working sounds of the piece being elevated, trained, sighted, loaded.

CPO: Sub-section C take post! (*Squelching of feet in mud. Muttering.*) Sub-section target: entrenched infantry. Aiming-point: farmhouse corner. Concentration and distribution: bring gun 80 degrees left. (*Gun being traversed through mud. Grunts. Handwheel working.*) Angle of sight: three zero. (*Ratchet.*) Nature of charge and fuse: cordite MD number 106. Cast-iron fuse. (*Man picking up ammunition.*) Method of ranging: right ranging. Nature of shell filling: gas. Range: one five zero zero. (*Ratchet.*) One round, load. (*Shell going into breech.*)

SETH: Every time I load my gun with mustard, Rouillé, I think of you, sending me into the blue. Heh-heh.

CPO: Order to shoot: Fire!

(*Click, explosion, whistle of shell, impact, pause, hiss of gas. Cries of gassed German soldiers stumbling around in panic.*)

SOLDIER: Meine Augen! Meine Augen!

STORYTELLER: He recalls a time when he'd been gassed himself, and met a French nurse in hospital. The Front, October 13th, 1918, the village of Werwick, near Wipers – Yprés to the uninitiated – with my grandfather erotically firing his 18 pound gun.

(*Edge in ward atmosphere.*)

Scene 2

SETH: Give us a kiss, darlin'.

(*Kiss.*)

SETH: D'you know what I think?

ROUILLE: No, Tommy, tell me. What do you think?

SETH: The British should be fighting alongside the Germans against the French.

ROUILLE: Cochon!

(*A slap.*)

STORYTELLER: My grandfather was not only the kind of
man who would have been a good Foreign Secretary. He
also had the makings of a sensitive artist, noting how
rays of sunlight came down through the rolling, yellow
cloud released by gas-shells, making a scene worthy of a
Baroque painting of the Ascension. Beneath the glowing,
fan-vaulted cloud, where earlier artists used to show the
suffering of the damned, were the trenches. Blindness.
Breathlessness. Confusion. Death.

(*Edge in cemetery atmosphere and birdsong.*)

STORYTELLER: 1984. Very hot out here, but green and
fertile. I'm standing with my mother beside my father's
grave in the war cemetery at Madjez-el-Bab, Tunisia. He
was killed during the Second World War, forty years ago.
She is unable to cry or pray.

RUSTY: He's not under there. Inside, I'm just a block of ice.

STORYTELLER: Surely you must feel something! TRY!

LOUIS ARMSTRONG: I gotta right to sing the blues,
I gotta right to feel low-down,
I gotta right to hang around,
Down among the riff-raff ...

(*Credits with song underneath. Cross from Armstrong into sound
of World War 2 aircraft in flight – Skymaster & P38 escort.*)

Scene 3

STORYTELLER: Early morning mist over the Black Sea.
A Skymaster military aircraft christened 'Sacred Cow',
escorted by P38 fighters, carries Franklin Delano
Roosevelt, President of the United States towards Saki
aerodrome. Twenty minutes behind him in a York
transport plane Winston Spencer Churchill, Prime
Minister of the British Empire, heads towards the same
destination. The twenty-five planes of this Allied
delegation made a night-time departure from Malta at
ten minute intervals, maintaining a constant airspeed
towards German-held Cyprus. There a ninetydegree turn
to port was executed before flying over the wine-dark

Aegean towards the coast of Thrace. At the time when dawn bloodies the night, Churchill pulls a leather flying-jacket closer round him and looks down on the Dardanelles.

CHURCHILL: (*To himself.*) Can't this thing go a bit faster?

STORYTELLER: Forty years ago, as First Lord of the Admiralty, in that other war, a suicidal campaign was launched to dislodge the Turks and Germans from this spot in order to open a line of communication with our Russian allies.

CHURCHILL: (*Musing.*) Let's hope it won't be so expensive this time.

STEWARD: Coffee, Prime Minister?

CHURCHILL: Gallipoli. Oh, dear, dear. The things they said about me. By then Uncle Joe'd already been in gaol six times for sedition and robbing banks. (*Laughs.*)

STEWARD: Yes, Prime Minister. Black?

CHURCHILL: Hot and strong. Hold it steady. Malt's good against typhus, lice and demons, all of which await us.

STEWARD: Yes, Prime Minister.

(*Flask being opened and whisky poured into coffee.*)

STORYTELLER: And where are all these planes taking Churchill and Roosevelt? Because Stalin, on the advice of his doctors, so he says, is refusing to leave the safety of the Soviet Union, a meeting vital to the world's future is to be held at Yalta in southern Russia. On both sides of the eighty-mile route from the airport to the conference venue stand young male and female Soviet soldiers, waiting in the icy wind to salute the re-conquerors of Europe – for Hitler is on his way OUT.

(*The winter wind. Stamping and slapping of people trying to keep circulation going.*)

STORYTELLER: Before the seven hundred-strong Allied delegation can touch down, the runway has to be checked for old cannonballs. This is the Crimea!/To the surface, frost sometimes sucks a souvenir/of the gentleman's war/ a hundred years before/Nightingale eggs. Heh-heh.

Scene 4

(*Aircraft landing one after the other.* (*World War 2 types.*) *Cross into whine of lift mechanism.*)

STORYTELLER: While Churchill waits in a cold wind, clutching his hat, watching sparks fly from his cigar, President Roosevelt is lowered to the ground in his wheelchair by a special lift mechanism ...

(*Forties 3-piece local dance band playing 'Knees Up Mother Brown' music fed into whine of lift mechanism.*)

STORYTELLER: A couple of time-zones to the rear, May Hammer is in the cloakroom of Tue Brook parish hall, Liverpool, struggling into a pair of voluminous Union Jack drawers, preparing to lead a folk-dance in honour of the goddess Mother Brown, to whom all knees must be raised.

(*Cheers and laughter as MAY enters.*)

STORYTELLER: With her three daughters and phlegmatic spouse/she once lived in tiny terraced house/in Everton's lovely vale. The family moved upmarket in 1935 because May's husband had been promoted and wished to erect a greenhouse for growing tomatoes in a non stone-throwing district of Liverpool. May found that she could not completely adjust to her change in status. Although by sheer force of character she inevitably became the life and soul of the party in Tue Brook, she found that it was a different party.

(*Laughter at the dance.*)

WOMAN: Oh, Mrs Hammer! How could you? That's the flag you're wearing!

MAY: Don't think I wouldn't die for it.

STORYTELLER: ... she says, stoutly. Later she will don a man's suit of tails, put on a toff's top hat, twirl a silver-topped cane, fill a clay-pipe with dog-ends from the dance-floor and sing a little defiantly:

MAY: I walk down the Strand! with my gloves in my hand! then I walk back again with them orf! I'm Bert, Bert! I haven't a shirt ...

STORYTELLER: ... the old music-hall hit. 'Burlington Bertie': followed by an impersonation of the American entertainer Al Jolson doing ...

MAY: (*Singing.*) Mammy, mammy, the sun shines east, the sun shines west! But I know where the sun shines best.

STORYTELLER: Resonance of this soul-searching between high and low, rich and poor, male and female, black and white, is made all the greater by Mrs Hammer's fifteen stone beauty, which suits her role as arch-priestess of parish fun, speaking in riddles, that betray all pre-war Liverpudlians' anxiety not to be overunderstood.

MAY: It wouldn't be a show without Punch! I'm going ashore for a loaf. We're short of nothing we've got. The rags round my arse are battering my brains out.

STORYTELLER: The meaning of much she says has been lost in the mists of the dispossessed mind. The same is true of Stalin who, with Hitler, has dispossessed socialism of all its meaning, but not in order to entertain.

MAY: If you're not Irish you must be.

STORYTELLER: The Soviet leader waits by a telephone to hear that the squadrons of his allies have arrived safely. However, he will not be at the airport to meet his guests.

Scene 5

(*Heard faintly behind the narration, a brass band strikes up with a few bars of 'Stars and Stripes', 'God Save the King', then the 'Internationale'.*)

STORYTELLER: Stalin wants the two western leaders to see the ruin of the land for themselves, the scorched earth, the wholesale destruction left behind by the Germans.

(*Motorcade and soldiers continuously saluting heard in car interior.*)

ROOSEVELT: My God, what a mess has been made of this place. Certainly makes me feel more bloodthirsty.

CHURCHILL: Barbarians! Wouldn't Bach and Beethoven be ashamed of them?

STORYTELLER: This journey is taking place in February 1945 with a cold wind whistling over the sea from the snowbound Caucasus.

(*Wind.*)

That chill air-stream flows west across a crucified continent to where, snug in his cubby-hole office on Liverpool's waterfront, May Hammer's half-her-weight husband, Seth, listens to a roll-call read out by Bags, his crippled warehouse clerk.

Scene 6

(*Edge in warehouse office atmosphere. Dock traffic – including steam lorries. Rumble of overhead railway. Ship's hooters.*)

BAGS: (*Reading.*) Artemis, Bella, Circe, Diana, Esther, Gloriana, Freya, Helen, Iris, Juno, HMS Warrington, The Arctic Star.

All in the Pool, waiting. Bring to mind those bad old days, boss, when most of them would have gone to the bottom.

SETH: We were better off, then. Didn't have to store the cargoes. Heh-heh.

BAGS: You'd rather work than be at home any day, Mr Hammer.

SETH: The trouble with you is you're like the man who shat himself. You know all about it.

BAGS: Sweating again, boss.

SETH: You know my ailment, Bags: the recurring malaria I got in the Land Between the Two Rivers. Heh-heh.

Scene 7

(*Cross into DOCTOR's surgery.*)

DOCTOR: Do I have to spell it out again, Mr Hammer? You can get dressed.

SETH: Keeps slipping my mind, doctor.

DOCTOR: If you carry on this way cirrhosis of the liver is a strong possibility.

SETH: Can't be worse than how I feel now. What symptoms should I look out for?

DOCTOR: Jaundice ... you've already got a sallow look ... black, sticky, evil-smelling motions ... your face and palms red ... projectile vomiting of blood ... quite impressive when it happens. I had someone in here – no names, no packdrill – who shot a mouthful from one side of the room to the other, splat! All over the wall.

STORYTELLER: Seth walks from the surgery, goes straight to the Black Lion via the Lamb and Flag to contemplate this danger. Afterwards, at home, in a hide leather armchair dotted with cigarette burns, he sits asleep dreaming that he's won the Tossing the Blood event at the Scotland Road Highland Games.

Scene 8

(*In the dance hall.*)

MAY: My husband? What a film-star! He's got one leg in the grave but he keeps jumping out again.

(*Laughter.*)

STORYTELLER: Night after peril-filled night my grandfather has spent in his armchair, railing against the German air force, and refusing to take refuge under the stairs. Bottles at his feet, Capstan Full Strength burning between his long, elegant, nicotine-stained fingers, he has poured contempt upon Goering's bomb-aimers for their failure to strike him dead.

SETH: Couldn't punch a buggering hole in a wet Echo!

STORYTELLER: The name of Liverpool's best-loved evening paper. But now the Luftwaffe come no more, and the V2 rockets don't have the range to reach Liverpool, which is a source of resentment to Mr Hammer, who likes to gamble with his attenuated life.

SETH: Ouch! Ooh!

STORYTELLER: During his doze, another cigarette has burned down to his fingers. Cursing, he flicks it into the fire, his bottle-end glasses magnifying blue, ball-bearing eyes, and the danger is past. But another threat rears up: on the mantelpiece a plaster figure of Dumbo, the flying baby elephant, accuses him with unblinking eye.

SETH: What are you looking at me for, Big Ears?

STORYTELLER: He reaches up, turns Dumbo's face to the wall, then subsides back onto his riddled throne.

(*Profound throaty snore.*)

STORYTELLER: Dreaming of death, he sleeps the sleep of a ghost. Although Seth Hammer clings to enough life not to be counted amongst the fifty million who have died in this worst-ever of conflicts, the Second World War, the casualty list he's always been on is twenty-five years old, and going yellow round the edges.

(*Very loud snore. Edge in BBC News for February 2nd 1945. Snoring continues.*)

MAY: (*Muttering.*) Oh, shut up, will you? I can't hear.

STORYTELLER: But is this the news? Perhaps her husband is right to sleep through because, apparently by common agreement, the real news in war is never told. The conference at Yalta cannot even be mentioned. Therefore, the question is begged: in what mind, where and how, is it really happening?

(*Radio volume is turned up. SETH starts, snuffles, grunts, coughs.*)

SETH: (*In his sleep.*) Ten Turkish? I know where I can get it for five.

(*He goes back to snoring.*)

MAY: (*Muttering.*) We don't want to hear about your foreign intercourse.

SETH: The one I want has projectiles you can hang your hat on.

MAY: Now you've made me drop a stitch!

STORYTELLER: In repose there is something vaguely Roman about his features. The love-poet Ovid, during his exile north-east of The Golden Horn, perhaps? No,

not Ovid. Seth's seamy grandeur is free of any softness
or sentimentality. Like the beautiful blurred features on
the Turin Shroud, his visage could have been made up
from all the war-beaten human faces in history
superimposed one upon the other.

(*Coughing. Spitting. Hiss of phlegm in the fire. Click of radio news
being turned off.*)

MAY: Hey, I was listening to that.

SETH: Next lot will be just the same.

MAY: You were having another nightmare.

SETH: No, now's the nightmare. Waking up here with you.

MAY: I've always said you're snotty but civil.

SETH: My arm's gone dead.

MAY: Rub it with a hot brick.

SETH: A one-armed husband wouldn't make much difference
to you. Heh-heh.

MAY: Don't talk like that. The boy's under the table. He
can hear everything.

SETH: Ach, he's not old enough to cotton on to what I'm
talking about. (*Lights up a cigarette.*)

STORYTELLER: Oh, but I am, I am! Carry on!

MAY: Seven's old enough to understand anything you
might come up with.

SETH: Lives in a world of his own, that one.

MAY: Who can blame him?

SETH: And he's thick.

STORYTELLER: True, O king. But I'm learning.

MAY: He's not thick. He can read which is more than you
can at the moment.

SETH: I can read!

MAY: But you can't hold the paper straight. Why don't you
make time to play with him? Go out with him now and
then.

SETH: They won't let kids in the pub. Whenever he's been
out with me he's ended up sitting on a cold doorstep
with a bottle of pop and a bag of crisps.

MAY: Then take him into the garden. Let him help in the greenhouse.

SETH: Too clumsy. He'd break things.

MAY: What's the use? I'll put your dinner on the table.

SETH: Can't face it.

(*Hawking and spitting.*)

MAY: If you've got to spit in the fire at least try and hit it.

SETH: Quack says I mustn't bend too much. (*Door opening.*) Heh-heh. (*Fades.*)

STORYTELLER: I lift the edge of the tablecloth and watch as my grandfather peers at the mess he's made in the polished hearth. Spitting is how he marks out the last of his domestic freedom. Everything in this room is kept spotless, scrubbed, clean, and in its proper place – except his mouth.

SETH: (*Fade in.*) I KNOW YOU'RE LOOKING, YOU GERMAN SPY. WHAT ARE YOU DOING UNDER THERE? TOSSING OFF? Heh-heh.

STORYTELLER: I'm only seven, Grandad.

Scene 9

STORYTELLER: The dinner is brought from the kitchen. Every night my grandmother has to plead with him to eat. This time she serves delicately-flavoured honeycomb tripe stewed in milk with onions, very gentle on the stomach.

(*Plate down on table with tablecloth.*)

SETH: (*Fade in.*) Don't want it.

MAY: Seth, you have to eat.

SETH: Can't cope with solid food at the moment. Give it to the cat.

MAY: She won't eat tripe.

SETH: Let the boy have it, then ... He'll eat anything. WON'T YOU?

MAY: Leave the lad alone.

SETH: All you ever think about is food. That's an insult to a man with half a stomach.

STORYTELLER: The whereabouts of the other half is a family mystery, but my gran believes that it may be in the possession of Rouillé, the French nurse who turned him inside-out in 1917.

SETH: Have you ever thought what the last five years have been like for me? All I've done is unload ships carrying food I can't eat. DID YOU CATCH THAT DOWN THERE, HUNGRY HORACE?

MAY: You should be glad the boy's got such a good appetite. There're millionaires who'd give everything they've got for it.

SETH: You're only feeding him up for the Army. They'll have him soon enough. Heh-heh.

MAY: Don't be so wicked! I go down on my bended knees every night to pray that never happens.

SETH: It will.

MAY: Oh, shut up and go to bed, you miserable bugger!

SETH: My arm's coming back to life. Doesn't half tingle. Why is it every time I come home Buggerlugs hides under the table?

MAY: He's scared of you. If I had any sense I'd join him.

SETH: You wouldn't fit. Heh-heh. HEY, YOU DOWN THERE! ONLY MICE LIVE UNDER TABLES, LOOKING FOR CRUMBS!

STORYTELLER: My gran was wrong. I wasn't scared. I was under the table to listen in case he came out with whether my father was definitely dead or alive, one or the other. I needed to know that. Because my grandfather was always drunk, he was most likely to let slip the truth. As for crumbs under that table, none ever survived. My gran used her Hoover like a flame-thrower. But, perhaps, there was a crumb. One crumb of comfort. A crumb of lead. I kept it in a matchbox, stuck in a space where the underparts of the table's folding leaves crossed. A chipped guardsman with a bent rifle and a red coat, but no face under the black battered bearskin because the pink paint had worn off. I'd worn it off, looking for my dad.

Scene 10

(*Doorbell.*)

MAY: Oh, God. Not visitors now.

RUSTY: (*Calling from upstairs.*) I'll get it.

MAY: I don't want anyone here with you like this. Please, Seth, try to behave.

SETH: It'll be the gang I invited home from the pub.

(*Doorbell again. RUSTY comes downstairs into the hall.*)

RUSTY: (*In her head.*) It's him. He's come back.

(*A long ring on the doorbell.*)

RUSTY: When I open the door, he'll be standing there. His face'll be sunburned. Some kind Arabs found him and took care of him at an oasis. 'Hello, Rusty', he'll say. 'Let's dance. '

(*Hall atmosphere. Door opening.*)

HUNT: Good evening. I was about to give up and go away.

RUSTY: I was upstairs.

HUNT: I thought I might have a word with the boys.

RUSTY: I'll get me mum.

MAY: (*As she comes into the hall.*) Who is it?

RUSTY: Mr Hunt.

SETH: (*From the living room.*) Bring the sod in here!

MAY: (*Shift of accent upmarket.*) Take Mr Hunt into the lounge, please.

(*Front door shutting. Best room door opening. Clock ticking.*)

HUNT: (*Softly, to RUSTY.*) We all have our crosses to bear.

MAY: Be with you in a minute. Look after Mr Hunt, Rusty.

(*Best room door shutting.*)

HUNT: I know it's inconvenient, but I am extremely concerned. Having thought about it, and sought some guidance, I knew I had to come.

RUSTY: My mum'll be here in a minute.

HUNT: I'm afraid I was walking past The Lamb and Flag
an hour ago when your father made his exit. Since then
I haven't been able to stop thinking about you, your
sons, and your predicament ...

(*Cross fade to living room.*)

Scene 11

SETH: I'm going in there!

MAY: You're not! The man isn't interested in you!
He comes to see the boys.

SETH: I'm a boy at heart. Heh-heh.

(*Swift cross back to best room.*)

Scene 12

HUNT: Don't worry. I'm not afraid of him.

RUSTY: My mum's coming. She won't be long.

HUNT: We have to think of those children. Someone must
tackle him.

RUSTY: My mum tackles him all the time.

(*Best room door opens.*)

MAY: (*From the hall.*) Don't go in there!

SETH: Good evening, sir. May blessings rain down on your
head like coco-nuts.

HUNT: Good evening, Mr Hammer. How are we?

SETH: We's all right. Far too well to need a visit from
you.

HUNT: Would it be possible for me to have a word with
the children – please?

RUSTY: John's asleep.

SETH: The other's hiding in his den. Go and drag him out,
Rusty.

HUNT: That won't be necessary. With your permission,
I'll go and talk to him.

SETH: You'll have to get down on your hands and knees; but you're used to that. As you're here, why don't we have a chat, man to man? If you've got something to say in this house you should say it to me.

HUNT: Perhaps it would be better if you told the boy I'd come to see him? I wouldn't want him frightened.

SETH: Him, frightened? Of you? Don't make me laugh. Beside, he's not frightened of anybody, especially priests, politicians and policemen. I've taught him that. Good advice for a lad growing up in these terrible times?

(*HUNT coughs nervously.*)

SETH: All right, ignore me. If you won't talk we could always sit and play the gramophone. I've got Giggly singing Tosti's *Goodbye* and *The Lost Chord*. (*Sings.*) 'Seated one day at the organ' ... (*Pause, then very coldly.*) No child of my blood is frightened of a buggering priest.

RUSTY: Dad! Stop it!

SETH: We breed men in this house, not dancing partners.

RUSTY: Take no notice, Mr Hunt.

SETH: He'd better take notice! He's in my house. (*Pause.*) I've no respect for your religion.

HUNT: I'm sorry to hear that.

SETH: We never go to church.

HUNT: That's not quite so. When your son-in-law ...

SETH: Ach, that doesn't count. All on the spur of the moment. Have some rum. (*Moving to bottle on table.*)

HUNT: It seemed to count then, Mr Hammer.

SETH: Thirty years ago I was left behind enemy lines in thick fog with ten lame horses and a load of frozen hay. No one thought: 'Where's he gone?' They just struck me off the list of the living and forgot I'd ever existed. The same will happen to my son-in-law, no matter what the women say. But faster than most they'll forget about useless articles like you.

HUNT: Though it saddens me greatly, I won't even try to argue with all that, Mr Hammer.

SETH: Because you bloody can't. My father was a lay-preacher, carried his bible everywhere, even to work. He was a gravedigger at Sefton Park.

HUNT: Really?

SETH: Cut the sod for one of my sisters, and he buried his own wife, my mother.

HUNT: That must have been a very painful experience for you.

SETH: Painful? Oh, yes, it was. He read a few words over her from the good book, patted her down with his shovel, then went off with Rosie, the charwoman from the cemetery office. (*Pause.*) Here, have a tot and cheer yourself up.

HUNT: No, thank you.

SETH: Don't sulk. Life's too short. D'you know what I've got in our coal-shed?

RUSTY: (*Calling.*) Mum! I can't manage.

HUNT: Your father and I are getting along very well, aren't we? So, tell me, what's this you've got in the coal-shed, Mr Hammer?

SETH: A Crucifixion I carved years ago out of a single piece of oak.

HUNT: How very interesting. I didn't know you were good at that kind of thing. May I change my mind about the rum? I'm quite fond of it, actually.

SETH: Good for you. I'm glad you've realised that I'm not as green as I'm cabbage-looking. But my art ended in tragedy: I knocked both arms off Jesus when I tried to carry him through the coal-house door to show everybody what I'd done. Heh-heh. Hey, what's going on here? What am I thinking about? I'm drinking with the cardinal-archbishop of Tue Brook and I've given him a glass the size of a thimble.

(*Glass cabinet being unlocked and opened. Chiming of glass.*)

RUSTY: I'll have to go and find my mum, Mr Hunt.

HUNT: I'll be perfectly happy here. There's no reason why your father and I shouldn't get on, is there?

SETH: No reason at all. We're both not Catholics.

HUNT: Do you still keep up with your sculpture? It must be a fascinating hobby. Perhaps you could do something for our church?

SETH: Why don't you shut your mouth and let us see who you are?

RUSTY: Dad!

(*Door opening and closing as RUSTY hurriedly goes out.*)

SETH: Stupid tart!

HUNT: (*Suddenly laying in to him.*) How dare you! Have you no shame? Your own daughter, a war-widow with two young children, trying to live with her grief, and all you do is insult her. Hasn't there been enough suffering in this house without you making it worse, intoxicated every day! Your poor wife cannot hold her head up in the street!

SETH: That's fighting talk. Ach, I can't be bothered. You always take the women's side. Very clever, that! Stops you getting clouted.

HUNT: Must I think of you as a wicked man?

SETH: Think of me how you like. You know nothing and whatever you say won't worry my soul-case.

HUNT: It's very difficult to be sympathetic with someone who's got so much pity for himself.

SETH: Listen, there're things you can't imagine and because you're only half a man I can't be bothered to tell them to you.

HUNT: Why am I only half a man?

SETH: Because you only want half the truth.

HUNT: I love the whole truth. Indeed, I love it more than life itself.

SETH: War and what it does to you is the whole truth, that's why it takes men to fight it, and the Devil to understand it.

HUNT: Pub-talk, Mr Hammer. Now, if you'll excuse me, I'm going to see if I can have a word with that child.

(*Door opening and closing.*)

SETH: And keep your hand off his knee. I know he'd let ya! Heh-heh. (*Gets up and lurches about.*) But you should stay here with me. This is the Best Room for the Best People. Hold on, I'll get you a bigger glass to go with your head. (*Fumbling of cabinet door. Breaking of glass as he falls against it. The falling glass is slowed down to a dreamy tinkle.*)

Scene 13

(*Cross into Russian folk choir, very softly. Muted, sleepy birdsong.*)

STORYTELLER: (*Voice over.*) The Big Three's Yalta conference got off to a slightly better start than Seth's synod. Held in the draughty ballroom of the Livadia summer palace, once the holiday home of the tsar, amenities have suffered because German troops looted everything they could lay their hands on, even down to taps and doorknobs, many of which have not been replaced. Senior diplomats are opening doors with dinner knives and having to urinate out of bedroom windows. And it's cold, but not as cold as outside. Hundreds of birds, having found their way into the Livadia for shelter, roost in the ornamental plasterwork.

(*Edge in palace ballroom atmosphere. Twittering of birds rises. Sporadic clanking of over-worked central heating system.*)

STORYTELLER: Fatigued and disoriented by their long journey, feeling the effect of Stalin's heavy-handed liquid hospitality, both Roosevelt and Churchill are having moments when they wonder: is this really happening?

STALIN: ... in the not-too-distant past, the Poles were happy enough to invade Russia when it suited them. And every time we're invaded from the west, be it French, German, they come through Poland. (*Pouring drinks.*)

ROOSEVELT: (*Shivering.*) I can't imagine anyone planning to invade Russia when this war's over.

STALIN: How can I take that for granted?

CHURCHILL: Have they been able to do anything about giving us more heat yet?

STALIN: You still cold? I don't feel it myself.

CHURCHILL: The temperature has dropped a lot, Joe, and the President must be kept warm.

STALIN: I gave orders to put everything on maximum. They said that the equipment is already at full stretch. (*Gets up.*)

(*Footsteps across ballroom.*)

ROOSEVELT: Then could we go to a smaller room that would be easier to keep warm?

STALIN: You want the three men who rule the world to meet in a broom-cupboard?

CHURCHILL: It's so cold I can't concentrate.

STALIN: All the radiators are on full blast.

ROOSEVELT: I'm getting too drowsy, Winston.

CHURCHILL: We really can't stay here, Joe. It's too big to heat.

STALIN: I'm comfortable, but then I'm used to a hard life. If you don't like it, blame the Germans. We've done our best to bring the old place back up to standard. I've brought all the best hotel staff in Moscow down here to look after you, and you're still not satisfied. Our country has nearly been destroyed. We suffer and we suffer, but we don't complain!

CHURCHILL: Please don't be offended, but I am very concerned for the President's health. Why don't we wander around and look for somewhere a little bit warmer? Anywhere will do.

ROOSEVELT: Are you against that idea, Joe? I have to admit that I am feeling the chill.

STALIN: I'm insulted, naturally, but what the hell? (*Roars with laughter.*)

(*Footsteps across ballroom floor – door opens – into a long corridor – wooden floor. Squeaking of wheel-chair.*)

STALIN: Everything I hear about the wonders of American technology – and your wheelchair needs oiling!

ROOSEVELT: I'd feel easier if I knew you could accept that no one's going to be in a position to threaten your security. This mess is going to take twenty years to clear up.

STALIN: And after twenty years? Also, you must remember Slavic peoples aren't like Germans, British and Americans. They don't like war. I don't want to ask them to fight again.

CHURCHILL: Where do you get the impression that we like war?

STALIN: The movies. John Wayne. Gary Cooper.

ROOSEVELT: Joe, Hollywood's a law unto itself and you're not talking to its sheriff. I can't ride in there with six-guns blazing wearing a big white hat.

STALIN: But if our interests collide later on, Hopalong Cassidy, you wouldn't hesitate to say to Hollywood – make old Joe the bandit in the big black hat. (*Laughs.*)

(*Squeaking stops.*)

CHURCHILL: A possibility? I'll peer in, shall I?

(*Opening of door.*)

Every window gone. Birdshit everywhere. Very depressing.

(*Door closing.*)

STALIN: Wait. We could try the games-room. I've got the billiard-table working. Darts for Winston.

ROOSEVELT: Too distracting. We must have a place where we can shut ourselves off and get down to work – quickly. Hell, I'm not even sure that we won't have to start over. Have we got anywhere so far? Perhaps we three old guys should begin again at the beginning?

(*Squeaking continues.*)

STORYTELLER: Down corridors, peering into ante-chambers, vestibules, living-, drawing-rooms, they search through the broken palace, looking for somewhere to settle, squabbling gently.

ROOSEVELT: We've been fighting side by side for a few years now. How is it you still don't trust us?

STALIN: Side by side? I'd say end to end.

CHURCHILL: Why not ask how can he make us trust him?

STALIN: The Soviet people have taken the brunt of this war. Compared to ours your losses are negligible. More Russians died in Leningrad than all your losses put together.

CHURCHILL: Have you counted our civilian casualties? The Blitz? The merchant seamen? We suffered greatly.

STALIN: Suffered! A gnat-bite! And neither of your countries has been fought over and occupied. You cannot hope to imagine what it does to the soul of the people.

CHURCHILL: These comparisons may be very edifying, but we will all three be the victors, and to all three victors should go the spoils. It's all very well playing the martyr, Joe, but who was it entered into a non-aggression pact with Hitler behind our backs?

STALIN: Must I mention Munich?

CHURCHILL: Nothing to do with me!

STALIN: You don't get away with it that easily, Winston. Neville Chamberlain was the British Prime Minister. His guilt is your guilt. That's democracy.

ROOSEVELT: Let's not go into all that. Take a step back. Give the whole business a thoroughgoing examination. Get a balanced view. Bearing in mind that the objective, our great responsibility, is for us to prepare a peace that will last, let's look at ourselves for a cool moment. Like it or not, worthy or not, we are the hope of the world.

CHURCHILL: I'm sure we've been past here before. Which turning did we take last time? Right or left?

(*They pause. Music. They move. Squeaking.*)

STORYTELLER: Under an arch between the news that was, and the news that wasn't, passed the Big Three into a very p-e-r-s-o-n-a-l kind of history.

(*Music stops. Squeaking of wheelchair stops.*)

CHURCHILL: At least there's a handle. Poke your head in, Joe.

(*Opening of glass door in greenhouse atmosphere.*)

Scene 14

STALIN: (*Sniffs up.*) Tomatoes! I love tomatoes!

SETH: Don't come in.

CHURCHILL: This will do.

SETH: I need time to myself. Wife's giving me hell, daughter's threatening to leave home, vicar's reporting me to Welfare, and the quack's condemned me to death.

CHURCHILL: Be a good chap and take the front end of the wheelchair so we can manage it down the step, will you? (*Pause.*) Get on with it, man!

SETH: Sah!

(*They carry ROOSEVELT over the greenhouse threshold. Closing of greenhouse door.*)

CHURCHILL: Thank God for some warmth! Where d'you get the fuel? The black market?

SETH: Black market? Me? I gather twigs! Bits of wood off bomb sites. Old boxes. Anything that'll burn.

CHURCHILL: Don't fret. No one's going to report you. We've got bigger fish to fry. Are you comfortable, Mr President?

ROOSEVELT: Not sure about that underlying smell, but I suppose I can live with it.

STALIN: Dried blood.

SETH: Got it off a friend. Not easy to find right now.

CHURCHILL: We've come to thrash out the post-war partition of Europe.

SETH: In my greenhouse?

STALIN: Needn't take long.

ROOSEVELT: Tell me, sir: to create the right conditions for a permanent peace amongst the nations, what would *you* do?

SETH: They wouldn't know peace if it jumped out of the gutter and bit them.

ROOSEVELT: It would help if an ordinary citizen like yourself would open his heart and tell us what he really thinks.

SETH: I'm not ordinary. What's ordinary? I don't know what ordinary is.

CHURCHILL: The man in the street. He on the Clapham omnibus. We need to understand.

SETH: I'm a man who hasn't been understood since 1918.

(*Dip greenhouse atmosphere. Bring in warehouse atmosphere.*)

SETH: (*On telephone.*) More cargo? Bring it over, sunshine. All the room in the world. (*Telephone down.*)

BAGS: But we haven't. The safety inspectors'll be onto us.

SETH: Jam everything in up to the ceiling. Make the floors bend and the walls bulge. Who cares? (*Drinks.*)

BAGS: Boss, we've got The Northern Rock and The Bolivar docking tomorrow ...

SETH: Invite them round. We can take anything they throw at us. It's twelve o'clock. Time for your dinner and my lunch. (*Going.*)

BAGS: Mr Les has been snooping round. Don't go in the Tug and Forelock. Oh, and your wife rang up.

SETH: She can't have done. The woman doesn't know how to use the phone.

BAGS: She said your boiler in the greenhouse is over-heating and she doesn't know how to turn it off. Says she's scared it'll blow up.

(*Dip warehouse office atmosphere.*)

STORYTELLER: While the Big Three perspire plentifully amongst Seth's tomatoes, and the docks and warehouses of Liverpool fill to danger-point, sweating scientists cram an entire universe into a container at Alamogordo American Air Force base, New Mexico, and Adolf Hitler finds room in his heaving brain to contemplate suicide. Seth hears this latter news straight from the Fuhrer's mouth while freeing the greenhouse boiler's rusted-up safety-valve.

Scene 15

(*Edge in greenhouse atmosphere. Tapping and hissing.*)

HITLER: Gentlemen, I have written my last political testament. You are the only people on earth whose editorial opinion I respect. Would you cast an eye over the manuscript for me?

ROOSEVELT: I'm not sure we've got time to dally.

(*Hiss from the boiler gets louder.*)

HITLER: When Communism has wrecked the future world I want people to read this little book and see how right I was.

(*Hiss from the boiler gets louder.*)

STALIN: Before you go, tell me how you got those camps of yours to be so efficient.

HITLER: Henry Ford.

ROOSEVELT: I can't let that pass!

HITLER: Pass, it has. Death is a motor-car on an assembly line going backwards.

SETH: If you gents don't mind, my dinner's waiting.

CHURCHILL: Leave the boy with us. He might learn something.

SETH: On your own head be it. Don't expect too much.

(*Greenhouse door opening and closing.*)

ROOSEVELT: After this war, two questions will arise: should leaders be given even the most trifling freedom to do their personal will? And: why should people want to be governed at all?

STALIN: Do you know how tomatoes make love, my son? When they're in flower, someone taps them with a cane.

Scene 16

(*Cross on hissing of boiler to living room atmosphere. Light music on the radio. Sewing machine working in the next room.*)

MAY: I said keep your eye on him for five minutes while I went to the shops. What d'you leave him in the greenhouse for? That place isn't safe.

SETH: I thought he'd like to stay there and play for awhile. (*Lights cigarette.*)

MAY: Why don't you tidy it up? It gets full of mice and they come into the house.

SETH: It's not full of mice now. (*Picks up newspaper.*)

MAY: I managed to get you a piece of Finnan haddock for your dinner. I've poached it with an egg on top. Is there any point in putting it on the table or shall I throw it straight into the bin?

SETH: I'll have a go, but I'm making no promises.

(*Door opening. Two-year old boy burbling.*)

RUSTY: I've made myself a new dress for the dance. D'you like it?

MAY: Oh, y-e-s. It's lovely.

RUSTY: Where's the queer feller.

MAY: Your father's left him in the greenhouse.

STORYTELLER: Rusty peers across the garden. The dirty, bemossed greenhouse glass is steamed up. Shapes behind could be plants, or a boy. She puts her new dress on a hanger, hooks it on the picture rail, then goes upstairs to bath the baby she was four months pregnant with when the news she has never been able to believe came from North Africa. To the other women of the family, superstitious and miracle-conscious as they are, this baby, when born, was its own father reincarnated. It is treated with a respect that borders on veneration. Every move it makes, every sound, has several meanings. Not the least of which is that Rusty's younger son is her husband and the boy-under-the-table's little brother is his father.

(*Running of bathwater. RUSTY hums 'When They Begin The Beguine'.*)

But Rusty refuses to fall into the trap set by this family myth. If she did it would mean that she accepted what the Army told her – that Jack, her husband, her dancing-partner for life, had been blown to smithereens on the side of a muddy road in Tunisia.

RUSTY: (*In her head.*) They never found him.

STORYTELLER: There was nothing to find.

(*Bath taps turned off.*)

Scene 17

(*Cross into greenhouse atmosphere.*)

ROOSEVELT: (*Fade in.*) Are you sure all the Czechoslovakians, Yugoslavians, Rumanians, Bulgarians, Hungarians, Estonians, Lithuanians, Latvians, not to mention the Poles, want to be Communists?

STALIN: Has anyone heard them saying they don't?

CHURCHILL: (*Muttering.*) And God help them if they did. (*Speaking up.*) Let's hear you promise free and democratic elections in all the countries liberated by Soviet forces.

STALIN: I promise, on my mother's grave.

CHURCHILL: Is she dead?

(*STALIN roars with laughter.*)

CHURCHILL: So what will the post-war Polish government look like, exactly.

STALIN: People might say I'm a dictator but I couldn't bring myself to discuss that without the Poles being present.

CHURCHILL: It was because of the Nazi invasion of Poland that we entered the war. We cannot therefore agree to anything that denies her complete democratic freedom.

ROOSEVELT: What do you say, Joe?

STALIN: That's guaranteed.

CHURCHILL: I've got to be sure that the people of Eastern Europe aren't merely exchanging one tyranny for another.

STALIN: Don't be so melodramatic. Franklin, is this what we're here to talk about?

ROOSEVELT: I know what he means. Joe, in all good faith, we accept the USSR's conquered all these territories at great expense. No one in his right mind wants to start the Third World War before we've finished the Second.

CHURCHILL: Hold on, there's a question ...

ROOSEVELT: (*Sharply.*) Give me a minute, will you? (*Pause.*) Joe, could we have an understanding between you and I that once emergency measures are no longer necessary, you'll ease up on some of the tougher practices?

STALIN: What do you mean?

CHURCHILL: The crushing of legitimate opposition by undemocratic methods. The use of terror, secret police! Mass deportations! Imprisonments and executions without trial! Disappearances!

ROOSEVELT: Winston, please don't put words in my mouth. I said 'tougher practices'. Joe knows what I mean.

STALIN: Of course I do. Even though it's an internal matter, I'll give you a personal promise, Franklin: as soon as it's practical we'll be much gentler with everybody.

ROOSEVELT: That's good enough for me.

CHURCHILL: (*Indignantly.*) How can Poland be an internal matter to Russia?

STALIN: Same way as India is to Britain.

ROOSEVELT: Joe, I'd like you to understand something. The US doesn't like empires. Anyone's empires. It's not in our tradition at all. And we're not in the business of either making or sustaining empires for other people. Okay, Winston? Now, let's move on, shall we? A framework for disarmament?

CHURCHILL: Yes, I'd like to hear what promises Joe's going to make about that!

ROOSEVELT: It's getting hot again. Give that valve another tap, will you, sonny?

(*A knock rings on the cast-iron of the boiler and is warped. SETH entering the greenhouse.*)

SETH: Sorted yourselves out?

CHURCHILL: This will take more time than we thought.

SETH: I'm looking for that boy I brought in here.

STALIN: He doesn't say much.

SETH: Father was killed two years ago and no one will tell him straight except the kids in the street.

STALIN: The street is where the truth lives.

CHURCHILL: Perhaps he's trying to work out who to believe, just as we are?

SETH: I reckon he knows.

ROOSEVELT: And your part in this?

SETH: His own mother, my eldest daughter, just won't accept the truth. If I tell him one thing and she another, who's he got to believe – eh?

CHURCHILL: How old is the little chap?

SETH: Seven.

CHURCHILL: Then you haven't a chance, I agree. His mother rules anything close to the heart.

SETH: And what if I did tell him? In his eyes I'd be reduced to the level of the kids in the street. We've been walking on eggs for a long time in our house. It's no way to live.

ROOSEVELT: What kind of future are we giving our young people if we lie to them about the simplest things? Do they have to look at the world in the mess it's in and also be denied the means of dealing with it? The truth!

SETH: Easily said. But my daughter won't have it. No matter what proof's put in front of her she says her husband's alive.

STALIN: The concealment of death isn't healthy. Let her heart break then let it heal. It will end up stronger. Then, next time she loses a husband, it won't be so painful.

SETH: But she's had it all in black and white! Telegrams, letters of condolence, her own letters returned by the Army rubber-stamped: ITEM COULD NOT BE DELIVERED. ADDRESSEE REPORTED DECEASED. But she keeps on writing, and they keep on sending them back.

RUSTY: (*Voice over.*) Dear Jack, It's exactly two years to the day since I last heard. Whoever's looking after you

or keeping you prisoner must be very tight not to let
you have a few sheets of writing-paper.

CHURCHILL: Hammer, this must be laid at your
door. A way could have been found to establish the
unpalatable fact with your daughter. Sounds to me as
though you've let things slide very badly.

ROOSEVELT: Your daughter seems to have been given all
the evidence she needs to prove her husband's dead. So,
she must have her own reason to behave as if he's not.
It may be a wrong reason, or a crazy reason, but it will
be a reason. Any idea what that might be, Mr Hammer?

SETH: Now you're asking.

ROOSEVELT: Yes, I am asking.

SETH: I don't know.

ROOSEVELT: If any daughter of mine ended up not being
able to face the truth, I'd want to know why.

STALIN: Heh-heh.

Scene 18

(*Cross fade greenhouse atmosphere into flashback street – on echo.
Atmosphere and Sunday church bells – 1937. Electric door bell heard
from outside. Door opened.*)

RUSTY: Oh, you're bang on time.

JACK: You told me to be.

RUSTY: Just a minute.

(*She pulls the door to so the lock touches but doesn't engage. They are on
the street side.*)

RUSTY: Jack, when you meet my dad I don't want you to
be afraid of him.

JACK: I won't be.

RUSTY: But I do want you to remember everything he's
been through. Think about your own dad and what
happened to him in the war. Mine survived, but only just.

JACK: Come on, Rusty, let's get on with it.

RUSTY: Don't be in too much of a hurry. He knows it's you
at the door. He's putting a tie on in your honour.

JACK: Now you've got me on edge. D'you think he'll like me?

RUSTY: He doesn't really like anybody so you won't feel left out.

JACK: This is getting worse by the minute!

RUSTY: Stand up to him, Jack, but in a nice way.

JACK: Is that what you do?

RUSTY: Just go over what you're going to say to him.

JACK: Sir, I love your daughter and I want to marry her.

RUSTY: He'll try to flummox you.

JACK: Flummox me? Why?

RUSTY: He does that. He likes flummoxing people. But don't let him do it to you. And, Jack ...

JACK: Yes?

RUSTY: Don't smile too much. He doesn't like that.

JACK: Sir, you miserable old bugger, I love your daughter very much and I want to marry her.

RUSTY: Why d'you love her so very much?

JACK: Because she can do the tango.

    (*Laughter. A kiss.*)

SETH: (*Inside.*) Come in if you're coming in, and shut that flaming door! There's a gale blowing through here.

RUSTY: Good luck. His bark's only as bad as his bite.

JACK: Thanks.

RUSTY: I love you.

    (*Door coming away from the lock, then being closed after they step through into the hall into the living room.*)

JACK: How d'you do, sir?

SETH: Your hand's clammy. Well, park your arse. You're overcrowding my eyesight.

JACK: Thank you, sir.

SETH: You're the one who's here to do the talking so get on with it.

JACK: Sir, I love her daughter and I want to marry you.

SETH: Have another go.

JACK: Sir, I love your daughter and I want to marry her.

SETH: Right. We've got that out of the way. Now, Nice Lad, I've got a few questions you'll have to answer. What does your father do?

JACK: He's dead.

SETH: What'd he die of?

JACK: He was killed in the last war.

SETH: So was I, near enough. What does your mother do?

JACK: She's a nurse in America.

SETH: America? What's she doing over there?

JACK: She went at the end of the war when I was three.

SETH: How long were you in Yankeeland?

JACK: Oh, I never went. She left me here.

SETH: Why did she do that?

JACK: The man she married didn't like other men's children.

SETH: Brought up in a home, were you?

JACK: My uncle and aunty looked after me.

SETH: What did their own kids think about that?

JACK: They're my father's brother and sister.

SETH: That's cosy. What does your uncle do?

JACK: Ironmongers shop in Rice Lane.

SETH: Protestant or Catholic?

JACK: Oh, me Uncle Charlie serves anybody.

SETH: Are you here in such a hurry because my daughter's expecting?

JACK: No.

SETH: But she will be – eh?

(*SETH spits in the fire.*)

Scene 19

(*Cross on the sizzle into greenhouse atmosphere.*)

SETH: Trouble is, gentlemen, she keeps on talking about him as if he's going to come back.

STALIN: Go out and find her another husband. Get another man between her legs. That'll make her think differently.

SETH: Hey, steady on. Besides, any feller who asks her out gets a flea in his ear.

ROOSEVELT: It's up to you to guide and help your daughter until she comes to terms with reality. Everyone has to adjust to new situations. It may be simply a matter of time and being patient. I can't see that there's anything we can do to help you. Now, if you'll forgive us, we must press on with this vexed question of reparations ... I'm getting tired again, Winston ... very sleepy.

SETH: You can't brush me under the carpet! If there wasn't a war this wouldn't have happened. Talk to the boy for me. Give us all a chance of getting back on an even keel. If he hears the truth from you, the Big Three, he'll make his mother understand. 'Out of the mouths of babes and sucklings ...', you know?

CHURCHILL: Hammer, we can't spend valuable time on specific cases like this. It will take another generation before people can completely believe what's happened to them in this war.

STALIN: Come on, Winston, do good when you have the chance. It shouldn't take long to convince the child. Let's get him in here and shout YOUR DAD'S DEAD! all together. (*Roars with laughter.*)

ROOSEVELT: On our agenda, your grandson will be item 115.

SETH: Thank you.

CHURCHILL: Under *Any Other Business.* Now, can we get on? Reparations.

ROOSEVELT: I have estimates that Germany's prewar wealth was $125 billion, reduced by the cost of the conflict to 75 billion. My people have calculated that 30% of a highly industrialised country's wealth can be siphoned off in reparations without inflicting gross hardship on the population. That puts $20 billion into the pot for us to share out three ways.

STALIN: I must have half.

CHURCHILL: Half? We're short of money as well, you know!

STALIN: Half is what I need to rebuild the Soviet Union from its ashes and half is what I must have!

Scene 20

(*Edge in doorbell ringing. Hall atmosphere. Running downstairs.*)

RUSTY: (*In her head.*) It's him! It's him! And here's me with me hair in curlers.

(*Door opened.*)

Oh.

TREVOR: It's Rusty, isn't it?

RUSTY: Yes.

TREVOR: I'm Trevor, friend of Jack's. I promised him I'd call. I'm sorry it's taken so long for me to come but it's the first real leave I've had ...

MAY: (*From the kitchen.*) Who is it?

RUSTY: Friend of Jack's! (*To TREVOR.*) Come in, come in.

TREVOR: Thanks. He always talked about you.

(*Door closing.*)

RUSTY: He mentions you in his letters.

TREVOR: We spent a lot of time together. Joined up on the same day. I recognised you straight away.

MAY: (*Arriving from the kitchen.*) God bless you, son. Come into the Best Room. Are you hungry?

TREVOR: No, thank you, not right now.

(*They move into the Best Room. Clock ticking.*)

MAY: Plump the cushions for Trevor! Come and be comfortable, son. Sit down and tell us all you can.

(*He runs a finger over piano keys.*)

TREVOR: Jack told me about the joanna, and the parties. You in top hat and tails and taking off Al Jolson.

MAY: We still do all that, don't we, Rusty? And *Burlington Bertie.* (*Sings.*) 'I'm Bert, Bert, I haven't a shirt. '

TREVOR: I've been going over and over in my mind what I could say ... first, he was my best mate ... took me a long time to ... (*Hurriedly.*) He didn't know anything about it, love – honestly.

RUSTY: About what?

MAY: (*Quickly.*) Where have you come from, son?

TREVOR: Warrington.

MAY: That's a long way.

RUSTY: He'll have to be careful not to miss his last bus.

TREVOR: A friend brought me over on the back of his motor-bike.

RUSTY: I think I'll get on with my sewing. You mustn't keep your friend waiting.

TREVOR: No ... He's gone for a walk for an hour ...

MAY: Rusty, this young man's come all the way from Warrington to see you. (*Pause.*) Make him a cup of tea, will you?

RUSTY: I'm in the middle of something. I've only got half a pattern for it and I'm having to make the rest up.

MAY: (*Firmly.*) Make the lad a cup of tea.

(*Pause. Door closes.*)

MAY: I'm sorry you had to go through that, son. You see, all we got was this telegram – 'Missing in Action' and we've heard nothing since.

TREVOR: Can't they get anything right? He was killed outright. How can they do things like that? Some bloody desk-wallah who couldn't care less. (*Pause.*) Sorry. I messed it up.

MAY: No, you didn't.

TREVOR: I should have trodden more carefully, got to know the situation before saying anything. I wasn't all that far from him when it happened. I was wounded myself.

MAY: I'm sorry to hear that, son. Did Jack suffer?

TREVOR: He never knew anything about it.

MAY: I hear they don't tell you much, even when it is to say they're dead. I wonder whether it wouldn't be better if they didn't just send a photograph of what's left and be done. Then we'd know.

TREVOR: You wouldn't have liked a photograph, Ma. I'd better go.

MAY: Don't think we're not grateful. I feel bad that you've
spent time and money coming so far to do your duty and
we haven't been able to treat you properly. But you can
see how things are.

TREVOR: All this time, keeping up such a pretence.
He wouldn't have wanted her to do that.
(*Treadle sewing machine working in other room.*)

MAY: With my daughter it will take longer than most. Jack
was the light of her life.

TREVOR: I know that. They were a couple of lovebirds.
I brought something for his kid ...

MAY: Kids.

TREVOR: I forgot.

MAY: One was posthumous.

TREVOR: Posthumous. (*Pause.*) You mean it was born after
you'd been told he was missing?

MAY: We'll get over it.

TREVOR: I'll leave what I've brought with you. (*Puts down
large envelope.*)

STORYTELLER: Leaving my grandmother caught out in
her protective lie, the bearer of such old bad news leaves
feeling as though his friend had died a second time.
Confused and upset, Trevor wanders the streets, not
knowing what to do with himself for the rest of the hour
he'd set aside for this encounter. Then, not wanting to be
alone, he goes into a nearby public house.

Scene 21

(*Pub atmosphere.*)

SETH: Hello there, soldier.

STORYTELLER: Sitting in the corner of the public bar,
cigarette in one hand, stout in the other, is a long-headed,
somewhat emaciated, sage who speaks kindly to him.

SETH: What are you having, then, soldier?

TREVOR: That's all right. I can't buy you one back so
I'll get my own.

SETH: Suit yourself. Coldstream Guards, eh? Six-footers. They died with their boots clean. Heh-heh.

TREVOR: All the way – North Africa to Germany.

SETH: Did you ever know a tall, dark lance-sergeant who fancied himself as a dancer ...

STORYTELLER: (*Voice over.*) Jack, Jack/Who never came back.

Scene 22

(*Edge in greenhouse atmosphere.*)

CHURCHILL: I think the French should also have a zone of occupation. De Gaulle is being hopelessly proud and difficult – and this would help the French salvage some self-respect.

ROOSEVELT: Not a bad idea. Out of kindness.

STALIN: No! No! No! They didn't do the fighting. They rolled over and lay down, finished! Now they're only bit players.

CHURCHILL: De Gaulle's such a prima donna. If France isn't recognised as a European power he'll be impossible to deal with ...

STALIN: She isn't a European power! She's a has-been!

CHURCHILL: Without a strong France and a free Greece and Italy, western civilisation is meaningless. I say that as an Englishman.

STALIN: A sentimental Englishman. Winston, you thrive on myths. On dreams! A free Greece! Why? Because you read Homer at school. This isn't school. This is the real world.

CHURCHILL: That's my cue. I give you a toast. To the proletarian masses of the world!

(*Clink of glasses.*)

CHURCHILL, ROOSEVELT and STALIN: To the proletarian masses of the world!

CHURCHILL: God bless them!

Scene 23

(*Cross on laughter into kitchen atmosphere. MAY is peeling potatoes. Kettle on stove.*)

RUSTY: We're going to have to think about leaving, Mum.

MAY: Don't say that.

RUSTY: My dad isn't fit to live with.

MAY: Give him another chance. I'll talk to him again. I'll be very firm this time. Fill that pan up with cold.

RUSTY: Talking won't help.

MAY: What else can I do?

RUSTY: (*Turning tap on – filling pan.*) Why should I have to sit here and listen to him going on about what he hears in the pub?

MAY: He doesn't understand your hope, love.

RUSTY: Making up stories like that. What gets into him? It's as if he wants us never to be happy.

MAY: No, love. It's not that. His brain's softening. Half the time he doesn't know his arse from his elbow. Pass me the salt, will you?

RUSTY: Then how does he hold down his job?

MAY: I think people help him on the sly. It won't be long before the firm will have to get rid of him.

RUSTY: What, with Uncle Les on the board of directors? And half the family working there. Never.

MAY: They've tipped me the wink. I don't know what we'll do when it happens. He'll disintegrate. That lad from Warrington left a present for the boys.

RUSTY: That's not all he left, the liar!

MAY: It's nothing much. Only a drawing Jack did of an Arab riding a camel.

RUSTY: That'll be a message for me.

MAY: Of course it will. It's very good. Very life-like. But he couldn't get the camel's feet in before the bottom of the paper.

STORYTELLER: A week later, responding to desperate notes from their mother, Rusty's two sisters have come to help persuade her not to leave. After a kitchen discussion of Seth's crimes, the four women move into the living-room, smoking furiously, their eyes hard and bitter on Seth as he sits slumped in his pockmarked chair, also screening himself with smoke. Clouds of tobacco fumes fill the room. The air swirls, acrid, choking, thick, like a battlefield. From beneath the table comes a cough.

Scene 24

(*Living room. A child's cough.*)

SETH: Time that one was in bed.

MAY: He's staying up. He wants to see his aunties.

SETH: He won't see much of them from under there.

RUSTY: He'd come out if you weren't around!

MAY: Don't talk to your father like that!

RUSTY: Oh, for God's sake!

MAY: You must treat your father with respect.

SETH: Save your breath. They don't know what it means any more. I'm getting out of here.

STORYTELLER: In an eerie, pre-figured silence, Seth's three daughters sit and watch as their father painfully pulls himself out of his chair, spits in the fire and misses, opens the French doors, gives the four women a fierce, sour glare then shambles down the garden to the haven of his greenhouse. With strange force their childhood fears of him return. Once he was master in this house, and of himself. His word was law. They watch him enter the house of glass. A match flares as he lights a cigarette. Then darkness except for one red dwarf star in his hand. They know his day has passed, Pity moves them.

Scene 25

(*Edge in greenhouse atmosphere.*)

SETH: (*Drawing on his cigarette.*) Peace. Peace.

STORYTELLER: Cradling a cluster of tomatoes in his beautiful, sensitive hands, he smells them.

SETH: Aaaah. From seed I did this.

STORYTELLER: Full of memories of first green shoots, he tends the boiler.

(*Furnace lid opened. Roar of fire.*)

For a moment he stares into the heart of the furnace, does not spit into it, feeds the inferno, then sits brooding, eyes on the moving square of scarlet flame/as if it were the Big Bang held for ever in a frame.

SETH: Sir, the stupid bitch won't even believe an eye-witness. And me wife lying in her teeth to cover up. Missing in Action! That's me she's talking about. Missing in Everything!

CHURCHILL: (*Aside whisper.*) For God's sake, Hammer, not now! I've got enough on my plate trying to keep Britain solvent sandwiched between usurious Americans on one side and rapacious Russians on the other.

SETH: My family are driving me up the wall, sir.

ROOSEVELT: I'd hope that lend-lease repayments could start dribbling through shortly. I have to satisfy Congress ... think of elections ...

CHURCHILL: We must have time. Our economy is shattered. You've taken all our gold reserves.

ROOSEVELT: A deal is a deal, Winston. The money has to come from somewhere.

CHURCHILL: Does it have to be from our absolute ruination?

ROOSEVELT: Come on, don't exaggerate. Once things get back to normal, you'll get back on your feet – economically.

SETH: That's what I want! Everything to be normal. Even ordinary!

STORYTELLER: Ignored by the Big Three this time, Seth takes refuge amongst the fragrant and familiar, his tall, trussed-up tomato plants. Financial finessing which reduces all life down to a sum he can do on the back of a fag packet, is usually music to his ear. But now it intrudes on a special sadness.

SETH: (*In his head.*) Let her believe what she likes. I can't be bothered.

STORYTELLER: Three hours later, the four women – the Big Four – have smoked themselves dry and talked themselves hoarse. Since his strategic retreat to the greenhouse, no one has mentioned the man of the fallen house. The women's moment of pity came and went in silence. Their talk has been of music, dancing, comedy shows on the radio, hair-dos, clothes, children, rationing. Meanwhile, with the Big Three droning round him like bees building the world's new hive, Seth has had four dreams: one of fame, one of joy, one of ecstasy, and one of power.

SETH: (*In his sleep.*) Oh, Michelangelo's mallet should be mine ... Up the Blues ... lend me your shirt, Dixie Dean ... Rouillé, fill it right up to the top, if you don't mind, darlin' ... I've got more hair than Atlee and my ideas for the future promise vigorous growth in the private sector.

STORYTELLER: When her sisters leave, Rusty goes to bed.

Scene 26

(*Edge in living room atmosphere.*)

RUSTY: (*At door.*) Night, Mum.

MAY: Good night, love. Another day over and not much learnt.

STORYTELLER: An impulse takes May out into the cool summer night. Standing thigh-deep amongst dahlias, she peers into the greenhouse. Seth is sitting bolt upright on a wooden Guinness crate, asleep, open-mouthed, garlanded with moon-silvered love-apples, a young smile on his face, one hand absently kneading his genitals.

MAY: (*In her head.*) Yes, and we know what you're dreaming about, you dirty sod.

STORYTELLER: But she's wrong. His four dreams of a greater self over, this one is now of her in the sweets and flowers shop where, one year before the Great War, she worked opposite the Empire Theatre in Lime Street. He sees himself again as he walks up and down the pavement rubbing shoulders with young men in top hat and tails as he plucks up courage to buy roses over her counter, then return them to her with a flourish.

(*1913 shop atmosphere – on echo.*)

SETH: Bought them for you, Bright-Eyes and I've got tickets for the royal stalls tomorrow night.

MAY: I'll have to see.

STORYTELLER: Oh, bliss! Her own stage-door johnny, her own Burlington Bertie, at last. But now, unlike that night of animal magic when her smile said yes, May turns her back on the sight of him. Full of anger, confusion and regrets, she re-enters the house. To calm her mind before she goes to bed, she mops the kitchen floor, prepares a potato-pie for the next day, pins the best room curtains straighter, polishes the walnut veneer sideboard, then locks up.

(*Yale lock.*)

MAY: (*In her head.*) The front.

(*Bolt being shot.*)

(*In her head.*) The side.

(*Large key in box lock.*)

(*In her head.*) The back.

(*Two bolts being shot.*)

(*In her head, viciously.*) The French!

STORYTELLER: Lying in bed with the door ajar, Rusty has listened to all this late-night restlessness, and knows the signs. As her mother reaches the top of the stairs, she goes out and helps unlace her corsets.

(*Laces being pulled out.*)

MAY: Oooh! That's better. They were cutting me in half.

RUSTY: You should leave him, Ma.

MAY: I have. Asleep in the greenhouse.

Scene 27

(*Cross on laughter into very loud dawn chorus.*)

STORYTELLER: At sunrise Seth is wakened by the birds – stiff and cold because the boiler has gone out. Lighting his first Capstan Full Strength of the day he leaves the greenhouse, crosses the dew-drenched garden and tries the back door. Finding it locked, he approaches the French doors but fails to gain entry. However, he can unbolt the side door. This brings him to the front door and the electric bell. Savagely he presses and holds his thumb on it.

(*Continuous ring of electric bell.*)

STORYTELLER: It's ten past five in the morning.

(*Electric door bell heard as in a dream.*)

RUSTY: (*In her head.*) Coming! It's him. It's him! I understood your drawing, sweetheart. The camel is long-lasting love. The hump is all the happiness stored up for us. You left out the hooves because they're cloven like the Devil's.

(*Running downstairs. Electric bell still ringing. Door unlocked and flung open. Burst of very loud dawn chorus of birds.*)

RUSTY: Jack! At last! (*Pause.*) Oh, it's you.

SETH: Your mother locked me out. I had to spend the night in the greenhouse.

RUSTY: Come in, Camel's-Feet!

(*Door slams.*)

Scene 28

(*Edge in living room.*)

SETH: He was there! The lad saw him die.

STORYTELLER: (*Voice over.*) I said the fly, with my little eye/I saw him die.

SETH: What other proof do you want?

RUSTY: He was making it up to please you.

SETH: Christ almighty! What d'you take me for?

RUSTY: Don't ask. This isn't getting us anywhere, Dad. I'll have to see if I can find somewhere else to live.

(*Fades.*)

STORYTELLER: Faced with his daughter's obstinate, self-inflicted blindness and the fear that she will actually leave this time – she has threatened to before but never had the heart or means to carry it out – Seth decides upon a policy of being nicer to his older, less reverberative grandson, persuading him to come out from under the table and help pick a few tomatoes.

Scene 29

(*Edge in greenhouse. Opening of furnace cover hawking and spitting.*)

CHURCHILL: If you've quite finished cleaning out your pipes, Hammer, we'd like to get on.

SETH: It was the mustard gas, sir. Two lots the Bosch gave me. Never been the same since. Will you be sure to have a word with the boy soon? It's getting urgent.

CHURCHILL: If we get round to it. We've still much to decide on post-war Europe.

SETH: Never mind post-war Europe! What about post-war our house?

(*Furnace lid slammed shut.*)

SETH: (*Muttering.*) What d'you care? When have you ever bloody cared?

ROOSEVELT: Hitler's 'Final Testament', Winston? So what d'you think?

CHURCHILL: Ravings of a criminal lunatic!

STALIN: I never realised how much he'd rather have worked hand-in-glove with Winston. If you Anglo-Saxons had played your cards right, you could have been the other half of the master-race. Heh-heh.

CHURCHILL: Some chance! I had him taped as a menace as soon as he came to power. How a sophisticated and civilised nation was so completely taken in by him is beyond my comprehension.

ROOSEVELT: It's no coincidence that Hitler's and Freud's ideas rose to prominence simultaneously. They were filling the same intellectual vacuum.

SETH: (*To himself.*) Listen to him. Thinks he's so clever. Bloody Yank!

ROOSEVELT: The Nazis brought the European superiority complex finally out of the Pit and let it loose.

SETH: (*To himself.*) Got brains he hasn't used yet.

(*A rustling among the tomato plants.*)

HITLER: May I hear your opinions of my work now?

CHURCHILL: Your mind is diseased. Your Nazi vision – a nightmare.

HITLER: Thank you. I apologise for referring to you in the text as a Jew-ridden, half-American drunkard. I may take it out. And you, Comrade Stalin? What did you think of my work?

STALIN: Swept me along, Comrade. By the time I'd got to the last page I was in an embarrassing position. On your side! (*Roars with laughter.*)

SETH: (*To himself.*) These people laugh when their arses are on fire.

HITLER: Praise from the red king of Moscow: once my ally, now my enemy; always ambiguous. I accept your plaudits for what they are.

STALIN: Adolf, your skull will stand on my desk as an ash-tray. When I knock the ash out of my pipe I'll remember how well you write.

HITLER: Come, come, we're brothers in thought. Although I can't take all the credit for advances in modern state practice, grant me some. But I have to acknowledge my greatest influences come from you three: the Soviet Union's total extermination of all political opposition; the British invention of the concentration-camp during the South African War; the United States' policy of exploiting and annihilating inferior races, to name but a few. As fair-minded people, you have to admit, it was I who most successfully fused these ideas together.

ROOSEVELT: Could someone open a window?

(*Moving around of CHURCHILL. Clattering.*)

CHURCHILL: They're stuck fast, painted over, I'm afraid. I'll open the door. Don't just sit there, Joe. Fan him!

ROOSEVELT: Sorry to be such a nuisance. Better get Item 115 on the agenda in here pronto.

CHURCHILL: Must we? Let's deal with him later. If you're getting tired again we can adjourn for a while ...

ROOSEVELT: Winston, I think my next adjournment is going to be a long one. When you haven't got much time, the young and the truth have to come first.

CHURCHILL: (*Edge back.*) Cap off! Stand up straight, boy! Stop fidgeting and picking your nose! Pin your ears back!

ROOSEVELT: Sonny, perhaps I'm the best person to give you this news straight because the journey your father took is one I'm setting out on shortly. I don't think you've got to choose between believing your daddy is dead or alive. If you hold him in mind he's around somewhere, like most fathers. And what you don't know about him, you can make up as you go along ... ah ... (*Pause.*) Joe, come closer ... listen ... Winston's a bit old-fashioned, but he's an honourable, kind man in a nineteenth-century cowboy kind of way.

STALIN: Don't worry. I'll look after him.

ROOSEVELT: And Winston ... Joe's a regular guy at heart. Give him a break. He's got plenty of problems, haven't you? Help each other ... (*Dies.*)

STALIN: Can you spare a couple of coins to put on his eyes?

CHURCHILL: Don't go, Franklin, I beg of you! Not with so many things left up in the air. Oh, lamentation! Where are we now? Who's going to hold us all together?

STALIN: Well, Adolf, you got your break. I got mine.

HITLER: I can't believe my luck!

Scene 30

(*Cross greenhouse into boy's bedroom.*)

RUSTY: You want to know what luck is, son? I gave your daddy a ring once and he left it behind in a dance hall cloakroom. He said he'd never have a moment's luck until he got it back. He never has.

(*Cross boy's bedroom into living room.*)

MAY: (*Fade in.*) Seth, if you drive Rusty and the kids out of here, I'm going with them.

SETH: I'm not driving them out! I've given them a home. I've fed them, put clothes on their backs ...

MAY: Don't give me that! Our Rusty works for her keep. And we have her war-widows pension which is 18/a week which I collect for her. She won't because she says she's not a widow. Work that one out. That's more than half what comes into this house. You earn five times what you give me to manage on. The rest goes on your booze.

SETH: I have to have some entertainment. There are a lot worse than me. Do I raise my hand to them? Do I? Never.

MAY: You haven't got the strength. And if you did, I'd flatten you. Anyhow, there it is. If they go, I go.

SETH: You wouldn't be able to manage.

MAY: Then we'll starve.

SETH: Get on with it, then!

MAY: I would rather starve than live here all by myself with you. (*Pause.*) I mean it, Seth!

SETH: How am I going to stop her going?

MAY: Talk to her.

SETH: She never listens to a word I say.

MAY: Tell her you're going to change.

SETH: Change into what?

MAY: Tell her you'll stop drinking. Tell her you can't handle it any more. Tell her you never could.

SETH: I'm not that terrible, am I.

(*Pause.*)

MAY: Every time you come through that door you cast a cloud. Promise Rusty you'll stop boozing. Promise her you'll stand in as a father to her boy as much as you can. Promise her you'll act like a decent man. Tell her anything you like, but keep her from going!

SETH: (*Lighting a cigarette.*) I don't know what all the fuss is about.

MAY: You've been told often enough. If you don't want to do anything about it, that's up to you.

(*Door opening and slamming shut.*)

SETH: (*To himself.*) Christ. (*Pause. Sighs.*) SON, ARE YOU UNDER THERE? ORDERS FROM ABOVE. WE'RE GOING TO HAVE TO GET CLOSER TOGETHER.

(*Panic noises from under the table.*)

OTHERWISE I'M SUNK. WE'RE BOTH SUNK. THERE'S NOTHING FOR IT. WE'LL JUST HAVE TO BE FRIENDS.

STORYTELLER: Not likely, Grandad! I put my matchbox in my pocket and headed for the door.

SETH: Hey, come back here!

(*Door opening and slamming. Succession of doors slamming with a crescendoing echo.*)

Scene 31

(*Edge in garden and birds. Two-year old CHILD coughing.*)

SETH: 'Oo's a pretty boy, den? 'Oo's grandad is kissing him all the time?

RUSTY: (*Coming into garden.*) Careful, you don't drop him, Dad!

SETH: I'm dandling him. And I'm kissing him!

RUSTY: He doesn't like having smoke blown in his face.

SETH: Everything is going to be different. What a perfect child! Jack stamped all over him. We'll make up for lost time now.

RUSTY: (*Taking the CHILD.*) You're an open book, Dad.

SETH: Don't leave, Rusty.

RUSTY: I left here a long time ago.

STORYTELLER: After Roosevelt's death his place at the conference is taken by the new president, Harry S Truman. The S doesn't stand for anything. It's just an S his parents gave him so he could call himself something he fancied in later life. I suppose once you've got a name like True Man, the rest can be taken light-heartedly.

SETH: Ssssssssssssh ...

(*A huge explosion.*)

SETH: Ssssh-i-i-i-i-i-t-e!

Scene 32

(*Edge in greenhouse atmosphere as explosion fades and debris falls.*)

SETH: Was it me boiler?

TRUMAN: As a controlled experiment we tied the first atomic bomb to a post in the New Mexico desert, triggering it by remote control. The Christians among the nearby Mescalero Apache reservation Indians thought it was the end of the world. The rest thought it was the Great Spirit finally cracking up. Only countable casualties were a few lizards.

SETH: The equivalent of twenty thousand tons of TNT! Made a crater big enough to get Birkenhead in.

CHURCHILL: The blast of this formidable weapon was colossal, turning the sands of the desert into glass.

STALIN: Boy, listen to me. Because America profits so much from the war, they feel guilty. To atone, they bomb themselves. (*Pause.*) Now, tell me about this weapon, Mr President. Who will you use it against?

TRUMAN: Depends.

STALIN: I think the Soviet Union will have to attack Japan. It's a matter of national pride. We lost the last war we fought against them, but that was under the Tzar.

TRUMAN: You're certainly a guy who chooses when to remember things. Godammit, all you're doing is inviting yourself to a turkey shoot. Once we drop that bomb ...

STALIN: Shooting turkeys, fish in a barrel, sitting ducks, I like.

SETH: Cover your faces for five minutes, gents. Have to dose the plants for spotted wilt, double streak, cucumber mosaic and stem rot.

(*Chemical spray being pumped.*)

SETH: (*While pumping.*) One of my brothers-in-law who works for me at the warehouse was out in China during the Great War and he's always said it's the best place he's ever been and he'd like to go and live there because they're so cruel and honest about it. Mr Reg another brother-in-law who's boss of my company can't stand anything east of Gibraltar because they're so honest and cruel about it. Where d'you go?

CHURCHILL: (*Mouth covered.*) Have you finished that dreadful business? We can hardly breathe.

(*Pumping stops.*)

STALIN: Mr Hammer, you have been most hospitable. But I have to impose even further. As host to the conference I feel moved to give a grand ball of peace and friendship which will also celebrate the birth of the atomic age. May I hold it here?

SETH: In my greenhouse?

STALIN: Preferably in your home.

Scene 33

(*Cross greenhouse into large palace ballroom.*)

VICTOR SYLVESTER: (*As MC.*) The band will now play 'I Gotta Right To Sing The Blues' which is a quickstep.

LOUIS ARMSTRONG: No, man. It's a slow-fox-trot. Slow-slow-quick-quick-slow. Slow-slow-quick-quick-slow.

(*The band plays. LOUIS ARMSTRONG sings.*)

STALIN: Rusty, may I have this dance?

RUSTY: The form round here is: Lend us your body for a struggle.

STALIN: Then – lend us your body for a struggle.

RUSTY: All right.

(*They dance.*)

STALIN: Rusty is an odd name for such a beautiful young woman.

RUSTY: That's my dad's fault, like most things. He had me christened Rouillé after a nurse he met, which is French for rusty. Don't ask me why.

STALIN: Why?

RUSTY: He said she'd saved his life after he'd been gassed in the trenches.

STALIN: Rusty doesn't suit you. You should change your name.

RUSTY: Not before you change the world.

(*Cross on music into buffet atmosphere and hum of conversation – the band plays on in the adjacent ballroom.*)

SETH: (*Fade in.*) I was saved from drowning in 1917 by a havildar-major ... that's the same as our sergeant-major ... of Indian troops.

STALIN: Perhaps you had better sit down?

SETH: It was on the shores of your Black Sea. I want to take Rusty there, take my daughter to show her the place where someone thought I was worth saving ...

STALIN: Now your daughter is happy dancing with all our young officers.

SETH: The one she's dancing with now isn't one of your officers.

(*Closer to the dancers. Echo on next section.*)

JACK: I was sitting there doing a quick sketch of this camel, sweetheart, when, as luck would have it, he does a big load right on top of a land-mine we'd just laid. I got knocked over by the blast and the camel landed on me with all its four feet blown off ... slow-slow-quick-quick-slow ...

RUSTY: I got your message.

JACK: I was crushed and couldn't shout for help. Thinking it was a general attack, our column moved off and left me behind.

RUSTY: And these Arabs came along on their way to market ...

JACK: That's right.

RUSTY: Kind Arabs!

JACK: Kind as you like. And they put me in a cart ...

RUSTY: Took you to an oasis!

JACK: Then it was all slow-slow-quick-quick-slow until I got you in my arms again.

RUSTY: Oh, Jack. You're such a wonderful dancer.

(*Cross music back to SETH and STALIN in the buffet.*)

SETH: (*Fade in.*) My daughter doesn't have any idea what I've been through. And she chooses to forget my good points. You know women: the sooner they can forget a man's decent actions, the more they like it.

STALIN: Suffer in silence is a sound working principle.

SETH: I've never told anybody else this, Joe. The reason I was drowning in your Black Sea was because I'd been to the mosque of Saint Sofia and seen the incredible statues of the mullahs, past and present. When I was saved by this Hindu who happened to be passing along the beach deep in contemplation, looking for driftwood – in Civvy Street he was a holy man, he told me later – I was trying to do myself in because I'd been overpowered by a terrible realisation that I'd never make a sculptor's arsehole.

STALIN: There are no statues in Saint Sofia.

SETH: There were the day I went.

STALIN: More vodka?

SETH: I better had.

(*A child's chuckle.*)

SETH: Where is he? He's here somewhere, eavesdropping! That spying little bastard never gives me a moment's peace.

STALIN: Why is he always watching you?

SETH: Doesn't want to miss it if I suddenly drop dead.

STALIN: Many people would like to see the end of Stalin, so, like you, I'm no stranger to reasonable paranoia. Whenever I get into a state about it, this is what I do: sit quietly to clear and settle the mind; rub oil of oregano behind the ears and do deep breathing. Read some poetry, Pushkin ... you know the one: 'I have put up a monument to myself/not built by human hand/' ... then Shakespeare, probably. I carry a book of his sonnets everywhere: 'Not mine own fears, nor the prophetic soul/ of the wide world dreaming on things to come/can yet the lease of my true lover control' ... After that, think about the wonders of Nature for a while, the flowers, the birds, the shapes of clouds. Then draw up the list.

SETH: What list?

STALIN: The list of those to be liquidated.

SETH: I can't put him on that. He's my grandson.

STALIN: So? (*Pause.*) Heh-heh.

(*Lift music then dip into:*)

HITLER: What a clean and orderly home you have, Mr Hammer. I admire the polish on your walnut veneer sideboard and the little flying elephant.

SETH: What's happened to you?

HITLER: After I was captured by Soviet troops in Berlin, Stalin gave orders that my moustache was to be shaved off and sent to him in a matchbox. When I was taken to Moscow and brought before him in chains, he was cleaning his teeth with a toothbrush whose bristles I recognised.

SETH: The world was told you'd blown your brains out, been doused in petrol and set on fire with Eva ... Eva, you know.

HITLER: My wife of one hour. How romantic, eh? That was a story Comrade Stalin put out so I could enjoy my retirement, incognito. You'd be surprised the number of times your name crops up in our conversations. May I sit down?

SETH: My personal chair but you can have it.

HITLER: Thank you. Ach, bullet-holes even here? (*Pause.*) Can you remember where you were on the night of 13th October, 1918.

STALIN: Yes, where were you? Adolf's always talking about you and this crucial moment in his life.

SETH: Me? What for?

CHURCHILL: Try to remember where you were, exactly.

SETH: I was in the Line.

TRUMAN: But where. Put your finger on it for us.

SETH: Just outside a place called Wervick near Wipers.

STORYTELLER: (*Whisper.*) Wipers, to the uninitiated,
Yprés. Which had been an old cloth-making town.

HITLER: And what were you doing in the Line at Wervick
near Wipers on that day?

(*Outburst of singing 'Knees Up Mother Brown' from the best room/
ballroom.*)

SETH: I can't think with all that row going on!

CHURCHILL: I'll close the door.

SETH: It's my wife, once she gets going ...

(*Door closes. Silence.*)

TRUMAN: Go on, Mr Hammer. Tell us. Try to remember.

SETH: I was lobbing it over.

STALIN: And what was it you were 'lobbing over' Comrade?

Scene 34

(*Edge in first world war front. Artillery fire in distance.*)

CPO: Right ranging. Nature of filling: gas. Range: one five
zero zero yards. One round. Fire!

(*Explosion of shell landing. Hiss of gas. Very faintly MAY can now be
heard singing 'Burlington Bertie' next door.*)

HITLER: You see, you changed the shape of the future
with that single shot. That day, I was in those trenches
opposite scribbling disorganised thoughts in my
notebook. The shell you fired made me go blind.

TRUMAN: That very shell?! Well, well.

HITLER: I was sent to hospital in Pomerania. There I had
time to sit in darkness and work out my ideas on how to
make the world a better place.

CHURCHILL: So it was an Englishman who helped you get
started? Oh, no, no! I can't have that. Dammit, I won't
have that! Liverpudlians aren't really Englishmen at all.

HITLER: Without Mr Hammer I would have remained no one.

TRUMAN: What a burden for you to carry, Mr Hammer. I thank God it's not on my shoulders.

SETH: That's not what happened at all! The wind changed and blew the gas back right in my face! Why d'you think I've only got half a stomach?

STALIN: Here is a man who breathes through his belly! (*Laughs.*)

(*Door opens to living room. MAY enters singing:*)

MAY: I'm Burlington Bertie
I rise at ten-thirty
And walk down the Strand
With my gloves in my hand,
Then I walk back again –
With them orf.

I'm Bert, Bert,
I haven't a shirt ...

HITLER: Bravo! Bravo!

(*MAY abruptly stops singing. Pause.*)

MAY: What are you doing in my house?

HITLER: Madam, I was invited.

MAY: Not by me, you weren't. Get out!

HITLER: Herr Hammer, your husband.

MAY: That's HIS chair. No one's allowed to sit in HIS chair but HIM!

HITLER: I beg your pardon. The chair is vacated.

MAY: I'm as house-proud as Bert's wife who hung herself with the dishcloth, so you'll have to go.

HITLER: Madam, I cannot follow you.

MAY: I'm the woman who knows the colour of the Red Sea and how the milk got in the coco-nut.

(*Rasp of blade being drawn from scabbard.*)

HITLER: I'm going! I'm going!

MAY: Before you do, grant me a favour. Look up my arse and see if my hat's on straight.

(*Lunge and skewering.*)

MAY: Take that and a pound a week!

    (*Cry from HITLER.*)

STORYTELLER: If my grandfather's medical records were as complete as I could make them, they'd show that Adolf Hitler, the Scourge of God, Europe, the World and the Imagination, actually met his death at the hands of my grandmother who, while impersonating an upper-class down-and-out, drew a blade from the swordstick prop of her act and ran the tyrant through the throat. Blood shot from his mouth, flew across the room and went splat! against the wall.

Scene 35

    (*Sound of splat. SETH howls in the terror.*)

SETH: I can't beat that for distance! Ooooh, don't you come near me with that stick!

MAY: What are you yelling about?

SETH: The ball's over. Get them out of here!

MAY: Get who? There's no one here except you and me.

SETH: Get them out!

    (*A struggle. MAY pushes SETH back into his chair. Sound of RUSTY running down the stairs.*)

MAY: Sit down and be quiet.

    (*Door opens quickly.*)

RUSTY: What's he done now?

SETH: You dirty bitch, I saw you giving the come-hither to half the Red Army. Have you no shame?

    (*Struggle as MAY keeps SETH in the chair.*)

RUSTY: Oh, God! His eyes have gone funny. They're like stones.

MAY: This was always coming. No one can drink so much and stay sane. See what you've done to yourself, you stupid, self-destructive sod! Rusty, get to the phone box. Call the doctor – quick now!

RUSTY: Yes, Mum.

MAY: Tell him your dad's seeing things.

SETH: I hope to Christ they're not burying Hitler in my greenhouse.

MAY: Hurry up!

RUSTY: Come out from under the table, son. Don't be afraid. Come on. Your grandad's not very well.

(*BOY hurriedly getting out from under the table and running to the door. Pause. A BOY's frightened breathing.*)

MAY: Take a threepenny joey out of my purse and take your mum to the telephone box. Look after her.

STORYTELLER: (*As BOY.*) I have to get someone I've left under the table, Gran.

MAY: Hurry up, then. Your mum's waiting.

(*BOY going under the table. Matchbox with lead soldier in it being shaken. Running of boy then front door opened and slammed. Pause.*)

SETH: (*Quieter.*) Once through the door, they take over the place. That's the kind of people they are.

MAY: Anything you say. (*Prays.*) Help him, God, Rouillé, anybody listening. You've taken everything else, but please don't take his mind. Not his mind.

SETH: I don't want them hanging around any more! Tell them to make themselves scarce, go back to where they slithered from. And they're never to come here again.

MAY: Of course, of course, love. Just you sit back ...

SETH: Why am I telling you to do this kind of job? It's man's work!

STORYTELLER: With demonic energy, he suddenly gets up, kicks the French doors open ...

(*French doors being kicked open.*)

STORYTELLER: ... and rushes down the garden to his greenhouse, picks up a spade he inherited from his gravedigger father, and proceeds to destroy all he's held sacred since his war. The temple of his pain. The temple of one hundred and fifteen panes. Of glass.

(*Greenhouse being broken up.*)

SETH: (*Yelling.*) How was I to know? All I did was what
  I was told! Never believe what you hear on the news!

HITLER: (*Voice over.*) Ah, such music. It takes me Bacht/to
  Kristallnacht. Heh-heh.

Scene 36

(*Solo trumpet and organ play Bach's 'Jesu, Joy of Man's Desiring' over
the breaking of glass.*)

STORYTELLER: I was number 115 on the agenda. 115 was
  the number of days between the liberation of Belsen and
  the dropping of the first atomic bomb: 115 days which
  imagination must defeat or we're lost. This Herculean task
  of out-imagining the truth was shouldered single-handedly
  by my grandfather. Although the psychiatrists in the
  hospital where he was sent did not know it, their thin,
  waxen patient, so shaken from within, so wan with care,
  was heroically out-dreaming the evils of the century for
  everyone's sake.

(*Cries and screams from SETH.*)

SETH: No more! No more!

STORYTELLER: Awestruck by the strength of his mighty,
  undiminishing hallucinations, the medical men decided
  that my grandfather's *delirium tremens* must have a physical
  cause that had been made worse by his colossal intake of
  alcohol. He was wheeled down to the operating theatre
  and a mask put over his face.

(*Hissing of gas.*)

SETH: Give me more! Give me more!

SURGEON: The man's capacity for anaesthetics is
  astonishing. He's still not gone under. Increase the
  flow, nurse ...

STORYTELLER: When they finally knocked him
  out under a cloudbank of ether and opened him
  up, the surgeon's scalpel went into the half of a
  stomach that wasn't there and ...

(*Scalpel strikes metal.*)

STORYTELLER: ... a ring that wasn't there was found. A lucky ring. An anti-existential sign/a part of some god's blind design/that mankind and my grandad might survive.

Scene 37

(*Edge in ward.*)

RUSTY: Hello, Dad. Any better today?

SETH: Same as every other day. What d'you bring him for?

RUSTY: He asked to come.

SETH: This is no place for a child. And don't let him tread on those tubes.

RUSTY: He's been asking why you broke up the greenhouse.

SETH: It was mine to break.

RUSTY: Mum says it might have been because of me. I hope it wasn't.

SETH: Don't let him get under the bed. He'll tie knots in me life-supply.

RUSTY: Mum says it might help you get better if I explain how I feel: Jack can't be dead till he's dead in my heart. That's all.

SETH: So you say.

RUSTY: I don't care about the facts. D'you know that Mum still has a note on a fag packet you sent her when you got back to your regiment after being missing in France? No one knew where you were. For a couple of weeks you were dead to everyone except her.

SETH: A couple of weeks isn't a couple of years. (*Gasps.*) Get your foot off, you little bugger!

STORYTELLER: My grandfather was the only man I had to model myself on in early life. With him as an example it's strange I should drink at all, but I do, and I've drunk to find visions like his, terrible ones, that go with the times. The worst I ever had was of myself, one-eyed and twice life-size, standing behind an open door and glaring over the top like the Cyclops. Shook me, but I carried on – like him – pouring a drink to get over it.

SETH: You – you've learned nothing, you overeducated gobshite!

STORYTELLER: The Black Pythagoreans reason thus: the 115 days –1 plus 1 plus 5 which equals 7. That is the number of days it takes to make or unmake a world.

SETH: My arse on you for a top hat and me legs for streamers!

STORYTELLER: In hospital he was supposed to be drying out, but cronies from the docks smuggled in bottles of drink when they visited. So the hallucinations continued, their violence unabated. He lost even more weight, dropping to six stone. Food was now little more than a nauseous memory. Then, with blackouts punctuating each day he was sent the father and mother of all nightmares, its scripts penned by the Archfiend himself.

Scene 38

(*Fade in hospital atmosphere.*)

NURSE: (*Fade in.*) Someone to see you, Mr Hammer.

CHURCHILL: Had to come. Election result has got me down. Did you vote for me?

SETH: I'm a superintendent of warehouses, aren't I?

CHURCHILL: What's got into them? I've been betrayed. Everything I've done for this country ...

SETH: They don't know they're born.

CHURCHILL: What does a chap have to do?

SETH: You know best, boss, but think on this: in our house I got voted out years ago. But somehow I'm still running the show.

CHURCHILL: Iron Curtain's come down like I said it would. Joe making a real nuisance of himself. Americans getting very arrogant. Money-mad. Our only hope's a united Europe. But I've decided to leave that to other men. Give up. Rest on my laurels. I've done enough. You never know, someone as good as me might come along.

SETH: Don't give up, Mr Churchill. We need you. The working-class Conservatives aren't dead, only sleeping. Co-operating with the socialist during the war has tired them out. But they'll make a comeback. They'll have to otherwise Labour will take Britain into the Soviet Union.

CHURCHILL: Your analysis is spot on, Mr Hammer.

SETH: What you've got to do is repair the slums and get them back on their feet again ... They're a hotbed of support for strong government. The less they have the more they like it. Did you bring your hip-flask?

CHURCHILL: A wee dram?

SETH: Can you empty the contents down that tube without spilling any?

(*Hip-flask being emptied down tube.*)

CHURCHILL: Steady as she goes.

SETH: This is easier than drinking. Me arm doesn't get tired. You see, sir, what's happening now is everyone's for change, like Hitler was. They don't understand it's his disease they've got. Before you build, you have to destroy, they say. And when they've wrecked everything good they had, they'll want it back. And that's the way they'll feel about you, mark my words, boss.

CHURCHILL: Ever thought of politics as a career?

SETH: Talk to my grandson. He handles my case now he's in the third form at primary school.

CHURCHILL: When you're better, pop down and look me up. And when you knock at the door/ bring me the obedience of the poor.

STORYTELLER: Eventually my grandfather was discharged and sent home. His bed was needed for other cases coming back to England now the war was over. Settling into his pockmarked chair, he spat in the fire, and said:

SETH: Well, I've to be up at sparrow fart and back to work tomorrow, thank God.

MAY: What d'you want in your sandwiches for work? And don't say nothing.

SETH: Corned dog'll do. Bags likes it.

STORYTELLER: But he started drinking again. This time my grandmother swallowed her pride and went down on her bended knees, begging him to stop. He agreed to try again, and again, and again.

(*Key in lock. Front door opening. Clanking of bottles in canvas bag. Hall atmosphere.*)

MAY: You're not bringing drink in here! You gave your absolute word.

SETH: It's pop for the kids. Honest.

(*Door closing.*)

MAY: They're out the back playing Dick Barton.

SETH: I feel rotten. I'm going straight to bed.

(*Slow footsteps on stairs.*)

MAY: Shall I bring you some tea?

SETH: No.

MAY: Don't drink all the cough-mixture in the bathroom cabinet. And no gin and Andrews in the morning.

SETH: (*Muttering.*) Aw, shut up. Leave me to suffer.

STORYTELLER: But never, never in silence.

(*A few bars of 'I Gotta Right to Sing the Blues' on LOUIS ARMSTRONG's trumpet.*)

STORYTELLER: He always went back to it, of course. And, in due time, aided and abetted by malaria, gas, Capstan Full Strength and democracy, it killed him.

Scene 39

(*A Liverpool street 1951. Trams passing.*)

SETH: Son, I want you to take me up to the polling station to vote for Mr Churchill. Just hold my hand. Eyes aren't so good these days.

(*Shuffling.*)

SETH: Hey, don't go so fast. I've only got two speeds these days. Dead slow and stop. Heh-heh.

STORYTELLER: It was my brother who led him, not me. By then he was the age I'd had been at the end of the war, and I was away at boarding school on a charity scholarship, having become a problem at home because I couldn't live in the same house as my grandfather any more.

SETH: God knows what they'll be doing to your brother down at that school. Your mother says his housemaster's an old artillery officer with a wooden leg. Heh-heh. He'll give him what for. Heh-heh. Forward the guns.

JOHN: I'm going to go to that school, Grandad.

SETH: No, you'll be better off staying here with me, sunshine. Go to the grammar school, then I'll fix you up with a good job. How d'you like to be a pox-doctor's clerk?

JOHN: I want to be like my brother.

SETH: Then you'll end up in gaol.

STORYTELLER: Long after my mother had come to terms with my father's death, my brother retained his magical meaning. The women in the street always made a fuss of him and said: 'God, isn't he lovely, God bless him.' Some even called him Jack/behind his back. Now, as he walked up the pavement with our grandfather, a housewife opposite who was cleaning her windows waved and called out ...

HOUSEWIFE: Hello there, son! Taking HIM for a walk, are you?

SETH: What d'you think I am, missus? A flaming poodle? AAH!

STORYTELLER: My brother's attention had been distracted. He walked my grandfather into a deep hole Council workmen had dug and left unguarded. But he didn't die straight away. His broken arm meant he was off work for months, the last straw for the warehouse company. He was retired early. So he sued the Council for loss of earnings. And won.

Scene 40

(*Edge in living room and MAY weeping.*)

RUSTY: What's up, Mum?

MAY: They've awarded him fifteen hundred pounds compensation.

RUSTY: Fifteen hundred! Oh, God! That's terrible!

STORYTELLER: Within six months he'd drunk the lot and was dead, having fallen down stairs after an all-day session celebrating Churchill's come-back. I'd had to go to the Black Lion and bring him home in his own wheelbarrow. But like the man with one leg in the grave, he jumped out again.

(*Edge in stairway atmosphere.*)

SETH: Look out! I'm coming down! Make way!

(*SETH tumbling downstairs.*)

MAY: (*In her head.*) God love us, what's happened now? Perhaps I shouldn't have mopped that top step until the morning.

SETH: Someone moved the universe. (*Dies.*)

STORYTELLER: I was given his gold watch chain which I sold for £8. My brother was given his penknife. Soon after the funeral he was sitting on the hearthrug, polishing the big blade, then the small blade, then the spike for getting stones out of horses' hooves. When he came to the badly bent corkscrew, my brother suddenly burst into tears and threw the penknife into the fire. It was as if he knew that his reincarnate magic had fled with his grandfather, its opposite, the first member of our family we'd witnessed being positively, visibly, and incontestably deincarnated. I don't believe any of these tears came from guilt for leading grandfather into the hole. Young as he was, my brother knew that had been waiting since 1918.

(*Music.*)

STORYTELLER: He left his body to medical science, thinking it might have curiosity value, but they said no thanks. There was no money for a stone so the

gravedigger's son lies under an unmarked hump of grass
and weeds. After his death, Burlington Bertie became
redundant.

Scene 41

(*Edge in living room atmosphere.*)

MAY: You asked if there was anything you could ever do
for me, son.

STORYTELLER: Yes, Gran.

MAY: I know why you're like you are. Some time, when
you've got a week to spare I'd like you to take your
mother out to Africa to see your father's grave.

STORYTELLER: If she agrees, it shall be done.

MAY: She will, one day. But you'll have to be patient.

STORYTELLER: My grandmother died after she'd shared
a quiet joint widowhood with my mother for thirteen
years, who always prevaricated on the visit to my father's
grave. Another fifteen years had to pass before she was
close enough to death herself fully to face the fact of his.
When we went I took two sons of my own to counter-act
the power of the Absence.

Scene 42

(*Muezzin cry. Fade in war cemetery atmosphere. Birdsong.*)

STORYTELLER: You sit down and I'll find it.

RUSTY: Could take hours.

STORYTELLER: I'll just keep walking up and down the
rows.

RUSTY: Those Arabs keep it very nice.

STORYTELLER: When I found him and his shining white
stone which read: '26606831 SJT, then his name, then
1st February 1943 aged 26, Coldstream Guards' followed
by a magically ambiguous quote from somewhere,
chosen by an anonymous hand: 'God proved him and
found him worthy of himself' the sky fused with the

earth and rolled me up in a wonderful fire. It didn't matter that nothing may have been in the coffin except rocks. It may even have been a matchbox down there, but I knew it as the one place sacred to him I could touch and receive the understanding of death. I put my hand out and felt the sun-warmed stone. Tears sprang but they were of liberation and gladness. Now I was in a real land under a real sun with real cemetery workers sitting under a real hedge smoking real cigarettes and waiting for a real tip. I went to the bench where I'd left my mother and brought her to the spot.

STORYTELLER: Here. (*Pause.*) Would you like to be left alone?

RUSTY: Son, you're watching me like a hawk.

STORYTELLER: Are you all right?

RUSTY: He's not under there. Inside, I'm just a block of ice.

STORYTELLER: Surely you must feel something! TRY! (*Pause.*) But that was all she'd say. The earth itself had failed to convince her. We drove back to the coast, a long car journey through hills with ruins of Roman cities porch-deep in brilliant spring flowers. She seemed strangely happy.

Scene 43

(*Edge in 1985 car interior on bumpy road.*)

STORYTELLER: Have you got anything to say to me?

RUSTY: What kind of a question is that?

STORYTELLER: Just wondered.

RUSTY: I always knew he wasn't out here. (*Lights up.*)

STORYTELLER: He was to me.

RUSTY: You were always one for imagining things. You get that off your grandfather.

STORYTELLER: Flattened, I said no more. She was happy because she'd kept the faith. She'd been right all along. He was yet to be found. Before she died a few months later, having been ill with chronic bronchitis – all that smoking – and no longer able to look after herself, my mother came to live near me in London. It was Christmas Eve. Her furniture was still in Liverpool and her flat wasn't quite ready. That morning I found her standing in the living room struggling to say the Lord's Prayer, and I knew that she was getting ready. By evening she was in the Whittington Hospital. I sat by the bedside, watching the monitor of her heartbeat, listening to the carollers in the corridors of that vast Victorian heap of stone.

(*Monitor bleeps. 'O, Come All Ye Faithful' by carol singers.*)

STORYTELLER: Suddenly the bright spot on the monitor leapt. She sat up and tried to run down the ward. Not away from death, but towards someone. Then she fell back and died, her mouth falling open with amazement that the bloody war could be over for her at last.

LOUIS ARMSTRONG: (*Grams.*) "Hey there, boy, what's the matter wit you? Don't you know I gotta right to sing the blues? Look out. One. Two. (*Sings.*) I gotta right ... "

Scene 44

(*Music starts but crosses immediately to jet aircraft take-off.*)

STORYTELLER: When my mother had gone, I had the last word on my father's whereabouts, however. I took her ashes out to Tunisia in a brown paper bag strapped up with Sellotape. My brother went with me.

(*Edge in air terminal sounds and atmosphere. Squeaking of baggage trolley.*)

STORYTELLER: At the Customs barrier we decided to go into the Red Channel, fearing that if our cases were spot-searched in the Green the bag would be suspect. Then we'd have to open it, with all that entailed. A young, rather fierce official took the bag and scrutinised it.

CUSTOMS OFFICER: Qu'est-ce que vous avez là-dedans?

JOHN: (*In rehearsed fifth-form French.*) Les cendres de nos mère.

CUSTOMS OFFICER: Notre mère. English?

JOHN: Oui.

CUSTOMS OFFICER: Why bring her here?

JOHN: Nous ... er ... portons cet sac ... er ... a la sépulcre ...

CUSTOMS OFFICER: I speak your language, don't I?

JOHN: We're taking her ... them to where our father's buried in the mountains. He was killed in the war.

CUSTOMS OFFICER: Ah, the war. Your war.

STORYTELLER: Yes, our war. (*Pause.*) He gave us a hard, bitter look. For a moment I thought he was going to insist we open the brown paper bag. If we did and they took a sample of those ashes to test, what would show up? What sparkling crystals of pure grief?/What structures of bright disbelief?/But the customs man merely shook his head, patted the brown paper bag, put it back into our hands and waved us through, saying:

CUSTOMS OFFICER: Go in peace.

STORYTELLER: So, we did.

LOUIS ARMSTRONG: (*Sings.*) I gotta right to sing the blues,
I gotta right to feel low-down,
I gotta right to hang around,
Down among the riff-ragg.
A certain gal in this old town
Keeps draggin' my heart around ...
(*Fade music.*)

The End.